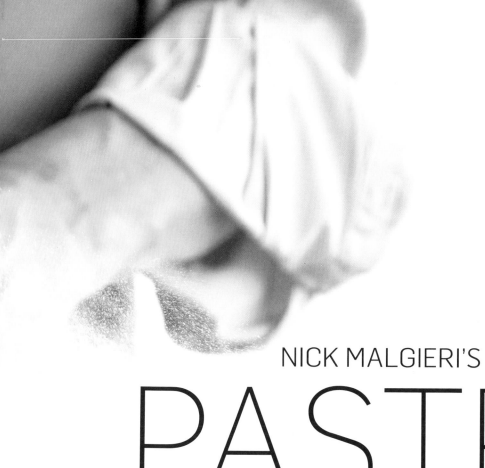

NICK MALGIERI'S
PASTRY

NICK MALGIERI'S
PASTRY

Foolproof Recipes for the Home Cook

Nick Malgieri

Photography by Romulo Yanes

KYLE BOOKS

For Phyllis Wender

Published in 2014 by Kyle Books
www.kylebooks.com
general.enquiries@kylebooks.com

Distributed by National Book Network
4501 Forbes Blvd., Suite 200
Lanham, MD 20706
Phone: (800) 462-6420
Fax: (800) 338-4550
customercare@nbnbooks.com

10 9 8 7 6 5 4 3 2 1

ISBN 978-1-909487-11-6

Text © 2014 by Nick Malgieri
Photography © 2014 by Romulo Yanes
Book design © 2014 by Kyle Books
Project editor Anja Schmidt
Designer Dirk Kaufman
Photographer Romulo Yanes
Food styling Paul Grimes
Prop styling PJ Mehaffey
Copyeditor Sarah Scheffel
Proofreader Liana Krissoff
Production Nic Jones, Gemma John and Lisa Pinnell

Library of Congress Control No. 2014934797

Color reproduction by Scanhouse
Printed and bound in China by 1010 International Printing Ltd.

CONTENTS

Introduction 5

Chapter 1: Ingredients & Equipment 7

Chapter 2: A Whole New Generation of Doughs 13

Chapter 3: Sweet Tarts & Tartlets 39

Chapter 4: Sweet Pies, Cobblers & Crisps 67

Chapter 5: Savory Tarts & Pies 99

Chapter 6: Strudel & Other Thin Doughs & Pastries 127

Chapter 7: Puff Pastry, Croissants & Other Laminated Doughs 153

Chapter 8: Brioche & Other Yeast-Risen Pastries 183

Chapter 9: Pâte à Choux or Cream Puff Pastry 203

Afterword 219

Bibliography 220

Index 220

Acknowledgments 224

INTRODUCTION

Baking is all I've ever wanted to do. I was a pretty good student in school, but I preferred dreaming about becoming a pastry chef. As a teenager, though, despite my passion for the craft, there were two things I steadfastly refused to do: whip egg whites and roll out dough.

Looking back, I understand my lack of success with the former—our home kitchen was equipped with plastic mixing bowls that always held slight films of grease. Any attempt to whip egg whites failed because they just won't foam up in the presence of fat. Rolling dough was a different story: my Italian grandmother, who lived with us, was a whiz at doughs—whether for pasta, pastry, or pizza. But she became ill before I could learn them from her. The first few times I tried working with dough on my own were dismal failures. Any recipe I followed only had the instruction to "roll the dough." Well, roll I did: the dough stuck to the surface, the rolling pin, or both. Or it tore or cracked. If I managed to get it into a pie pan in one piece, it usually shrank in the oven. I happily baked cakes and cookies and an occasional fancy dessert—but no whipped-up egg whites, and definitely no dough.

I softened toward the egg whites first. After watching Julia Child whipping egg whites in a copper bowl, I went to the Bazar Français in New York City. The copper bowls were way beyond my budget, but the friendly owner, Mr. Ruegger, showed me a stainless steel bowl and then picked out a large balloon whip. I still use that bowl often, though I did eventually buy a copper one.

Next came the dough. I watched my aunt, the official American baker in our family, roll her pie dough made with vegetable shortening between two sheets of wax paper and gave it a try. My crust for a lemon meringue pie turned out pretty well, but my parents commented on the awful taste the shortening imparted. My grandmother had always used lard for her pastry, as is still the custom in southern Italy. So I tried making the crust with butter—it was a little more work but the crust tasted a lot better. Eventually, because I practiced a lot, even rolling became easier.

Over the years, I've shared many pastry dough recipes, from ridiculously easy to quite elaborate. In this book I've given you a range of doughs, as well as step-by-step photos, about how to prepare, roll, shape, and bake them. If you have a bad case of pastry-phobia or a fear of rolling, I can't guarantee a magic cure, but I can promise that if you follow the simple instructions here, you'll be able to tackle any pastry project you like.

Nick Malgieri, New York City, January 2014

CHAPTER 1

INGREDIENTS & EQUIPMENT

While keeping calm and practicing often are the keys to mastering pastry doughs, it's still important to use the correct ingredients and equipment if you want the recipes you try to turn out well. The building blocks of pastry doughs are flour, butter or occasionally oil or lard, and liquids that might be water, eggs, or even sour cream. Sugar, flavoring, and yeast also play an important part in some doughs, and the following brief descriptions of commonly used ingredients can guide you in purchasing the correct ones to use.

Equipment falls into two categories: The first covers equipment needed to prepare doughs and work with them, while the second, and equally important, pertains to the pans used for baking pastries. Pie and tart pans, large and small, flat baking pans for individual free-standing pastries, and alternative molds, such as muffin pans and gratin dishes, fall into the second category.

A steady hand, good ingredients only as far away as a local supermarket, and basic equipment available inexpensively in a hardware or cookware shop are all you need to successfully prepare all the recipes in this book.

INGREDIENTS

Flours

A wheat berry consists of three parts: a starchy endosperm, used to make white flour; an outer covering, or bran; and an oily germ. To produce flour, berries are milled and then sifted. Flour is made from either soft or hard wheat—the designation refers to the kernel's density. Hard wheat has a higher proportion of the proteins that will eventually form strong gluten in a dough. For this reason, flours made from hard wheat are referred to as strong flours. Soft wheat has a lower percentage of gluten-forming proteins and is used to make weak flour. Bread flour is a strong flour; cake flour, a weak one. All-purpose flour falls between the two.

All-purpose flour: All-purpose flour (standard white flour) is a mixture of strong and weak flours that has a 10.5 to 11.5 percent protein content. As its name implies, it's suitable for almost all uses and may be bleached or unbleached. Stored at room temperature in an airtight container, all-purpose flour will keep for at least one year.

Plain flour: Used in the UK, this has a lower protein content than American all-purpose flour, though it functions well in recipes for pastry doughs and cake and cookie batters.

Pastry flour: Pastry flour has a low protein content and a high starch content and is similar to the plain flour milled in the UK. In my experience, pastry flour is used in large quantity recipes for pastry doughs, because the increased mixing time required by the larger quantity might make a dough made with all-purpose flour begin to toughen.
For small quantities, it's not necessary to use pastry flour.

Bread flour: Bread flour is higher in protein, around 12 percent, which is desirable when making bread, other yeast doughs, and some doughs that are stretched or rolled paper thin, like strudel. Bread flour develops strong gluten, trapping gases formed during fermentation in bread and providing needed structure in paper-thin doughs.

High-gluten flour, as its name indicates, has a very high protein content, about 14 percent, producing doughs with very strong gluten. In this book it's used for yufka and baklava doughs.

Sugars

To make sugar, sugarcane is ground, then pressed to release its juice. This liquid is heated and centrifuged to produce sugar and molasses. The sugar is redissolved and purified with granular carbon, which is then filtered out along with the impurities it traps. Once purified, the sugar is processed to form crystals. The crystals are dried to remove any remaining moisture. Finally, the sugar is passed through a succession of sieves to separate the coarse crystals from the fine ones.

Sugar must be stored as airtight as possible, as it absorbs moisture from the air. It will last indefinitely, but if not properly stored, it will harden into a solid chunk.

Granulated sugar: All recipes in this book use granulated sugar—regular white sugar—unless otherwise specified. Granulated sugar is added gradually to most preparations, especially egg mixtures. Unbeaten egg yolks to which sugar is added quickly may lump and "burn," meaning the sugar absorbs so much of the yolk liquid on initial contact that the remaining yolk components harden, preventing the sugar from dissolving completely. Also, when you whip egg whites with sugar, a large quantity of sugar falling on the egg whites at one time can force air out of them.

Brown sugar: Brown sugar is made by blending refined sugar in its liquid form with molasses. The amount of molasses determines whether the sugar is light brown or dark brown. Brown sugar can dry out and harden into a block if left uncovered. Once you open the package, store it tightly covered, preferably in a plastic bag, in the refrigerator. If it hardens, you can place it in the microwave for a few seconds to soften it.

Turbinado sugar: Turbinado is a partially refined sugar that may be used interchangeably with light brown sugar.

Confectioners' sugar: Also known as powdered sugar or 10X sugar (because it is ten times finer than granulated sugar), confectioners' sugar is made from granulated sugar that has been ground to a powder. The confectioners' sugar sold in the United States includes a tiny amount of cornstarch, which prevents caking, but means it cannot be used in any kind of cooked sugar solution, as the cornstarch may burn. Confectioners' sugar is also not used in whipped cream, as it will turn the mixture chalky. Always sift it after measuring to eliminate lumps.

Salt

I prefer fine sea salt, and I use it when baking. For coarse salt I use additive-free kosher salt, or a specialty salt such as French fleur de sel or English Maldon salt. Check the side panel of any salt you buy: it should list only salt as an ingredient; anticaking agents impart a bitter taste and should be avoided.

Leaveners

Leaveners cause a dough or batter to rise by creating carbon dioxide. Below are the most common leaveners used in baking.

Baking powder: A chemical leavener, this is a mixture of bicarbonate of soda (baking soda, see below) and an acid element. In the past, tartrate baking powder included cream of tartar, a powerful acid. Today, most baking powder utilizes phosphate elements as the acid component. Starch, usually cornstarch, is also mixed in to stabilize the powder, as well as to absorb the excess moisture in the air, which would cause caking and lack of potency. Almost all baking powder available today is double-acting, meaning that it creates two chemical reactions that promote rising: first when combined with liquid, and second when exposed to heat. Keep baking powder in a dry spot and replace every six months. When I open a can, I write the date on the lid with a permanent marker.

Baking soda: Baking soda, or sodium bicarbonate, is an alkali, so it needs an acid to begin the leavening process in a dough. Such acids include buttermilk, yogurt, sour cream, molasses, honey, cocoa, chocolate, and cream of tartar. Always use only the amount of baking soda called for in the recipe, sift it over the other dry ingredients, and stir it in well to avoid pockets of undissolved baking soda, which will form lumps with an unpleasant chemical aftertaste. Any batter made with baking soda needs to be placed in a preheated oven fairly quickly, because baking soda reacts on contact with moisture and immediately begins producing the carbon dioxide that will leaven what you're making. Wait too long and you won't get nearly the impact you expect. Keep baking soda in a cool, dry spot and replace every six months. Baking soda also absorbs odors, so seal it tightly.

Yeast: A fungal leavener, yeast is suited to elastic, gluten-forming doughs that accommodate its slow development of carbon dioxide. Most recipes call for active dry yeast, which is granulated and comes in bulk packages of a pound or more, small jars, or individual envelopes, which contain 2¼ teaspoons (¼ ounce or 7 grams). Yeast is also available in small moist cakes and in instant form, which is faster-acting because of its finer granulation. All packaged yeast has an expiration date and should be kept in the refrigerator or freezer.

Fats

Fats have a bad reputation in our society, but there are few pleasing baked items without at least some fat in them. The choice of fat affects both the flavor and the texture of the finished product.

Butter: When it comes to butter, freshness is key. To test a stick of butter for freshness, scratch the surface with the tip of a table knife. Butter that has oxidized will be lighter on the inside than on the outside, and whatever you bake with it will taste stale. Store butter in the freezer and for long-term storage, keep it in its wrapper, sealed in plastic wrap and then foil. Always use unsalted butter for baking. While higher fat European-style butters are becoming more available, in this book I used only regular butter from the supermarket.

Oils: Oils are used in baked items in place of or in addition to butter, and frequently to coat pans. When vegetable oil is called for, safflower, peanut, and canola oils will all work. Look for "cold-pressed" oil—although US manufacturers are permitted to label oil as they wish, so the term has less meaning here than it does in Europe, where it's regulated. You will also see oils labeled "expeller-pressed," which means they have been expressed without chemical agents, but does not necessarily mean the oil was brought to a high temperature during processing, which can destroy its flavor. (It can also make the oil resistant to high heat, desirable at times for cooking but rarely for baking.) Experiment a little, find a brand you like, and use it.

Several recipes call for olive oil. It's fine to use whatever olive oil you habitually have on hand, whether extra-virgin or pure.

Lard: The best lard to use for baking is rendered from leaf lard, a layer of hard fat from the belly area of a pig. An old-fashioned butcher shop or a farmers' market vendor who sells pork products are the only places you'll find leaf lard. Most lard you find in the supermarket is rendered from pork fat in general and is softer than leaf lard. Outside the United States, lard is used in pastry dough preparation and cooking in general. Good-quality lard is a lot better tasting and more healthful than chemically rendered oils and solid shortenings.

Liquids

Liquids are an essential part of most pastry doughs, water being the most common.

Water: Today we don't give much thought to water, but it does have a taste, and the water used in baked goods does impart flavor and affect the results. If you live in an area with particularly hard water, meaning it has a high mineral content, you may want to consider using bottled water for baking. Unless otherwise specified, water added to pastry dough should always be chilled.

Milk and other dairy products: Cow's milk and its derivatives—butter (see page 9), milk, cream, sour cream, yogurt, and cheese—make up the baker's dairy ingredients. For baking, choose whole (full-fat) milk; this goes for other dairy products as well. Throughout the Western world, the milk sold in stores is pasteurized to kill bacteria. Most milk is also homogenized to keep the cream from separating to the top. While convenient, this does remove some of the flavor.

Buttermilk: Low in fat yet rich in texture, buttermilk lends moisture and tenderness. Originally, buttermilk was the liquid left over after slightly fermented cream was churned into butter; the ferments in the cream imparted a tangy flavor to the buttermilk. Now buttermilk is created by combining low-fat milk with cultures similar to those used in yogurt.

Cream: Heavy whipping cream has a fat content of 36 percent, which is why it whips to a silky and luxurious consistency. When I call for half-and-half, I mean traditional half-and-half (about 18 percent butterfat).

Sour cream: Again, use only full-fat sour cream. Nonfat versions will not yield the same results. Sour cream in the United States is made from half-and-half and has the same fat content.

Eggs

Eggs are the workhorses of the pastry kitchen. With few exceptions, it would be almost impossible to bake classic pastries without them. Sometimes the whole egg is used, and sometimes just the yolks or whites. No matter how eggs are used, they bind other ingredients like flour, sugar, and butter; act as leaveners; enrich and moisten; thicken mixtures; emulsify liquids; and glaze pastries and doughs.

The egg white, or albumen, makes up about two-thirds of the total weight of the egg, providing over half the protein. When whipped, the white will increase in volume six to eight times. The yolk accounts for the remaining third of the total weight of the egg and contains all the fat and a bit less than half the protein.

Eggs are categorized by grade and size. Grade is based on the inner and outer quality of the egg, while size is determined by the average weight per dozen. A dozen eggs graded US large weigh 24 ounces. However, within the dozen there may be variations. Some recipes, notably those for certain meringues, call for heating egg whites without completely cooking them. If you are concerned about eating uncooked eggs, substitute pasteurized egg whites.

Buy eggs with clean, uncracked shells. (There is no difference in quality or nutrition between brown and white eggs.) Store eggs large ends up in their cartons in the refrigerator and use them before their expiration date. Also, eggs absorb odors, so keep them away from strong-flavored foods. Extra egg whites can be kept covered in the refrigerator for up to ten days. To store yolks, sprinkle them lightly with water, press plastic wrap on the surface, and refrigerate for no longer than two days.

A final note: Crack your eggs one at a time into a small cup before adding them to the other ingredients. Encountering a rotten egg is fairly rare (and you'll recognize one immediately when it turns up), but if one egg is bad and you've cracked it into the main bowl, you'll have to toss the entire mixture.

EQUIPMENT

Pans

Tart pans: Tart pans have removable bottoms and fluted sides; sometimes these are labeled "French tart pans." They will be of various diameters, but the sides should be 1 inch high.

Pie pans: I always prefer a Pyrex pie pan, because the glass makes it easier to see the degree of doneness on the bottom crust, and glass heats better than metal, ensuring a well-baked pastry. If you're going to buy only one, choose a 9-inch pan with sloping sides.

Individual and mini tart pans: This is one place where you can substitute. Ramekins and muffin pans can stand in for these smaller-sized pans.

Baking pans: Baking pan size might seem flexible, but in most cases it's not. A smaller pan may not hold all the dough and filling to be baked, and a larger one will cause it to be spread too thin. Cake layer pans are round pans that are 2 inches deep, sometimes slightly shallower in Europe. For rectangular pans, I use 9 x 13 x 2-inch pans, 10 x 15 x 1-inch jelly-roll pans and 12 x 17 x 1-inch commercial half-sheet pans. In addition to baking cookies, flat unrimmed cookie sheets are useful for moving dough and cake layers and for chilling pieces of dough. If you find your oven gives off strong heat from the bottom, insulated cookie sheets are worth the expense (but use them only on that bottom shelf). You can also stack two pans for a similar effect.

Tools

Rolling pins: I prefer the dowel type of rolling pin without handles—it's basically a straight cylinder of wood, about 16 inches long and 2 inches in diameter. Nylon rolling pins can also be useful, because dough won't stick to them as easily. For rolling yufka and baklava dough, I use a ⅞-inch diameter dowel that is 24 inches long (dowels are usually 48 inches in length, so one dowel will make two rolling pins). A 5/16-inch diameter dowel is used for forming one of the baklava pastries here.

Scrapers: A bench scraper is a rectangular stainless-steel blade—usually about 3 x 5 inches—set in a wooden handle. It is used for keeping the work surface free of stuck dough and for cutting dough into pieces. A bowl scraper, made from rubber or plastic, is a useful tool for cleaning out the inside of a mixing bowl, filling a pastry bag, or smoothing a batter or filling with a flat edge.

Cutters: Cutters are used to punch regularly shaped pieces out of rolled doughs. Though they may not seem dangerous, cookie cutters are just as sharp as knives, so work with them carefully. They are usually made from tinned steel or good-quality hard plastic. Sets of graduated sizes of round cutters come in plain and fluted styles.

Pizza wheels: Pizza wheels are useful for cutting various doughs. They come with either straight or serrated wheels, and some are two-in-one, meaning they have a wheel of each type on either end of the handle.

CHAPTER 2

A WHOLE NEW GENERATION OF DOUGHS

For this book, I've developed new doughs alongside some of my old favorites that are as easy to prepare as they are to use. Whether you do this by hand or use a stand mixer or food processor, these doughs are ready quickly. And while most of them benefit from a short rest in the refrigerator before being rolled and formed into a crust, some can be rolled out immediately after mixing.

I like to categorize doughs in two ways: those that have a visible internal structure and those that are merely smooth pastes. The former are the flaky doughs that have tiny pieces of fat randomly sprinkled throughout; when the dough is rolled, the pieces of fat become irregular layers that fill with steam and puff slightly in the oven. The latter are the doughs based on liquid fats or in which solid fat is smoothly mixed with the rest of the ingredients, as for sweetened doughs.

All simple pastry doughs, whether flaky or smooth, should be tender after baking. A large part of that tenderness is due to the proportions of the ingredients, but it is also important to handle the dough minimally during mixing and allow the rolled-out crusts to chill before baking.

If you've had difficulties with pastry doughs in the past, try these recipes; I know you'll be successful with them.

OLIVE OIL DOUGH

Makes enough for 1 large tart or single-crusted pie (double the quantities for a double crust), or 8 or 9 individual 4½-inch tarts

1½ cups/200 grams unbleached all-purpose flour (spoon into dry-measure cup and level)

1 teaspoon fine sea salt

1 teaspoon sugar

1 teaspoon baking powder

¼ cup/80 grams olive oil

2 large eggs

PLANNING AHEAD
This dough keeps well in the refrigerator for up to 3 days.

VARIATIONS
Use a vegetable oil such as organic, cold-pressed safflower oil for a milder flavor.
Double all the ingredients for a two-crust pie.

This is my new favorite dough for savory tarts and pies—it is easy to prepare, rolls out like a dream, and bakes to a tender texture. There's just enough olive oil flavor to complement the filling it surrounds. It's a perfect example of the fact that baking doesn't have to be complicated to be good. You can substitute this dough for Flaky Buttery Dough in any of the savory tart or pie recipes.

1. Use a fork to stir together the flour, salt, sugar, and baking powder in a medium bowl.

2. Make a well in the center of the dry ingredients and add the oil and eggs. Use the fork to beat the eggs and oil together, then gradually draw in the dry ingredients a little at a time until the dough starts to hold together.

3. Scrape the contents of the bowl to a lightly floured work surface (it's okay if there are still some dry bits) and fold the dough over on itself 4 or 5 times, gently kneading it smooth. Kneading too much might make the oil separate from the dough.

4. Wrap the dough in plastic and keep at a cool room temperature if you're using within a few hours; refrigerate for longer storage.

FLAKY BUTTERY DOUGH

Makes enough for 2 single-crusted pies or 1 double-crusted pie

2⅓ cups/315 grams unbleached all-purpose flour (spoon into dry-measure cup and level)

½ teaspoon fine sea salt

1 teaspoon baking powder

8 ounces/2 sticks/225 grams unsalted butter, chilled and cut into ½-inch pieces

2 large eggs

PLANNING AHEAD
This dough keeps well in the refrigerator for up to 3 days.

To maximize flakiness and get as much delicate buttery flavor as possible, you need to use enough butter in a dough. If you remember to chill this dough after mixing it and again after rolling it, you'll enjoy both a superior texture and flavor. To keep from melting the butter and creating an excessively soft dough, this is best mixed in the food processor.

1. Combine the flour, salt, and baking powder in the bowl of a food processor; pulse several times at 1-second intervals to mix.

2. Add the butter and pulse again 3 or 4 times. Use a metal spatula to scrape the side of the bowl and mix the butter pieces throughout the flour.

3. Pulse again 3 or 4 times.

4. Using a fork, beat the eggs to break them up, then add to the bowl. Pulse again until the dough almost forms a ball; avoid pulsing too much, or the pieces of butter needed to make the dough flaky will become too small.

5. Invert the dough onto a lightly floured work surface, carefully remove the blade, and quickly press the dough together.

6. Divide the dough into 2 pieces, form into thick disks, and wrap each in plastic. Chill for a couple of hours before rolling.

FLAKY DOUGH USING LARD

Since I grew up on southern Italian food that used lard in both cooking and baking, I've never had an aversion to it. And while I support anyone's desire to avoid pork products for religious reasons, I don't quite understand the general aversion to lard. It certainly tastes better and is much healthier than chemically rendered vegetable shortening with or without trans fats. Even if you only have access to lard from the supermarket, try this recipe for a savory tart or pie or something simple and rustic like an apple pie, and you'll see why many people swear by lard for pie dough. This dough is best mixed by hand and you can substitute it for Flaky Buttery Dough in any savory recipe. It also works well in some less delicate sweet tarts and pies, such as the Apple & Cheddar Pie on page 88.

Makes enough for 2 single-crusted pies or 1 double-crusted pie

2 cups/270 grams unbleached all-purpose flour
(spoon into dry-measure cup and level)

½ teaspoon fine sea salt

1 teaspoon baking powder

⅓ cup ice water

12 tablespoons/170 grams lard, chilled and cut into ½-inch pieces

1. Use a fork to stir together the flour, salt, and baking powder in a medium bowl.

2. Pour the water into a small bowl or cup, and then measure ¼ cup of it, leaving the rest in the bowl. Set both aside.

3. Add the lard to the dry ingredients and use both hands with your fingers apart to reach to the bottom of the bowl and lift upward through the pieces of lard ① so that they're all coated with flour and evenly mixed throughout.

4. Gently rub the pieces of lard into the flour using your fingertips, occasionally repeating the motion in step 3, until the lard is reduced to ¼-inch pieces, about 30 seconds ②.

5. Pour the ¼ cup water all over the surface of the flour and lard mixture ③, then use the fork to toss upward from the bottom of the bowl, until the water is evenly mixed throughout ④. If there are a lot of dry bits in the dough, use some of the remaining water a little at a time, repeating the tossing motion with the fork, until the dough starts holding together easily ⑤.

6. Invert the dough onto a lightly floured work surface and quickly press it together.

7. Divide the dough into 2 pieces and wrap each in plastic. Chill for 2 hours before rolling.

VARIATION
FLAKY DOUGH MADE WITH LARD AND BUTTER: For a milder flavor, replace half the lard with an equal amount of butter, adding the butter first and rubbing it in a little before adding the lard.

PASTY DOUGH

Makes enough for 6 large pasties or 12 small

3¾ cups/500 grams unbleached bread flour (spoon into dry-measure cup and level)

1½ teaspoons fine sea salt

10 tablespoons/1¼ sticks/140 grams unsalted butter, cold, cut into ¼-inch cubes

¾ cup + 2 tablespoons/200 grams cold water

This unusual dough is reserved exclusively for making Cornish-style pasties on page 125. While most of the recipes that pasty makers have revealed call for vegetable shortening, I was bent on using only butter, but I was afraid that butter might not survive the vigorous mixing that the dough needs. Fortunately, butter held its own, resulting in a dough with the right degree of elasticity for making pasties as well as excellent flavor.

1. Stir the flour and salt together in the bowl of an electric mixer. Stir in the butter and place the bowl on the mixer fitted with the paddle attachment. Mix on the lowest speed until the butter is finely worked into the flour, 3 to 4 minutes.

2. Scrape the bowl and beater and attach the dough hook. Start mixing on the lowest speed and pour in the water in a stream. Mix until the dough is evenly moistened and masses around the hook. If some dry bits remain unmoistened at the bottm of the bowl, add up to a tablespoon more water, a little at a time, until no dry flour remains.

3. Increase the speed to low/medium and beat until smooth and elastic, 2 to 3 minutes longer.

4. Transfer the dough to a floured work surface and knead by hand for a minute or two. Divide the dough into six 5-ounce/140-gram pieces or twelve 2 ½-ounce/70-gram pieces and round them smoothly. Wrap individually in plastic wrap, place in a bowl, and chill for several hours before rolling.

SOUR CREAM DOUGH

Makes enough for the top crust of a large savory pie or sweet cobbler or 8 empanadas

2 cups/270 grams unbleached all-purpose flour (spoon into dry-measure cup and level)

½ teaspoon fine sea salt

8 ounces/2 sticks/225 grams unsalted butter, chilled and cut into 20 pieces

⅔ cup/150 grams sour cream

My dear late friend Sheri Portwood ran a Dallas catering business for years and was constantly trying to perfect her recipe for rugelach, which uses this dough. I've included recipes for rugelach in several other books, but I love this dough as the top of a deep-dish savory pie, a cobbler (especially when it's cut into separate overlapping disks for the top crust), or for any top-crust-only pie. It's flaky, extremely tender, and delicate, almost like puff pastry. A food processor does the best job of mixing this.

1. Combine the flour and salt in the bowl of a food processor and pulse several times at 1-second intervals to mix.

2. Add the butter and pulse until it's finely mixed into the flour and no visible pieces remain.

3. Spread the sour cream all over on the top of the flour and butter mixture (rather than adding it all in one spot). Pulse 3 or 4 times; if the dough is already starting to form a ball, stop pulsing; if not, pulse a few more times but don't overmix or the flaky quality of the dough will be lost.

4. Invert the dough onto a lightly floured work surface. Shape into a disk and wrap in plastic.

5. Chill the dough for 2 to 3 hours or overnight before using.

YEAST-RISEN DOUGH FOR EMPANADAS

This dough is similar to that used for the Spanish pie or empanada Gallega in my bread book. Although the empanada in the original recipe is a large pie, this also works very well for turnover-type empanadas. A half recipe of this dough can also make an excellent single crust for a savory pie or tart. You can use this dough for any of the empanada recipes.

1. Mix the flour with the sugar and salt and set aside.

2. Whisk the water and yeast together by hand in the bowl of an electric mixer, then whisk in the oil and egg. Use a large rubber spatula to stir in the flour mixture.

3. Place the bowl on the mixer fitted with the dough hook and beat on the lowest speed until fairly smooth, about 2 minutes. Remove the dough from the mixer and knead for a minute.

4. Place the dough in a lightly oiled bowl and turn it so that the top is oiled. Cover the bowl with plastic wrap, and let the dough ferment until it doubles in bulk, 30 to 45 minutes.

5. Divide the dough into twelve 2-ounce/60 gram pieces. Form into even disks, place on a floured pan, cover with plastic wrap, and chill until they are firm enough to roll, about 1 hour.

Makes about 1½ pounds/675 grams, enough for about 12 empanadas

3 cups/400 grams unbleached all-purpose flour (spoon into a dry-measure cup and level)

1½ teaspoons sugar

1½ teaspoons fine sea salt

¾ cup/170 grams room-temperature (about 75°F) tap water

2¼ teaspoons fine granulated active dry or instant yeast

½ cup/100 grams olive oil, plus more for brushing

1 large egg

CORNMEAL DOUGH

Makes enough for 1 large tart or single-crusted pie

⅔ cup/90 grams unbleached all-purpose flour (spoon into dry-measure cup and level)

⅔ cup/112 grams stone-ground yellow cornmeal

1 teaspoon fine sea salt

1 teaspoon sugar

1 teaspoon baking powder

8 tablespoons/1 stick/112 grams unsalted butter, chilled and cut into 12 pieces

1 large egg

PLANNING AHEAD

This dough keeps well in the refrigerator for up to 3 days.

The slightly sweet and nutty flavor of cornmeal pairs well with many savory or sweet fillings. I also love this dough because it bakes to a slightly crunchy but tender texture. It's especially good as a cobbler topping. Please be sure to use stone-ground cornmeal for this; it's both more finely milled and has much more corn flavor than the typical degerminated cornmeal available in the supermarket. You can substitute this dough for Flaky Buttery Dough in any of the savory tart or pie recipes.

1. Combine the flour, cornmeal, salt, sugar, and baking powder in the bowl of a food processor and pulse several times at 1-second intervals to mix.

2. Add the butter and pulse again repeatedly until it is finely mixed into the dry ingredients.

3. Add the egg and pulse again until the dough just starts to form a ball.

4. Invert the dough onto a lightly floured surface and quickly press it together.

5. Form the dough into a disk shape and wrap in plastic. Refrigerate until needed.

VARIATION

CORNMEAL DOUGH WITH CHEESE OR HERBS: Add ½ cup coarsely grated Gruyère or cheddar and/or 1 tablespoon chopped flat-leaf parsley, cilantro, or finely snipped chives, along with the butter.

SWEET PASTRY DOUGH MADE WITH OIL

Makes enough for 1 large tart or single-crusted pie

1¼ cups/170 grams unbleached all-purpose flour (spoon into dry-measure cup and level)

2 tablespoons sugar

½ teaspoon baking powder

¼ teaspoon fine sea salt

3 tablespoons expeller-pressed safflower oil, preferably organic

2 tablespoons water

1 large egg

PLANNING AHEAD

This dough keeps well in the refrigerator for up to 3 days.

This dough is a fraternal twin to both the unsweetened olive oil dough (page 14) and the butter-based sweet pastry dough opposite. It has the advantage of being really easy to prepare and to roll, and is ready to go immediately after it's mixed. I always use an organic expeller-pressed safflower oil to make this. Other easily available oils, especially ones that have fat chemically extracted from seeds or nuts, give an off taste to a delicate dough like this. I experimented with using nut oils, but since the nut flavor almost entirely dissipates while the dough is baking, I couldn't justify the added expense involved in using them. You can substitute this dough for the Sweet Pastry Dough made with butter that follows.

1. Use a fork to stir together the flour, sugar, baking powder, and salt in a medium bowl.

2. Make a well in the center of the dry ingredients and add the oil, water, and egg. Use the fork to beat the liquids together, then begin to draw in the dry ingredients a little at a time until the dough starts to hold together.

3. Scrape the contents of the bowl (it's okay if there are still some dry bits) onto a lightly floured work surface and fold the dough over on itself 4 or 5 times, gently kneading it smooth. Kneading too much might make the oil separate from the dough.

4. Wrap the dough in plastic and keep at a cool room temperature if you're using it within a few hours, or refrigerate for longer storage.

SWEET PASTRY DOUGH

This is the same recipe as my sweet dough from *BAKE!* and several other books that I've been using successfully for over thirty years and have taught to thousands of people. I thought of doing something different just for the sake of having something new but then decided that the ease of preparation and handling, plus the tender quality of this dough after baking, can't be improved upon. Below are the food processor instructions, and after the recipe, you'll find instructions for working by hand and for using a stand mixer.

1. Combine the flour, sugar, baking powder, and salt in the bowl of a food processor; pulse several times at 1-second intervals to mix.

2. Add the butter and pulse again until the butter is finely mixed throughout the dry ingredients and no visible pieces remain.

3. Use a fork to beat the eggs enough to break them up, and add to the bowl. Pulse again until the dough almost forms a ball; avoid pulsing too much or the dough might become too soft.

4. Invert the dough onto a lightly floured work surface and gently knead together 3 or 4 times to make it smooth.

5. Divide the dough into 2 pieces, form them into disks, and wrap each in plastic. Chill for a couple of hours before rolling.

6. Before rolling the dough, place it on a floured surface and gently knead until smooth and malleable. Form into a disk again before beginning to roll.

VARIATIONS

To mix the dough by hand, stir the dry ingredients together in a medium mixing bowl. Add the butter and use your fingertips to rub the butter into the dry ingredients, occasionally using your hands to scrape the bottom of the bowl and incorporate any unmixed flour. Once the butter is finely mixed throughout and no visible pieces of butter remain, use a fork to beat the eggs to break them up; add them to the bowl. Use the fork to scrape up from the bottom of the bowl and incorporate the eggs. You can also stir with the fork while using the other hand to move the bowl back and forth on the work surface. Once the dough starts holding together, continue with step 4.

To mix the dough in a stand mixer, combine the dry ingredients in the mixer bowl and place on the mixer fitted with the paddle attachment. Mix on the lowest speed for a few seconds, then add the butter and mix until it begins to break down into smaller pieces, about 30 seconds. Stop and scrape the bowl and beater, then repeat 30 seconds of mixing, followed by stopping and scraping, until the butter is finely worked into the dry ingredients and no visible pieces remain. Whisk the eggs to break them up; add to the bowl and mix again on the lowest speed until the dough begins to hold together, then continue with step 4.

Makes enough for 2 single-crusted pies or tarts or 1 double-crusted pie

2 cups/260 grams unbleached all-purpose flour (spoon into dry-measure cup and level)

⅓ cup/75 grams sugar

½ teaspoon baking powder

¼ teaspoon fine sea salt

8 tablespoons/1 stick/112 grams unsalted butter, chilled and cut into 12 pieces

2 large eggs

PLANNING AHEAD

This dough keeps well in the refrigerator for up to 3 days.

FRENCH-STYLE COOKIE DOUGH (PÂTE SABLÉE)

Makes enough for 2 large tarts or a dozen individual 4½-inch tarts

8 ounces/2 sticks/225 grams unsalted butter, slightly softened

1 cup/112 grams confectioners' sugar, sifted after measuring

2 teaspoons vanilla extract

½ teaspoon lemon extract, optional

2 large egg yolks

2½ cups/340 grams unbleached all-purpose flour (spoon into dry-measure cup and level)

PLANNING AHEAD

This dough keeps well in the refrigerator for up to 3 days.

There's nothing better for a tart assembled in a fully baked sweet crust than this type of cookie dough. It's sweet, slightly crumbly, and perfectly complements the filling—usually tangy citrus curd or velvety pastry cream topped with delicate fruit and berries. Good cookie dough is soft; it's not so easy to work with but provides a crisp and delicate crust for many sweet tarts both large and small.

1. Beat the butter and confectioners' sugar on the lowest speed in a stand mixer fitted with the paddle attachment until well mixed, then increase the speed to medium and beat until lightened, about 3 minutes.

2. Add the extracts, then the egg yolks, one at a time, beating after each addition until the mixture is smooth.

3. Use a rubber spatula to scrape the bowl and beater and beat in the flour on the lowest speed.

4. Scrape the dough onto a lightly floured work surface and gently knead it together 3 or 4 times to make it smooth.

5. Divide the dough into 2 pieces, form them into disks, and wrap each one in plastic. Chill the dough for a couple of hours before rolling.

ALMOND COOKIE DOUGH

Makes enough for 2 large tarts

2 cups/270 grams unbleached all-purpose flour (spoon into dry-measure cup and level)

1 cup/112 grams finely ground blanched almonds, sifted

12 tablespoons/1½ sticks/170 grams unsalted butter, slightly softened

1 cup/112 grams confectioners' sugar, sifted after measuring

2 teaspoons vanilla extract

½ teaspoon lemon extract, optional

2 large egg yolks

PLANNING AHEAD

This dough keeps well in the refrigerator for up to 3 days.

Most cookie doughs enhanced with ground nuts don't have enough added to make much of a difference in the dough's taste or texture. This dough is loaded with ground almonds, so it has great flavor and a crumbly quality that sets it apart. While any ground nuts would work, blanched almonds are my choice for the delicate flavor and texture they impart.

1. Stir the flour and ground almonds together and set them aside.

2. Beat the butter and confectioners' sugar on the lowest speed in a stand mixer fitted with the paddle attachment until well mixed, then increase the speed to medium and beat until lightened, about 3 minutes.

3. Add the extracts, then the egg yolks, one at a time, beating after each addition until the mixture is smooth.

4. Use a rubber spatula to scrape down the bowl and beater and beat in the flour mixture on the lowest speed.

5. Scrape the dough onto a lightly floured work surface and gently knead it together 3 or 4 times to make it smooth.

6. Divide the dough into 2 pieces, form them into disks, and wrap each one in plastic. Chill the dough for a couple of hours before rolling.

SWEET COCOA DOUGH

This is a slight variation on my favorite, Sweet Pastry Dough (page 19), and is just as easy to prepare and use. I like alkalized (Dutch-process) cocoa best for this because it has a more chocolaty color and delicate flavor than natural cocoa. Follow the instructions in the Sweet Pastry Dough recipe if you want to mix by hand or in a stand mixer.

1. Combine the flour, cocoa, sugar, baking powder, and salt in the bowl of a food processor; pulse several times at 1-second intervals to mix.

2. Add the butter and pulse again until the butter is finely mixed throughout the dry ingredients and no visible pieces remain.

3. Use a fork to beat the egg enough to break it up, then add it to the bowl. Pulse again until the dough almost forms a ball; avoid pulsing too much or the dough might become too soft.

4. Invert the dough onto a lightly floured work surface and gently knead it together 3 or 4 times to make it smooth.

5. Form the dough into a disk and wrap it in plastic. Chill it for a couple of hours before rolling.

6. Before rolling the dough, place it on a floured surface and gently knead until smooth and malleable. Form into a disk again before beginning to roll.

Makes enough for 1 large tart or single-crusted pie

1 cup/135 grams unbleached all-purpose flour (spoon into dry-measure cup and level)

3 tablespoons alkalized (Dutch-process) cocoa, sifted after measuring

3 tablespoons sugar

½ teaspoon baking powder

¼ teaspoon fine sea salt

5 tablespoons/70 grams unsalted butter, chilled and cut into 8 pieces

1 large egg

PLANNING AHEAD

This dough keeps well in the refrigerator for up to 3 days.

CHOCOLATE COOKIE DOUGH

This dough has real chocolate flavor and an extremely delicate texture after baking, making it particularly well suited to individual and miniature tarts. Use the best quality chocolate you can get, but be sure it's labeled semisweet; darker chocolate might make the dough too bitter.

1. Stir the flour and confectioners' sugar together and set aside.

2. Place the butter in a bowl and use a large rubber spatula to beat it smooth. Scrape in the chocolate and stir it into the butter (if the chocolate is still warm, the butter will melt and the dough will be ruined).

3. Add the flour mixture and stir it in to form a soft dough.

4. Scrape the dough out onto a piece of plastic wrap and cover it with more wrap. Press the dough with the palm of your hand to make it about ½ inch thick. Slide the dough onto a plate or cookie sheet and refrigerate until it is firm, 1 to 2 hours.

5. As this dough becomes very hard when chilled, soften it for 20 to 30 minutes at room temperature, then knead it together until malleable.

NOTE

The butter has to be softened to the consistency of mayonnaise—if it's firmer, it won't mix evenly with the cooled chocolate. If you forgot to soften the butter, cut it into small cubes and microwave it for no more than 3 seconds at a time until it is very soft. Don't let the butter melt, or the dough won't have the right texture.

Makes enough for 2 large tarts or single-crusted pies or 12 individual 4½-inch tarts or at least 36 tartlets or barquettes

2½ cups/340 grams unbleached all-purpose flour (spoon into dry-measure cup and level)

½ cup/60 grams confectioners' sugar, sifted after measuring

8 ounces/2 sticks/225 grams unsalted butter, very soft (see Note)

6 ounces/170 grams semisweet chocolate (no more than 60 percent cocoa solids), melted and cooled to room temperature

PLANNING AHEAD

This dough keeps well in the refrigerator for up to 3 days.

NUT BISCUIT BATTER (FOR COOKIE DOUGH CRUSTS)

Makes enough for a 10-inch tart

2 tablespoons unbleached all-purpose flour

2 tablespoons sugar

1 large egg

Pinch of salt

½ teaspoon vanilla extract

¼ cup/about 1 ounce ground nuts

2 tablespoons unsalted butter, melted

This buttery batter is spread on the bottom of a cookie dough tart crust before it's baked. It adds richness, a note of flavor, and most of all, prevents the crust from softening by absorbing any liquid draining from fruit or other filling in the tart.

1. Whisk the flour and sugar together in a medium bowl; add the egg and whisk smooth.

2. Whisk in the salt and vanilla, then use a small rubber spatula to fold in the nuts and butter.

3. Follow steps 1 through 3 in Baking an Empty Crust for a Tart or Pie (page 37), using the cookie crust and tart pan of your choice. Spread the nut biscuit batter into the crust. Do not line the crust with paper and beans; instead, skip to step 6 and bake the crust until it is completely baked through, 20 to 25 minutes.

Using Scraps of Dough

While all the pastry dough recipes in the previous pages are calculated to provide the right amount of dough for the pan size required, you may still accumulate some dough scraps after trimming a crust once it's safely in its baking pan. If you have just a couple of tablespoons of dough scraps, you can reroll them and use a round or decorative cutter to make a few decorations for the top of a double-crusted pie. But if you have a handful of scraps, use one of the procedures below to make some little treats from them.

USING SCRAPS OF UNSWEETENED DOUGH: These may be treated the same way as the sweet dough scraps below or used to make a savory snack. Form the scraps into a square and wrap and chill if the dough has become soft. Place the square of dough on a floured surface and flour it; roll it to a rectangle twice as long as it is wide. Spray or brush the dough with water and sprinkle some grated dry cheese, fresh or dried herbs, or even some coarse salt and freshly ground pepper on the bottom half of the dough. Fold the top half of the dough down to enclose the seasonings and press well. Roll again to almost the original size and use a pizza wheel to cut the dough into ¼-inch-wide strips. Transfer them to a parchment-covered pan and bake them at 350°F until golden and dry, about 15 minutes.

USING SCRAPS OF SWEETENED DOUGH: Proceed as above, rolling the dough to a rectangle and spraying with water. Use some cinnamon sugar with or without the addition of ground nuts to cover half the dough. Fold, roll, cut, and bake as above.

Gluten-Free Doughs

These recipes were both shared by Michelle Tampakis, our gluten-free baking expert at the Institute of Culinary Education and a friend and colleague for more than thirty years. After discovering her gluten allergy, she plunged wholeheartedly into working with alternative flours and has developed delicious recipes in every category of baked goods—her rice flour pasta and her gluten-free brioche are both outstanding. She now owns and operates Whipped Pastry Boutique, a gluten-free bakery.

Chances are that if you have wheat sensitivities of any kind, you won't be reading this book, but many readers might be inspired to prepare a pie or tart for someone who is gluten intolerant. There are quite a few pie and tart fillings that contain no flour, which would pair well with these doughs. Please remember, though, that if you decide to bake for someone who can't have wheat, you'll have to scrupulously clean all your vessels, utensils, and work areas; even a minuscule amount of flour could cause a life-threatening reaction in someone with a severe allergy.

Both the following doughs bake up crisp and flavorful. The unsweetened dough is best when fully baked and finished with a filling that needs little or no subsequent baking. The sweet cookie dough is similar but, because of its particularly inelastic nature, is best suited for individual or miniature tarts. With these limitations in mind, substitute these doughs in any recipes that have gluten-free fillings.

UNSWEETENED GLUTEN-FREE DOUGH

Makes enough for 1 large tart or single-crusted pie

- ⅔ cup/75 grams brown rice flour
- ⅓ cup/38 grams potato starch
- ¼ cup/15 grams white rice flour
- ¼ cup/15 grams tapioca flour
- 1 tablespoon sugar
- 1 teaspoon fine sea salt
- 8 tablespoons/1 stick/112 grams unsalted butter, chilled and cut into 12 pieces
- 3 tablespoons ice water
- 1 teaspoon distilled white vinegar

1. Combine all the dry ingredients in the bowl of a food processor and pulse several times at 1-second intervals to mix.

2. Add the butter and pulse again until the ingredients are finely blended but still mealy.

3. Mix the water and vinegar together and add to the bowl. Pulse again until the dough forms a ball.

4. Invert the dough onto the work surface. Mold the dough into a disk, wrap in plastic, and chill until firm, about 1 hour.

PLANNING AHEAD
This dough keeps well in the refrigerator for up to 3 days.

GLUTEN-FREE COOKIE DOUGH

Since this dough is sweetened with confectioners' sugar, be sure to read the side panel of the package: Some confectioners' sugar might contain wheat starch and therefore not be entirely gluten free. This keeps in the refrigerator for up to 3 days.

Makes enough for 2 large tarts or 10 to 12 individual tarts

- 1½ cups/170 grams sorghum flour
- ¾ cup/85 grams brown rice flour
- ¼ cup/30 grams tapioca flour
- 2 tablespoons/15 grams potato starch
- ¼ cup/50 grams granulated sugar
- ¼ cup/25 grams confectioners' sugar, sifted after measuring
- ½ teaspoon fine sea salt
- 12 tablespoons/1½ sticks/170 grams unsalted butter, chilled and cut into 20 pieces
- 1 large egg
- 1 large egg yolk
- 1 teaspoon vanilla extract

1. Combine all the dry ingredients in the bowl of a food processor and pulse several times at 1-second intervals to mix.

2. Add the butter and pulse again until the ingredients are finely blended but still mealy.

3. Mix the egg, egg yolk, and vanilla together and add to the bowl. Pulse again until the dough forms a ball.

4. Invert the dough onto the work surface. Mold the dough into a disk, wrap in plastic, and chill until firm, about 1 hour.

ROLLING GLUTEN-FREE DOUGHS & FORMING TART CRUSTS

BAKING GLUTEN-FREE TART CRUSTS

See the instructions for blind-baking tart crusts on page 37. Be careful not to overbake a gluten-free crust, or it will become very hard.

Unlike most pastries, you can't dust the surface of gluten-free doughs with any sort of flour for rolling—the sticky nature of these doughs only makes them absorb more and more of it as you roll. Because of this, they have to be rolled between pieces of parchment or wax paper and chilled before being transferred to the pan.

1. Have two large squares of parchment paper and a thin cookie sheet or flexible cutting board ready before beginning to roll.

2. Place one of the squares of paper on your work surface and center the chilled dough on it. Cover it with the second piece of paper ①.

3. Press gently with your rolling pin in successive strikes that are parallel to each other and to the edge of the work surface. Turn the whole package of dough and paper 30 degrees and repeat.

4. After the dough has softened slightly, roll it as for any other dough ②, from 6 o'clock to 12 o'clock and back again without rolling over the edges and rotating the dough 30 degrees after every set of rolls.

5. Once the dough is large enough for your pan ③, slide the package of dough and papers onto your cookie sheet and chill until it is firm, 15 to 20 minutes.

6. Once the dough has chilled, spray your tart pan with vegetable cooking spray. Carefully peel off the top paper and quickly invert the dough ④, centering it over the pan.

7. Peel away the second paper and gently ease the dough into the bottom and against the side of the pan all around ⑤, allowing any extra to hang over the top edge.

8. Roll over the top of the pan with your rolling pin to remove any excess dough ⑥. Finish off the top edge of the crust by pressing against the side of the dough with your thumb and down from the top at the same time.

9. For individual tart crusts, roll the dough to a square, then use scissors to cut it into squares large enough to cover the bottom and sides of your pans. Follow steps 6 to 8 with the individual squares of dough.

ROLLING SIMPLE PASTRY DOUGHS

Rolling dough is easy; millions—probably billions—of people can do it, and so can you. Over the years, I've developed some specific methods for teaching people how to do it successfully, and they are listed here.

1. Always start with chilled dough; the only exception is dough that's made with oil.

2. Flaky doughs and cookie doughs need to soften briefly at room temperature before being rolled, but be careful not to wait too long if the room is warm.

3. Sweet doughs have to be floured and kneaded briefly until malleable.

4. Before rolling any dough, ease it into the shape needed for the pan. For a round pan, form it into a rough disk shape ①; for a square or rectangular pan, form it into a square. Only press in on the sides of your piece of dough; don't fold it over on itself or roll it into a ball. The only exception is the sweet dough.

5. Once you have the shape you need, flour the work surface with pinches of flour and place the dough on it. Flour the top of the dough. Using pinches of flour means that you are much less likely to add too much flour while you're rolling. Never use handfuls of flour on the surface or the dough.

6. Before beginning to roll, flatten your piece of dough by pressing it with the rolling pin in a series of lines parallel to the edge of the work surface. Turn a round piece of dough 30 degrees or a square piece 90 degrees and repeat. You'll see that the dough starts getting slightly softer and thinner but keeps the shape you've eased it into. Remember to renew the pinches of flour under and on top of the dough even as you're pressing it out.

7. When you roll, imagine that the dough is the face of a clock and roll from 6 o'clock to 12 o'clock and back again, stopping short of rolling over the edges in both directions ②.

8. Turn a round piece of dough 30 degrees or a square 90 degrees ③ and repeat ④, remembering to flour the surface and the dough.

9. Repeat steps 7 and 8 until the dough is the correct size for your pan. Have your pan nearby so that you can compare the size of the dough to it. For a tart pan, the diameter of the dough should be the diameter of the pan plus twice its depth plus an inch. For a pie pan, the size should be 3 inches wider than the top of the pan.

PREROLLED TART OR PIECRUSTS

Having rolled crusts ready in the refrigerator or freezer takes little time and makes assembling tarts and pies a snap.

1. Follow the directions for rolling on page 26.

2. Calculate the diameter of your prerolled crust; it should be a few inches larger than the pan you'll eventually bake it in.

3. Cut a pattern from stiff cardboard or use a cake cardboard to trim the first piece of dough to the required size.

4. Transfer the dough to a cookie sheet covered with plastic wrap.

5. Cover the dough round with plastic wrap and stack the next crust you roll on top of it, continuing for however many crusts you're making.

6. Wrap and refrigerate the pan and use the prerolled crusts within a day or two.

7. Alternatively, you can freeze the crusts: let them rest in the refrigerator overnight first. Then place the pan in the freezer until the crusts are frozen solid, slide them from the pan to a piece of cardboard, and wrap them well in plastic. They will keep for a month or two.

8. To use your prerolled crust, whether refrigerated or frozen, slide it to the work surface still on its base of plastic wrap. While the dough is still relatively stiff, slide your hands between the crust and plastic, palms up, and center it on the pan you're using. Let the dough soften slightly so that there is no danger of tearing it.

9. Form the tart or piecrust according to the instructions on pages 28 and 29.

LINING A PAN FOR A TART OR PIE

1. For a tart pan, once the dough is in the pan, lift the edges and ease the dough into place from the edge inward. Never stretch dough to conform to the shape of the pan, or it will shrink back while baking.

2. Press the dough against the bottom of the pan and then gently press with a fingertip into the angle where the side meets the bottom of the pan.

3. Gently press the dough against the side of the pan and let the excess hang over the rim of the pan.

4. For sweet doughs and cookie doughs, roll over the top of the pan with a rolling pin to remove the excess dough.

5. For flaky doughs, use scissors, a bench scraper, or the back of a paring knife to trim all but ½ inch of the excess dough ①. Fold this dough back into and against the side of the pan to reinforce it and to provide a little extra dough to make up for eventual shrinkage ②.

6. If you are making a tart with any type of dough or a pie with a cookie crust, even off the top edge of the crust by pressing it in against the side of the crust with your thumb and down with your index finger at the same time ③.

7. For a pie, unfold the flaky or sweet dough into the pan and press well against the bottom and sides of the pan. If you are making a single-crust pie, see the instructions on page 36 for finishing the edge. For a double-crusted pie, you do not need to do anything more to the bottom crust; see pages 32 to 34 for instructions on forming the top crust.

8. Chill the crust until firm. If you're going to keep it refrigerated for more than a few hours (overnight is best, especially with a flaky dough), wrap the chilled crust in plastic.

FORMING INDIVIDUAL TART CRUSTS

The pans I use for individual tarts are 4½ inches in diameter. They make a generous individual serving, whether savory or sweet. If you know you're going to be making individual tarts, the process starts right after mixing the dough.

1. Once your dough is mixed, shape it into a fat cylinder, wrap it, and chill it. This makes it easy to cut round slices of dough for lining the pans. The sweet, cocoa, and chocolate doughs are the exception, since they have to be kneaded to make them malleable enough for rolling before being shaped into a cylinder.

2. Weigh your dough and calculate how many tarts you can make with it—you'll need a 2-ounce/60-gram piece of dough for each pan. Mark the dough into the corresponding number of equal-sized pieces. Once it is marked, use a bench scraper to cut the dough.

3. Roll and form the small pieces of dough in exactly the way described for a tart crust on page 26 and at left.

4. Arrange the tart pans on a jelly-roll pan and chill them before baking. If you're going to keep the crusts chilled until the next day, wrap them in plastic once they're firm.

FORMING MINI ROUND TART CRUSTS

The pans I use for these are slope-sided and 2½ inches in diameter at the top. If you have new ones, wash them well and dry them, then bake them at 375°F for 30 minutes and allow them to cool. Heating them seasons the surface, much as you might do with a new omelet pan. Coat the pans with vegetable cooking spray the first few times you use them; after that, it will no longer be necessary. Once you start baking with the pans, only wipe them well after each use; don't wash them in soapy water, or dough might stick in them. Be especially careful not to overfill the tarts, especially with anything custardy that might overflow and glue the crust to the pan.

1. Divide the dough you're using for miniature tarts into three or four pieces and work with one piece at a time, keeping the remainder wrapped and chilled.

2. Roll as appropriate for the specific dough you're using, keeping it about ⅛ inch thick.

3. Use a plain or fluted round cutter that's slightly larger in diameter than the top of your pans to cut the dough. As each disk is cut, center it in one of the pans and gently press into place, making sure that the edge of the dough reaches the top of the little pan all around.

4. Arrange the tins on a jelly-roll pan and chill them before baking.

5. Before you roll out the next piece of dough, incorporate the scraps from the previous piece under it so as to avoid having a large pile of scraps too soft to reroll when you're finished.

LINING A MUFFIN PAN

Make sure to prepare the cavities of your muffin pan with a heavy coat of soft butter or vegetable cooking spray ①.

1. Follow steps 1 through 3 in Forming Individual Tart Crusts, opposite.

2. After rolling, each piece of dough should be a little more than 5 inches in diameter (the cavities in a standard muffin pan are about 2 inches in diameter at the base and about 1½ inches deep).

3. Gently fold the piece of dough in half and slightly curve the folded edge upward on each side. Open out the piece of dough and let the center of the disk fall into the bottom center of the cavity in the pan ②.

4. Use your fingertips to press it in place against the bottom and sides of the cavity, then use the point of a paring knife to trim the edge of the dough even with the top of the cavity ③.

FORMING MINIATURE RECTANGULAR, SQUARE, OR BARQUETTE CRUSTS

Miniature pans that come in other than round shapes are easy to line with dough.

1. Start with steps 1 and 2 as for Forming Miniature Round Crusts (page 29) and slide the dough to a lightly floured flexible cutting board or cookie sheet.

2. Cut off a scrap of excess dough and use it to make a little tool for pressing the dough into the pans: Form the dough into a ball and flour it well. Pinch the top to make a little upright handle ① and press it into an extra one of the pans ②; and pull the dough from the pan ③.

3. Arrange the pans on the work surface in approximately the same shape as the piece of dough, but keep the arrangement of pans an inch or two smaller in all directions. Coat the pans with vegetable cooking spray.

4. Slide an inch of the dough off the far end of the cookie sheet, tilt the sheet at about a 45-degree angle to the work surface and, beginning with the arrangement of pans farthest from you, slide the dough onto the pans ④. If the dough fails to cover all the pans, slide the ones that are only partially covered out from under the dough.

5. Gently press with a fingertip in the center of each little pan to begin molding the dough to the shape of the pan. Use the tool to press the rolled dough into each pan ⑤.

6. Lightly flour the top of the dough and run your rolling pin over the surface to cut off the excess ⑥.

7. Arrange the lined pans on a jelly-roll pan; chill them before baking.

8. Incorporate the scraps into the next piece of dough to be rolled and continue until all the pans are lined.

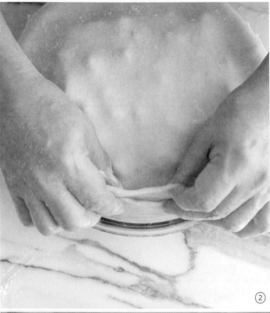

TOP CRUSTS FOR DOUBLE-CRUSTED PIES

A whole top crust is made from a disk of dough a little wider than the top of the pie pan or other pan to allow for some dough to be turned under the edge of the bottom crust to prevent juices from leaking out. Top crusts are pierced or slashed in several places so steam can escape during baking; otherwise, the steam will burst through the weakest place on the side of the pie, causing a leak.

Lattice crusts are made from strips of dough that are arranged in a diagonal or perpendicular pattern over the filling. In general, roll the dough for lattice crusts a little thinner than you would for a whole top crust, since the strips tend to sink a little into juicy fillings and thicker strips, once they get soaked with juice, do not bake through well.

Before making the top crust, prepare the bottom crust as described in Lining a Pan for a Tart or a Pie on page 28, and fill the pie as directed in your recipe.

FULL TOP FOR A PIE

1. Roll the dough for the top crust about 1 ½ inches larger in diameter than the top of the pie.

2. Brush the edge of the bottom crust with water.

3. Fold the dough for the top crust in half, line up the fold with the diameter of the pan, and unfold it to cover the filling ①.

4. Gently press the edge so that the top and bottom crusts adhere to each other ②.

5. Trim away all but ½ inch of excess dough from the top of the pie.

6. Use the blunt edge of a table knife to lift a piece of the bottom crust and fold the edge of the top crust under it so that it is even with the rim of the pan ③; repeat all around the pie.

7. Flute the edge of the pie as in the instructions on page 36.

DIAGONAL LATTICE TOP FOR A PIE

1. Roll the dough for the top crust a little larger on a side than the diameter of the pan's top.

2. Use a sharp pastry wheel, plain or serrated, to cut the square into strips ½ inch wide.

3. Arrange one of the strips across the center of the filled pie ①.

4. Place more strips parallel to the first one and equidistant from each other on both sides of the center strip ②.

5. Turn the pie 45 degrees and arrange another strip across the diameter, at an angle to the first strips ③.

6. Repeat step 4.

7. Use a bench scraper or the back of a knife to sever the strips at the edge of the pan.

8. Use your thumb to press the ends of the strips securely against the edge of the bottom crust, then use a bench scraper or the back of a knife to even up the rim.

9. Flute the edge of the pie as described on page 36, if you wish; I think it looks better when left plain.

PERPENDICULAR LATTICE

In step 5, give the pie a quarter turn so that the second set of strips is laid at a 90-degree angle to the first.

①

②

③

WOVEN LATTICES

I make perpendicular woven lattices both open, with spaces between the strips, and closed, with the strips next to each other. The procedure is the same for both.

1. Lightly dust with flour a cardboard round or a tart pan bottom a couple of inches wider in diameter than the top of your pie.

2. Follow steps 1 and 2 in the diagonal lattice on page 33, arranging parallel strips on the cardboard, instead of the pie. If you want an open lattice, space the strips 1 to 2 inches apart; for a closed lattice, use twice as many strips and place them right next to one another.

3. Fold back every other strip at its midpoint ①.

4. Insert a perpendicular strip up against the folds.

5. Unfold the strips so that they cross over the perpendicular strip.

6. Fold back the strips that are underneath the perpendicular strip, positioning the folds 1 to 2 inches from the perpendicular for an open lattice ② or leaving no space for a closed lattice.

7. Insert another perpendicular strip and unfold the strips to cross over it.

8. Repeat steps 6 and 7, until you reach the edge of the cardboard.

9. Turn the cardboard 180 degrees and repeat steps 3 to 8 ③.

10. Chill the lattice for a couple of minutes. Brush the edge of the bottom crust with water, then slide the lattice onto the top of the filled pie ④. Trim the strips at the edge of the pan and use your thumb to press the ends of the strips securely against the edge of the bottom crust. Use the bench scraper or the back of a knife to even up the rim.

11. Flute the edge of the pie as described on page 36, if you wish; I like it better left plain.

FINISHING A PIECRUST (FOR A SINGLE-CRUST PIE)

Preparing a single piecrust requires finishing the edge (when preparing the same crust for a double-crusted pie, the edge is simply trimmed even with the top edge of the pan). Fluting is easy to do, especially if you follow my method of shaping the edge and then going back over the pattern to make it more distinct.

1. Follow steps 1 through 3 on page 28 to line the pan for a single-crust pie ①.

2. For a single-crust pie, use scissors or the back of a knife to trim away all but ½-inch of dough at the top edge of the pan ②.

3. Evenly fold the extra dough under at the edge of the pan.

4. Lightly flour your fingertips; position the thumb and index finger of one hand together on the outside of the crust's edge.

5. Gently pinch while using the index finger of the other hand to push from inside the crust ③.

6. Continue all around the crust.

7. Flour your fingertips again and repeat.

8. Chill the crust before baking.

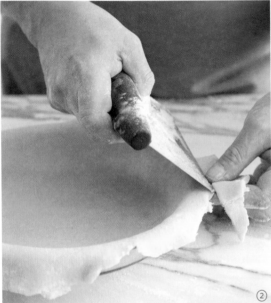

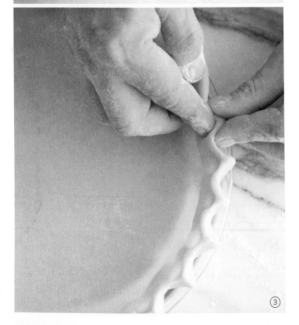

BAKING AN EMPTY CRUST FOR A TART OR PIE

Baking a tart or piecrust "blind," or unfilled, provides a crisp crust and is often done for pies that will have a creamy filling. It's easy but requires a little advance planning, because your crust should be baked and cooled before you proceed with the remaining steps of the recipe.

1. Chill your crust—ideally, overnight—before you start the process.

2. When you're ready to bake, set a rack at the middle level in the oven and preheat to 375°F.

3. For a large pie or tart, pierce the dough at 1-inch intervals all over with the tines of a fork.

4. Line the dough with a disk of parchment paper or lightweight foil. If you use foil, spray the surface that will come in contact with the dough to avoid any possibility of sticking. Never use heavy-duty foil—a fold in the foil can easily cut through the dough.

5. Fill the lined pastry shell with dried beans. You'll need a couple of cups for a large pie or tart, or about ⅓ cup beans per 4½-inch pastry shell. For small individual tartlet crusts about 2½ inches in diameter, you can cut down cupcake paper liners to line the pans; alternatively, if you have enough extra little pans, spray the backs of some and use them inside the dough-lined ones. Set individual tarts or tartlets on a jelly-roll pan.

6. Place the tart, pie, or loaded jelly-roll pan in the oven and decrease the temperature to 350°F.

7. For large tart or pie crusts, bake until the dough is set and no longer shiny and raw looking when you lift the paper to look, about 15 minutes. Carefully remove the paper and beans and continue baking until golden, about 15 minutes longer.

8. Individual and miniature crusts take much less time to bake and might be completely done in less than 15 minutes. Begin checking them after 8 to 10 minutes.

CHAPTER 3

SWEET TARTS & TARTLETS

While it's possible to argue the differences between tarts and pies, I like a simple definition of a tart or tartlet: a large tart is straight-sided, single-crusted, and served unmolded from its baking pan. Individual tarts are the same, but may also be slope-sided. That's it. You can add a top crust to a tart, but in this book I've confined top crusts to sweet or savory pies baked in pie pans or layer-cake pans.

This chapter starts with recipes that don't require blind-baking the crusts, perhaps the easiest and quickest way to make a tart. Each has specific instructions about placement in the oven and the temperatures to use to make sure both crust and filling bake to perfection. If you follow them exactly, you'll have excellent results.

Tarts in blind-baked crusts follow; there are several ways to keep the crust from becoming soggy after filling in this type of tart, and they all work well. Remember, though, that a tart like this is always best on the day it's assembled.

Individual tarts and tartlets round out the chapter. I use specific-sized molds for both, though a lot of variation in size is possible.

ORANGE & ALMOND TART

Makes one 10-inch tart, 8 to 10 servings

One 10-inch tart crust made from Sweet Pastry Dough (page 19)

TART FILLING

4 large navel oranges, about 1½ pounds, divided use

¼ cup water

7 tablespoons sugar, divided use

6 ounces canned almond paste

1 large egg

6 tablespoons/¾ stick unsalted butter, very soft

1 large egg yolk

1 teaspoon vanilla extract

¼ cup unbleached all-purpose flour (spoon into dry-measure cup and level)

¼ teaspoon baking powder

FINISHING

¾ cup apricot preserves, heated and strained before measuring

¼ cup lightly toasted sliced almonds for finishing

VARIATIONS

The upper tart in the photo is made with red-fleshed Cara Cara oranges. Blood oranges would be a flavorful and visually striking choice too. A couple of small and very sweet white or pink grapefruit would make a lovely tart, but don't use the zest, which is too bitter.

Flavorful oranges are available all year long, but this tart is especially welcome in early winter, when there is little fresh fruit besides imports available. Lightly poaching the oranges controls the amount of juice that exudes from them during baking and makes for a neater and more intensely flavored tart. Almost any fruit can be adapted to this type of filling and crust—see Variations for suggestions.

1. Finely grate enough zest from the oranges to make 2 teaspoons, and set it aside for the almond filling. Use a sharp paring knife to remove the skin and white pith completely from the oranges, and then halve them from stem to blossom end. Cut the oranges into ¼-inch-thick slices and set them aside.

2. Bring the water and 4 tablespoons sugar to a boil in a nonreactive sauté pan large enough to hold the orange slices in a shallow layer; remove the pan from the heat and add the slices.

3. Bring the oranges to a boil over medium heat, then let them cool in the syrup. When you're ready to assemble the tart, transfer the orange slices to a pan lined with paper towels and reserve the syrup.

4. Set a rack at the lowest level in the oven and preheat to 350°F.

5. Beat the almond paste and remaining 3 tablespoons sugar on low speed in the bowl of a stand mixer fitted with the paddle attachment until reduced to fine crumbs. Add the whole egg and beat until the mixture is completely smooth, a minute or two. Beat in the butter until smooth, then stop and scrape the bowl and beater. Beat in the reserved orange zest, egg yolk, and vanilla. Quickly mix the flour and baking powder together and fold them into the filling using a rubber spatula.

6. Spread the filling into the prepared crust and smooth the top. Arrange the orange slices, overlapping, in concentric rows over the almond filling. Gently press the oranges into the filling.

7. Bake the tart until the crust is baked through and golden and the almond filling is set, 30 to 40 minutes.

8. While the tart is baking, bring the syrup to a boil and allow it to reduce until slightly thickened, 4 or 5 minutes; don't reduce it too much, or it will solidify. Let it cool.

9. For the apricot glaze, combine ¼ cup of the reduced syrup with the apricot preserves. Bring to a boil, lower the heat to a simmer, and cook until thickened, about 5 minutes.

10. Cool the baked tart on a rack and unmold it. Slide the tart to a platter. Lightly brush the oranges with the apricot glaze, reheating it first if necessary, immediately before serving; sprinkle the edge of the tart with the sliced almonds.

APPLE & CALVADOS CREAM TART

One 10-inch tart crust made from Sweet Pastry Dough (page 19)

APPLE FILLING

2 tablespoons unsalted butter

3 tart apples such as Granny Smith, about 1½ pounds, peeled, halved, cored, and cut into ½-inch dice

3 tablespoons turbinado sugar or light brown sugar

¼ teaspoon ground cinnamon

CALVADOS CREAM

¼ cup granulated sugar

2 tablespoons unbleached all-purpose flour

2 large eggs

½ cup heavy whipping cream

1½ tablespoons Calvados or applejack

Confectioners' sugar for finishing

Apples and custard cream make a rich and satisfying tart filling, especially when flavored with Calvados, French apple brandy. In the United States, applejack will be easier to find; feel free to substitute it for the Calvados.

1. For the apple filling, melt the butter in a wide sauté pan over medium heat and add the apples. Sprinkle with the turbinado sugar and cinnamon and toss. Reduce the heat to low and cook the apples until they exude water; raise the heat to high and, stirring frequently, let the excess juices reduce. Test the apples for doneness: If they still seem hard, turn the heat down and cook until tender, up to 5 minutes more. Scrape the filling onto a plate to cool. The filling can be prepared in advance and covered and refrigerated for a day or two.

2. Set a rack at the lowest level in the oven and preheat to 350°F.

3. For the Calvados cream, combine the sugar and flour in a medium bowl and whisk them thoroughly together. Add the eggs and whisk smooth. Whisk in the cream and Calvados.

4. Spoon the cooled apple filling into the crust without pressing it. Set the tart on the stovetop or close to the oven to avoid spills when moving it and gently pour in the Calvados cream, filling the crust only to within ¼ inch of the top. If the crust is too full, the custard cream will overflow while the tart is baking.

5. Carefully transfer the tart to the oven. Bake until the crust is baked through and the custard cream has set, 30 to 40 minutes.

6. Cool the tart on a rack. Lightly dust the edge with confectioners' sugar. Unmold the tart and slide it onto a platter; serve the tart on the day it's baked.

VARIATIONS

APPLE CREAM TART: Omit the Calvados or applejack and substitute 2 teaspoons vanilla extract.

PEAR TART: Substitute well-drained diced poached pears for the sautéed apples. Omit the butter, turbinado sugar, and cinnamon. Sprinkle the pears with a few pinches of nutmeg after arranging them in the tart crust. Instead of using Calvados, flavor the custard cream with vanilla or substitute pear eau-de-vie.

PEACH TART WITH ROSE GLAZE: Instead of making the apple filling, use 2 to 2½ pounds ripe peaches, peeled, pitted, and cut into quarters or sixths, depending on their size. Arrange the peach wedges in the crust peeled side down and perpendicular to the edge of the tart. Flavor the custard cream with vanilla only and fill and bake the tart as above. Brush the cooled tart with a glaze made from ⅓ cup apricot preserves, ⅓ cup Turkish rose petal jam, and 2 tablespoons water, brought to a boil, reduced slightly, and strained.

APPENZELL HAZELNUT TART (APPENZELLER HASSELNUSSFLADE)

The town of Appenzell and its surrounding two half cantons are a land of dairy farms, excellent cheese, and traditional pastries and honey cakes. This hazelnut tart is more like a coffee cake than a dessert tart, but it's delicious nonetheless. The best way to "chop" hazelnuts is to place them on a jelly-roll pan and rock a small saucepan back and forth over them to crush them.

1. Set a rack at the lowest level in the oven and preheat to 350°F.

2. Put the whole hazelnuts and sugar in the bowl of a food processor and pulse repeatedly at 1-second intervals until the nuts are finely ground.

3. Add the flour, baking powder, spices, eggs, yolks, and butter to the work bowl and pulse again until the mixture is smooth, about 10 or 12 one-second pulses.

4. Use a thin-bladed metal spatula to scrape down the side of the bowl; add the milk and pulse again until smooth.

5. Remove the blade and scrape the filling into the prepared crust. Sprinkle the chopped hazelnuts on the filling.

6. Bake the tart until the crust is baked through and the filling has set, 30 to 40 minutes.

7. Cool the tart on a rack. Unmold it to a platter and dust confectioners' sugar over the top immediately before serving.

Makes one 10-inch tart, 8 to 10 servings

One 10-inch tart crust made from Sweet Pastry Dough (page 19)

HAZELNUT FILLING

1 cup/4 ounces whole natural hazelnuts + 3 tablespoons coarsely chopped hazelnuts

¾ cup granulated sugar

¾ cup unbleached all-purpose flour (spoon into dry-measure cup and level)

½ teaspoon baking powder

½ teaspoon ground cinnamon

½ teaspoon freshly grated nutmeg

Large pinch of ground cloves

2 large eggs

2 large egg yolks

8 tablespoons/1 stick unsalted butter, very soft

⅓ cup whole milk

Confectioners' sugar for finishing

VARIATION

APPENZELLER ZIMTFLADE (CINNAMON TART): Reduce the hazelnuts (or substitute the same amount of walnuts or almonds) to ½ cup. Increase the cinnamon to 1 teaspoon, the nutmeg to 1 teaspoon, and the cloves to ¼ teaspoon. Omit the chopped nuts on top.

PINEAPPLE & COCONUT TART

I love pineapple, but supermarket pineapples are frequently disappointing, so I developed a pineapple confit to sweeten and concentrate the fruit for this tart. The confit takes some time to prepare, but it's worth the extra effort.

1. Set a rack at the lowest level in the oven and preheat to 350°F.

2. Combine the sugar and flour in a medium bowl and whisk them thoroughly together. Add the eggs and whisk smooth. Whisk in the coconut cream and vanilla.

3. Cut the wedges of pineapple confit into ¼-inch-thick slices and arrange them overlapping on the prepared crust.

4. Gently pour in the coconut cream, filling the crust only to within ¼ inch of the top. If the crust is too full, the coconut cream will overflow while the tart is baking. Sprinkle the top of the tart with the shredded coconut.

5. Carefully transfer the tart to the oven. Bake until the crust is baked through and the coconut cream has set, 30 to 40 minutes.

6. Cool the tart on a rack. Unmold the tart and slide it onto a platter; serve it on the day it's baked.

Pineapple Confit

If you live in Hawaii or Puerto Rico, you can buy a perfectly ripe, sweet pineapple, but most of us have to contend with ones that are underripe and lacking in sweetness. Several years ago, I experimented successfully with roasting pineapple before using it in a tarte tatin; this recipe takes the process a step further and adds some butter and sugar to enhance the pineapple's flavor, with excellent results.

1. Set a rack at the middle level in the oven and preheat to 300°F; if you have a convection setting, preheat to 275°F.

2. Trim the top and bottom from the pineapple and halve it lengthwise. Cut each half into 4 long wedges, then trim the core and peel from each, being careful to cut away any eyes that remain on the skin side.

3. Sprinkle the bottom of a small roasting pan with a third of the butter and a third of the sugar and arrange the pineapple wedges on it peeled side down. Sprinkle with the remaining butter and sugar.

4. Bake the pineapple until it softens and starts to color a little, about 1½ hours, using tongs to turn the wedges every half hour.

5. Increase the temperature to 425°F (400°F convection) and continue baking the pineapple until the sugar caramelizes. Watch carefully to be sure the sugar doesn't darken too much.

6. Allow the pineapple to cool for a few minutes, then use tongs to transfer it to a shallow bowl.

7. Place the pan over low heat and let the sugar start to melt. Add the water and use a silicone spatula to scrape up any caramel stuck to the pan. Let the juices reduce slightly and pour them over the pineapple.

8. Cool the pineapple completely. For the best flavor, refrigerate it before using.

Makes one 10-inch tart, 8 to 10 servings

One 10-inch tart crust made from Sweet Pastry Dough (page 19)

COCONUT CREAM FILLING

¼ cup sugar

2 tablespoons unbleached all-purpose flour

2 large eggs

½ cup unsweetened Thai coconut cream

1 teaspoon vanilla extract

Pineapple Confit (recipe follows)

½ cup sweetened shredded coconut

PINEAPPLE CONFIT

Makes about 18 ounces, enough for 1 large tart

1 large pineapple, 2 to 2½ pounds

4 tablespoons unsalted butter, melted

¾ cup sugar

¼ cup water

VARIATION

Substitute light brown sugar or turbinado sugar for a third of the white sugar.

One 10-inch tart crust made from Sweet Pastry Dough (page 19)

FILLING

4 large eggs

2 cups McIntosh Applesauce (recipe follows)

1 teaspoon finely grated lemon zest

1 tablespoon lemon juice, strained before measuring

⅔ cup heavy whipping cream

⅓ cup granulated sugar

⅓ cup turbinado or light brown sugar

½ teaspoon ground cinnamon, plus more for sprinkling

Lightly sweetened whipped cream for serving, optional

MCINTOSH APPLESAUCE

Makes about 2 cups

2½ pounds McIntosh apples, peeled, halved, cored, and sliced

½ cup water

OLD-FASHIONED APPLESAUCE TART

My dear friend Ann Amendolara Nurse shared this recipe that she used to make every fall when McIntosh apples are in season. The original calls for sweetened condensed milk, but I've changed it to use a combination of cream and both white and brown sugars.

1. Set racks in the lowest level and upper third of the oven and preheat to 350°F.

2. For the filling, whisk the eggs in a bowl until frothy, then whisk in the applesauce.

3. Whisk in the lemon zest, juice, cream, sugars, and cinnamon.

4. Pour the filling into the prepared crust and sprinkle with several pinches of cinnamon.

5. Bake the tart on the bottom rack until the crust is baked through and the filling is set, about 30 minutes. Move the tart to the upper rack until the filling is fully set and slightly puffed, another 15 minutes.

6. Cool the tart on a rack and unmold it to a platter. Serve it with whipped cream if you wish.

McIntosh Applesauce

1. Combine the apples and water in a nonreactive saucepan over medium heat; bring to a boil.

2. Decrease the heat to maintain a simmer and cook until the apples are reduced to a chunky puree and most of the water has evaporated, 15 to 20 minutes. If the apples remain firm, add ¼ cup more water and continue cooking until they soften.

3. Use a potato masher to smooth out the applesauce—it's not necessary to puree it in a blender or food processor.

4. Scrape the applesauce into a container, cool it, and store it covered in the refrigerator for up to 3 days.

5. Bring the applesauce to room temperature before using it in the recipe above.

SWISS EASTER RICE TART (OSTERFLADE)

More a pastry shop specialty than a dessert prepared by home cooks, this rice tart—a sort of rice pudding baked in a crust—is popular throughout Switzerland. The key to getting the right consistency for the filling is to overcook the rice from the outset. It needs to be smooth and creamy to puree well later on. The ground almonds add richness and flavor.

1. For the rice filling, bring a large pot of water to a boil and add the rice. Stir occasionally until the water returns to a full rolling boil. Reduce the heat to maintain a low boil and cook the rice for about 15 minutes—the grains should be split at the ends when the rice is properly cooked. Drain the rice, but do not rinse it.

2. Combine the cooked rice with the milk, sugar, butter, and salt in a large, heavy saucepan. Bring the mixture to a boil over medium heat. Decrease the heat to low and cook until it is reduced and thickened, about 20 minutes. Cool the mixture, then puree it in a food processor.

3. Pour the pureed rice into a bowl and stir in the lemon zest. Mix the ground almonds and flour, then stir them into the rice. Add the eggs one at a time, stirring smooth after each addition.

4. Set a rack at the lowest level in the oven and preheat to 350°F.

5. Pour the rice filling into the prepared crust and smooth the top.

6. Bake until the crust is baked through and the filling is set and golden, 30 to 40 minutes.

7. Cool the tart on a rack. Unmold and slide it onto a platter to serve. Sprinkle lightly with confectioners' sugar right before serving.

Makes one 10-inch tart, 8 to 10 servings

One 10-inch tart crust made from Sweet Pastry Dough (page 19)

RICE FILLING

½ cup long-grain rice, such as Carolina

3 cups whole milk

½ cup granulated sugar

1 tablespoon unsalted butter

¼ teaspoon salt

2 teaspoons finely grated lemon zest

½ cup/2 ounces blanched almonds, finely ground in a food processor

1 tablespoon unbleached all-purpose flour

3 large eggs

Confectioners' sugar for finishing

Makes one 10-inch tart, 8 to 10 servings

One 10-inch tart crust made from French-Style Cookie Dough (page 20) spread with 1 batch Hazelnut Biscuit Batter (page 22), fully baked

LEMON CREAM

1 cup whole milk

⅓ cup sugar

2 tablespoons cornstarch

¼ cup lemon juice, strained before measuring

2 large egg yolks

1 cup Lemon Curd (recipe follows)

MERINGUE

4 large egg whites

¾ cup sugar

Pinch of salt

LEMON CURD

8 tablespoons/1 stick unsalted butter

5 large egg yolks

1 cup sugar

⅓ cup lemon juice, strained before measuring

2 teaspoons finely grated lemon zest

FRENCH LEMON MERINGUE TART (TARTE AU CITRON MERINGUÉE)

This is based on a similar tart made by Philippe Conticini at his Pâtisserie des Rêves shop in Paris. I was struck by a photo of the tart topped with a wave of meringue. Fortunately M. Conticini was forthcoming with his method for achieving this unique effect.

1. For the lemon cream, whisk the milk and sugar together in a small saucepan and bring to a boil over low heat. Meanwhile, whisk the cornstarch, lemon juice, and yolks smooth in a small bowl. When the milk boils, whisk it into the lemon mixture. Strain back into the pan, and cook over low heat, whisking constantly, until it thickens and boils for 2 minutes. Scrape into a small bowl, press plastic directly against the surface, and chill thoroughly. This can be prepared up to 3 days ahead.

2. To assemble the tart, pipe the lemon curd in a spiral on the hazelnut biscuit. Cover with the lemon cream, filling the crust to the top; use a metal spatula to spread the top smooth and flat. Cover and freeze the tart solid.

3. Finish the tart at least 6 hours before serving. Set a rack at the middle level in the oven and preheat to 375°F.

4. For the meringue, combine the ingredients in a mixer bowl and set it over a pan of boiling water; whisk until all the sugar has dissolved. Whip on medium-high speed until the egg whites have risen in volume but are still creamy and not dry.

5. Scrape the meringue onto a cookie sheet, forming a 10-inch disk. Invert the frozen tart into the meringue and gently press to adhere. Pull the tart away sideways, leaving a tall point at one side. Bake until the meringue is golden, 7 to 8 minutes, then keep the tart at room temperature until fully defrosted.

6. Unmold and slide the tart onto a platter. Use a thin, sharp knife to cut it, and wipe with a wet cloth between cuts.

Lemon Curd

This makes more than you need for the lemon tart, but it keeps for weeks if tightly covered and refrigerated (use it for the Traditional Vanilla Mille-Feuille Variation on page 161). An enameled small Dutch oven is perfect for preparing it.

1. Melt the butter in a medium nonreactive saucepan. Off the heat, whisk in the egg yolks, sugar, lemon juice, and lemon zest.

2. Set the pan over medium heat and whisk until the curd gets hot and steam starts to emerge. Decrease the heat to low and continue whisking until the curd thickens. Take care not to let the curd come to a boil; move the pan on and off the heat as needed.

3. Strain into a stainless-steel bowl or clean plastic container, press plastic directly against the surface, and chill until cold.

STRAWBERRY & RASPBERRY TART WITH MINT

While I hate the indiscriminate use of mint leaves as a decoration for desserts in general, the flavor of mint in moderation is wonderful with berries. Right before serving this tart, I like to scatter tiny mint leaves on it, then lightly dust it with confectioners' sugar. If you only have large mint leaves, then stack them and cut them into fine ribbons.

1. For the pastry cream, combine the milk, cream, and half of the sugar in a small saucepan and whisk. Place the pan over low heat and bring it to a full boil. Meanwhile, in a bowl, whisk the yolks and then whisk in the remaining sugar. Sift the flour over the yolk mixture and whisk it in.

2. When the milk mixture boils, whisk it into the yolk mixture. Strain it back into the pan and place it over medium heat. Use a small, pointed-end whisk to stir constantly, being sure to reach into the corners of the pan, until the cream comes to a full boil and thickens. Continue to cook, whisking constantly, for 30 seconds. Remove the pan from the heat and whisk in the vanilla.

3. Scrape the cream into a glass or stainless-steel bowl and press plastic wrap directly against the surface. Chill it thoroughly.

4. No more than 4 hours before you intend to serve the tart, unmold the cooled, baked tart crust and slide it onto a platter. Spread the cold pastry cream into the crust.

5. Randomly scatter the strawberries and raspberries on the pastry cream or arrange in concentric rings, gently pressing them so they adhere, and covering the cream completely.

6. Immediately before serving, sprinkle the tart with the mint leaves, followed by a light dusting of confectioners' sugar.

Makes one 10-inch tart, 8 to 10 servings

One 10-inch tart crust made from French-Style Cookie Dough (page 20) spread with 1 batch Almond Biscuit Batter (page 22), fully baked

PASTRY CREAM

¾ cup whole milk

¼ cup heavy whipping cream

¼ cup sugar

3 large egg yolks

2 tablespoons unbleached all-purpose flour

1 teaspoon vanilla extract

1 pint tiny height-of-season strawberries, rinsed and hulled

2 half-pint baskets fresh raspberries, picked over but not washed

3 tablespoons tiny mint leaves or larger leaves stacked and cut into thin ribbons

Confectioners' sugar for finishing

NOTE

The 9-inch square pan in the photo has approximately the same volume as a 10-inch round pan.

SOUR CHERRY TART WITH ALMOND MERINGUE

Makes one 10-inch tart, 8 to 10 servings

One 10-inch tart crust made from French-Style Cookie Dough (page 20) spread with a double batch of Almond Biscuit Batter (page 22), fully baked

CHERRY FILLING

1 quart/2 pounds sour cherries, rinsed, stemmed, and pitted

⅓ cup sugar

¼ teaspoon almond extract

2 tablespoons cornstarch

2 tablespoons water

ALMOND MERINGUE

3 large egg whites

Pinch salt

½ cup sugar

1 cup/about 3 ounces sliced almonds, divided use

VARIATION

Substitute a 1½-pound jar of sour cherries packed in water. Drain the cherries over a bowl and reserve the juice. In a nonreactive saucepan, whisk ½ cup of the cherry juice with the sugar and cornstarch. Set over low to medium heat and whisk until it thickens and comes to a full boil. Off the heat, fold in the drained cherries and the almond extract. Resume the recipe at step 3.

Cherries and almonds are an easy flavor combination; they're botanically related, though distant cousins, and the perfume of almonds is a perfect complement to the tartness of sour cherries. Where I live in New York City, sour cherries are available for a only a few weeks in mid- to late July; out of season I like to use sour cherries that come packed in water in a 1½-pound jar. See the Variation at the end of the recipe for using these.

When baking the cookie dough crust, don't let the nut biscuit get more than lightly golden; the tart needs to bake again to crisp the meringue topping.

1. For the cherry filling, combine the cherries, any accumulated juices, the sugar, and almond extract in a nonreactive saucepan and bring the mixture to a boil over medium heat. Mix the cornstarch and water and stir in ½ cup of the hot cherry juices. Remove the pan from the heat, then stir the cornstarch mixture into the filling.

2. Return the pan to medium-low heat and cook, stirring, until the filling thickens, comes to a boil, and turns clear, about 2 minutes.

3. Scrape the filling into a bowl, press plastic directly against the surface, and cool it to room temperature. For advance preparation you can chill the filling for up to 2 days, but bring it to room temperature before using it.

4. Set a rack at the middle level in the oven and preheat to 325°F.

5. For the almond meringue, half-fill a medium saucepan with water and bring it to a boil over medium heat. Meanwhile, whisk the egg whites, salt, and sugar together by hand in the bowl of an electric mixer. Place the mixer bowl over the pan of boiling water and whisk gently but constantly until the egg whites are hot (140°F) and the sugar has dissolved, 2 to 3 minutes.

6. Using an electric mixer fitted with the whisk attachment, whip the meringue on medium-high speed until the egg whites have risen in volume but are still creamy. Overwhipping will make the meringue dry and grainy.

7. While the meringue is whipping, spread the cooled cherry filling into the tart crust.

8. Once the meringue is whipped, fold in all but a tablespoon of the sliced almonds. Spread the meringue over the cherry filling, making sure to touch the meringue to the side of the tart crust all around. Sprinkle with the reserved almonds.

9. Bake the tart until the meringue is crisp, 20 to 30 minutes.

10. Cool the tart on a rack, unmold it, and slide it onto a platter to serve.

MANGO LASSI TART

This light and delicate tart filling is based on the popular Indian drink that's not unlike a mango smoothie. In India, mango lassi is sometimes perfumed with a few pinches of ground cardamom. If you'd like to try that combination, just sprinkle a little on the tart right before serving or pass some ground cardamom in a tiny bowl for the guests to add on their own if desired.

1. Use a fork to stir the gelatin and water together in a small heatproof bowl. Let the mixture stand for 3 to 4 minutes while you half-fill a small sauté pan with water and bring it to a boil. Once the gelatin has softened and absorbed all the water, set the bowl in the hot water off the heat and wait another 5 minutes for the gelatin to melt.

2. Combine the yogurt, mangoes, and sugar in a blender jar and puree it. Once the gelatin has melted completely, add it to the blender jar and puree again.

3. Pour the mango puree into a mixing bowl. Rewhip the whipped cream if it has gone liquid during chilling, then quickly fold the cream into the mango mixture.

4. Pour the filling into the tart crust and refrigerate until it sets, at least 3 hours.

5. Unmold the tart and slide it onto a platter to serve. Sprinkle it very lightly with the cardamom if you like.

Makes one 10-inch tart, 8 to 10 servings

One 10-inch tart crust made from French-Style Cookie Dough (page 20) spread with 1 batch Almond Biscuit Batter (page 22), fully baked

1 tablespoon unflavored granulated gelatin

¼ cup cold water

1 cup Greek yogurt, any fat content you like

12 ounces peeled mangoes (about 3 large Indian mangoes or 4 to 5 Mexican ones), cut into ½-inch pieces

¼ cup sugar

1 cup heavy whipping cream, whipped to a soft peak and chilled

Ground cardamom for garnish, optional

NOTE

Large, round Indian mangoes are perfect for this; smaller, yellow, flat Mexican mangoes are also very flavorful.

CHOCOLATE RASPBERRY TART

Makes one 10-inch tart, 8 to 10 servings

One 10-inch tart crust made from French-Style Cookie Dough or Chocolate Cookie Dough (pages 20 or 21), fully baked

GANACHE FILLING

1 cup heavy whipping cream

2 tablespoons light corn syrup

10 ounces dark chocolate (60 percent cocoa solids), melted and cooled

4 tablespoons/½ stick unsalted butter, very soft

2 to 3 half-pint baskets fresh raspberries, picked over but not washed

Confectioners' sugar for finishing

Cocoa powder for finishing

I used to make this tart with an elaborate chocolate mousse filling. Now I prefer it with a simple and flavorful ganache under the berries. Be sure to use premium chocolate, since there's nothing to camouflage its flavor.

1. For the ganache filling, whisk the cream and corn syrup together in a small saucepan. Bring to a slight simmer over low heat, then pour it into a bowl and cool to room temperature.

2. Pour the cream mixture over the chocolate and vigorously whisk them together. Whisk in the butter and immediately pour the ganache into the baked tart crust. Be careful: if the butter isn't as soft as mayonnaise, it won't mix easily with the chocolate and cream and might leave lumps.

3. Arrange the raspberries on the ganache, either symmetrically or in a generous-looking pile.

4. Just before serving, dust the raspberries with confectioner's sugar and a bit of cocoa.

NOTE

This tart can sit several hours before serving; just don't refrigerate it, or both the crust and filling will harden.

Individual Tarts

Individual removable-bottom quiche pans are 4½ inches in diameter, ⅞ inch deep, and hold about 6 fluid ounces. Once lined with dough, the capacity will decrease to around 4 fluid ounces, depending on the dough's thickness. If you don't want to invest in them, you could substitute individual aluminum foil pie pans, but they're usually a lot deeper.

If you want to convert one of the large tart recipes to individual quiche pans, as a general rule, the dough and filling of the large tart should be enough for 6 to 8 individual pans.

Small slope-sided tartlet pans are about 2½ inches in diameter and ½ inch deep. Too small for one to be an individual dessert, these are best served with tea or coffee in the afternoon or alongside a simple dessert such as a fruit salad.

Mini muffin pans can substitute for small tartlet pans, especially when the filling is baked in the crust. Just be careful to brush them with soft butter and then coat the buttered surface with vegetable cooking spray so that they unmold successfully.

INDIVIDUAL APPLE TARTS WITH ALMOND CRUNCH

The crisp topping on these tarts—almonds, sugar, and butter caramelized together while the tarts are baking—is delicious, and a welcome change from crumb topping.

1. For the apple filling, melt the butter in a wide sauté pan over medium heat and add the apples. Sprinkle with the turbinado sugar and cinnamon and toss to combine. Decrease the heat to low and let the apples cook until they exude some water; increase the heat to high and, stirring frequently, let the excess juices reduce. Test the apples for doneness: if they still seem hard, decrease the heat and cook until tender, up to 5 minutes longer. Scrape the filling onto a plate to cool. The filling can be prepared in advance and covered and refrigerated for a day or two.

2. When you're ready to bake the tarts, set a rack at the lowest level in the oven and preheat to 400°F. Arrange the tart pans on a jelly-roll pan.

3. For the topping, butter or spray a 2-quart heatproof bowl and set it aside. Melt the butter in a small saucepan and stir in the honey and sugar. Bring the mixture to a full rolling boil over low heat, then remove it from the burner and stir in the almonds. Scrape the topping into the prepared bowl and let it cool slightly.

4. Spoon the cooled apple filling into the crusts without pressing it. Spoon some of the cooled topping onto each tart, distributing it evenly.

5. Place the tarts in the oven and decrease the temperature to 350°F. Bake until the crusts are baked through and the topping has caramelized, about 30 minutes.

6. Cool the tarts on a rack. Unmold and serve on individual dessert plates.

Makes 6 individual tarts

Six 4½-inch tart crusts made from Sweet Pastry Dough (page 19)

APPLE FILLING

2 tablespoons unsalted butter

4 tart apples such as Granny Smith, about 2 pounds, peeled, halved, cored, and cut into ½-inch dice

¼ cup turbinado sugar or light brown sugar

¼ teaspoon ground cinnamon

ALMOND CRUNCH TOPPING

6 tablespoons/¾ stick unsalted butter

¼ cup honey, light corn syrup, or golden syrup

¼ cup granulated sugar

1 cup/about 3 ounces blanched sliced almonds

SALTED CASHEW CARAMEL CHOCOLATE TARTLETS

Makes 12 to 18 tartlets

Twelve 2½-inch tartlet crusts made from Flaky Buttery Dough or French-Style Cookie Dough (page 14 or 20), fully baked. It's best to chill the tartlet crusts overnight before baking to reduce shrinkage.

CARAMEL CASHEW FILLING

2 tablespoons water

⅔ cup sugar

1 tablespoon honey

⅓ cup heavy whipping cream

½ cup (about 2½ ounces) roasted, salted cashews, rubbed in a paper towel to remove excess salt, chopped into ¼-inch pieces

CHOCOLATE TOPPING

3 ounces dark chocolate (60 percent cocoa solids), melted and cooled

½ cup heavy cream

1 tablespoon light corn syrup

Coarse salt such as fleur de sel or crushed Maldon salt for finishing, optional

Salty nuts and caramel are a delicious combination—and when you add a chocolate topping, you get a candy bar in a tart crust. By the way, roasted and salted cashew halves are much less expensive than whole ones—in the recipe they're chopped anyway. Roasted salted almonds are also delicious in these tartlets.

1. For the filling, combine the water and sugar in a medium saucepan and stir to mix. Cook the mixture over medium heat and stir occasionally until the syrup turns to a deep amber caramel.

2. Meanwhile, stir the honey into the cream in a small saucepan and bring it to a slight simmer over low heat; cover and set aside.

3. When the sugar mixture is ready, remove the pan from the heat and begin pouring in the hot cream and honey mixture, a little at a time, to avoid having the caramel boil over. If the caramel hardens, return the pan to the heat and cook, stirring until the caramel is smooth, no more than a few seconds. Stir in the cashews.

4. Evenly divide the filling among the baked tartlet crusts, filling them with about a tablespoon of the cashew caramel, to within ¼ inch of the top.

5. For the chocolate topping, place the chocolate in a mixing bowl and bring the cream and corn syrup to a simmer in a saucepan. Pour the cream over the chocolate and whisk smooth.

6. Spoon some of the topping onto each of the tartlets, using an offset spatula to spread it smooth and flat if necessary.

7. Let the glaze set at a cool room temperature. If you like, sprinkle each tartlet with a tiny pinch of salt before serving.

INDIVIDUAL RASPBERRY & PISTACHIO TARTS

Makes 8 individual tarts

Eight 4½-inch tart crusts made from Sweet Pastry Dough (page 19)

3 large egg whites

Pinch of salt

⅔ cup granulated sugar

6 tablespoons/¾ stick unsalted butter, melted

1 tablespoon kirsch or white rum

1 teaspoon vanilla extract

⅔ cup/about 2½ ounces very green pistachios, skins removed, finely ground in the food processor (see Note)

¾ cup unbleached all-purpose flour (spoon into dry-measure cup and level)

2 half-pint baskets/12 ounces fresh raspberries, picked over but not rinsed

Confectioners' sugar for finishing

The pistachio filling in these tarts is very much like the small French cake known as a financier. Less rich and more flavorful than the typical nut-based tart filling called frangipane, it creates a moist and subtle background for the berries. A spoonful of lightly sweetened whipped cream would be good with these.

1. Set a rack at the lowest level in the oven and preheat to 400°F. Arrange the tart pans on a jelly-roll pan.

2. Whisk the egg whites and salt by hand in a mixing bowl and whisk in the sugar.

3. Whisk in the butter, followed by the kirsch and vanilla.

4. Use a rubber spatula to fold the pistachios and flour in at the same time.

5. Pour a scant ¼ cup of the batter into each of the tart crusts. Arrange the raspberries in a couple of concentric circles on each tart, keeping them about ¼ inch apart. Gently press so that the raspberry bases are embedded about ¼ inch deep in the filling.

6. Place in the oven and decrease the temperature to 350°F. Bake until the crust is baked through and the filling has set, 30 to 35 minutes. Cool the tarts on a rack, then unmold them. Dust lightly with confectioners' sugar before serving.

NOTE

To remove the skins from pistachios, cover them with water in a saucepan and bring to a rolling boil. Drain, then rub the pistachios in a towel to loosen the skins. If you're not using right away, place the nuts on a jelly-roll pan and dry them out in a 300°F oven for 10 minutes. After they cool, store in the freezer.

MORAVIAN CITRON TARTLETS

Don't get scared—these aren't made with candied citron. Here the word is a corruption of *Zitrone*, the German word for lemon, used by the nineteenth-century German-speaking Moravian settlers of the Winston-Salem area in North Carolina. I learned about these years ago from Beth Tartan, the pen name of Elizabeth Hedgecock Sparks, who was for many years the food editor of the Winston-Salem paper and an expert on the cooking of the region. This is adapted from her book *North Carolina and Old Salem Cookery*, a classic of American culinary literature. Though similar to the lemon-scented chess pies also popular in the area, the filling for citron tarts is distinguished by the fact that the ingredients are chopped together, not beaten smooth.

1. Set a rack at the lowest level in the oven and preheat to 375°F. Arrange the tartlet pans on a jelly-roll pan.

2. Combine the egg yolks, butter, brown sugar, lemon zest, and juice in the bowl of a food processor fitted with the metal blade. Pulse repeatedly at 1-second intervals until the butter is broken down into 1/8-inch pieces. Don't try to make a smooth mixture.

3. Pour the filling into a bowl; pour a measuring tablespoon of the filling into each tartlet crust, stirring up the filling as you do to maintain an even distribution of the ingredients.

4. Bake the tartlets until the crust is baked through and the filling is set, 20 to 25 minutes. Don't overbake or the filling will start to simmer, overflow, and cause the tartlets to stick to their pans.

5. Cool the tarts on a rack and serve them the day they are baked.

Makes 12 tartlets

Twelve 2½-inch tartlet crusts made from Sweet Pastry Dough (page 19), see Note

3 large egg yolks

2 tablespoons unsalted butter, cut into 20 pieces and chilled for 5 minutes in the freezer

½ cup light brown sugar, firmly packed

Finely grated zest of 1 medium lemon

1 tablespoon lemon juice, strained before measuring

NOTE

Normally Sweet Pastry Dough is rolled about 1/8 inch thick. For these tartlets, roll the dough thinner because they bake so quickly. Use your thumb to press the dough firmly against the side of each little pan to raise the crust about 1/8 inch above the rim to allow for shrinkage and to prevent the filling from coming in direct contact with the pan or it will stick there.

LESLEY'S INDIVIDUAL DOUBLE CHOCOLATE TARTS

Makes 8 individual tarts

Eight 4½-inch tart crusts made from French-Style Cookie Dough (page 20), fully baked

CHOCOLATE CUSTARD FILLING

½ cup whole milk

1⅓ cups heavy whipping cream

½ cup sugar

4 large eggs

3 ounces dark chocolate (60 percent cocoa solids), cut into ¼-inch pieces

GANACHE GLAZE

6 ounces dark chocolate (60 percent cocoa solids), cut into ¼-inch pieces

1 cup heavy whipping cream

These ethereal chocolate tarts come from my friend Lesley Chesterman, restaurant critic and food writer at the *Montreal Globe*, Quebec's premier English-language newspaper. Her recipe originally produced a single large tart, but I like this as an individual dessert.

1. Set a rack at the middle level in the oven and preheat to 350°F. Arrange the tart pans on a jelly-roll pan.

2. For the custard filling, whisk the milk, cream, and half of the sugar together in a saucepan and bring the mixture to a boil over medium heat.

3. Whisk the eggs with the remaining sugar. Place the chocolate in a separate bowl.

4. Once the cream mixture boils, pour a quarter of it over the chocolate and whisk until smooth and melted. Whisk in the remaining cream mixture, then whisk the chocolate and cream mixture into the eggs. Pass the filling through a fine-mesh strainer.

5. Fill the tart crusts to within ¼ inch of the top with the chocolate cream. Carefully place the tarts in the oven and decrease the temperature to 325°F. Bake until the chocolate cream has set, about 20 minutes.

6. Cool the tarts on a rack.

7. For the ganache glaze, place the chocolate in a mixing bowl and bring the cream to a simmer in a saucepan. Pour the cream over the chocolate and whisk smooth.

8. Pour an eighth of the ganache on one of the tarts and tilt it to cover the surface evenly and entirely with ganache. Repeat with the remaining tarts. Let the glaze set at a cool room temperature and serve the tarts the day they are baked.

MEXICAN CHEESE TARTLETS (TARTAS DE REQUESÓN)

In Mexico these tarts are both sold and consumed with *panes dulces*, Mexican sweetened breads that are eaten for breakfast and later in the day for *merenda*, the late afternoon meal. The cheese used in Mexico is *requesón*, which is very similar to Italian ricotta, as it is made from whey rather than milk. But it's usually clotted at a higher temperature, making the curds harder than ricotta, and has a higher salt content. Part-skim-milk ricotta is a perfect substitute.

1. Set a rack at the lowest level in the oven and preheat to 350°F.

2. If the ricotta is very coarse, press it through a strainer into a bowl. Stir in the salt and sugar.

3. Beat in the vanilla, then the egg and egg whites, one at a time.

4. Spoon the mixture into the prepared muffin pan, filling each crust only to within ¼ inch of the top to allow for expansion. Sprinkle the filling with a pinch or two of cinnamon.

5. Bake until the filling is set and slightly puffed, 30 to 35 minutes.

6. Cool the tarts in the pan. To unmold them, invert a jelly-roll pan on the muffin pan and flip the whole stack. Lift off the muffin pan and turn the tarts right side up. If it's cool in the kitchen and you've used soft butter for greasing the pan, it will be easier to unmold the tarts if you place the pan in a hot oven for a minute or two to melt the butter.

Makes twelve 3-inch tarts

One 12-cavity muffin pan lined with Sweet Pastry Dough (page 19)

3 cups/1½ pounds part-skim-milk ricotta

¼ teaspoon salt

½ cup sugar

1 teaspoon vanilla extract

1 large egg

2 large egg whites

¼ teaspoon ground Mexican cinnamon (see Note)

NOTE

Mexican cinnamon, also known as Ceylon cinnamon or "true cinnamon," is sweeter and less intense than other varieties and is used liberally in Mexican sweet baking.

CHAPTER 4

SWEET PIES, COBBLERS & CRISPS

Cakes, cookies, and other simple sweets can create pleasurable memories of home-baked treats, but nothing connotes home baking better than a juicy homemade pie. Whether piled high with fruit or loaded with rich, creamy filling, pies—and cobblers and crisps, their close relatives—are perfect for simple meals and family gatherings.

All the pies in this chapter are baked in a standard slope-sided glass pie pan. For readers outside the United States, this pan fortunately has approximately the same volume as a 10-inch/ 25-cm round French tart pan with 1-inch/2.5-cm-high sides, and it can easily be substituted.

Cobblers and crisps are easy to prepare in almost any baking dish, but my preference runs to dishes no more than 2 inches deep. A deeper baking dish provides proportionately less surface area for the topping, and the filling takes longer to bake.

Pies and cobblers may be topped in a variety of imaginative ways; use the photographs of top crusts in chapter 2 as a guide.

CRANBERRY PECAN PIE

Makes one 9-inch pie, about 8 servings

One 9-inch piecrust made from Sweet Pastry Dough (page 19)

6 cups fresh cranberries, about 1½ pounds, rinsed, picked over, and drained

⅓ cup granulated sugar

⅔ cup turbinado or light brown sugar

1 tablespoon finely grated peeled fresh ginger

Finely grated zest of 1 large orange

½ cup fresh orange juice, strained before measuring

4 tablespoons/½ stick unsalted butter, cut into 5 or 6 pieces

½ teaspoon ground cinnamon

¼ teaspoon ground ginger

1 cup coarsely chopped pecan pieces

VARIATIONS

Substitute walnuts for the pecans. Or use the crumb topping on page 85 instead of just the nuts (you can stir those into the crumb topping before you sprinkle it on).

Warning: this pie has a tart and tangy filling that might not be sweet enough for some people. That said, I love the tangy quality of this filling and wouldn't want it to be any other way. By the way, since the filling is cooked before the pie is baked, you can taste it and add a little more sugar if you want. My late friend Joseph Viggiani shared this recipe years ago; I have no idea where he might have found it.

1. Combine the cranberries with the rest of the ingredients except the pecans in a large nonreactive saucepan. Bring the mixture to a simmer, stirring often, and cook at an active simmer until slightly thickened, about 5 minutes. Don't overcook, or the filling will be hard after the pie is baked. Let cool.

2. Set a rack at the lowest level in the oven and preheat to 375°F.

3. Stir half of the pecans into the filling and pour it into the prepared piecrust. Smooth the surface and scatter the remaining pecans on top.

4. Place the pan in the oven and decrease the temperature to 350°F. Bake until the crust is baked through and the pecans are toasted, 35 to 40 minutes.

5. Cool the pie on a rack and serve it at room temperature.

MOLASSES PECAN PIE

Makes one 9-inch pie, about 8 servings

One 9-inch piecrust made from Sweet Pastry Dough (page 19)

⅓ cup unsulfured (mild) molasses

¼ cup water

1 cup sugar

4 tablespoons/½ stick unsalted butter

4 large eggs

¼ teaspoon fine sea salt

2 tablespoons bourbon, optional

2 cups/8 ounces pecan halves, or a mixture of halves and pieces

Lightly sweetened whipped cream for serving

VARIATION
TRADITIONAL PECAN PIE: Substitute 1 cup dark corn syrup and ⅔ cup sugar for the molasses, water, and sugar; use 3 eggs instead of 4. Everything else is exactly the same.

Molasses lends an old-fashioned flavor to a rich pecan pie, in addition to cutting back on the intense sweetness that the typically used corn syrup brings. For traditionalists, see the Variation for my standard pecan pie recipe.

1. Set a rack at the lowest level in the oven and preheat to 400°F.

2. Stir the molasses, water, and sugar together in a saucepan and bring the mixture to a boil over medium heat. Remove from the heat, add the butter, and let it melt into the hot syrup.

3. In a medium bowl, whisk the eggs with the salt and bourbon if using. Stir the butter and syrup mixture, and slowly pour it into the egg mixture while whisking.

4. Let the filling stand for 10 to 15 minutes, then skim any foam from the surface.

5. Stir in the pecans and pour the filling into the prepared crust.

6. Place the pie in the oven and decrease the temperature to 350°F. Bake until the crust is baked through and the filling is set and slightly puffed, 45 to 50 minutes.

7. Cool on a rack and serve at room temperature with some whipped cream.

OSGOOD PIE

I first heard of this pie when Bennie Sue Dupy, a native of Mart, Texas, near Waco, shared its recipe, suggesting that it would also make a good bar cookie. I did adapt the recipe for my cookie book—and now here it is in its original form. Many versions of this pie—also referred to as raisin pecan chess pie—have vinegar as a flavoring. I've decided to use gentler lemon juice instead, and it certainly brightens the flavor of this quite sweet filling.

1. Set a rack at the lowest level in the oven and preheat to 400°F.

2. Beat the butter and sugars together by hand using a rubber spatula. Add the egg yolks, one at a time, beating smooth after each addition.

3. Stir in the lemon juice, pecans, and raisins.

4. Whip the egg whites and salt in a stand mixer on medium-high speed using the whisk attachment. Continue whipping until the egg whites hold a soft peak—don't overwhip.

5. Use a rubber spatula to fold the egg whites into the filling.

6. Scrape the filling into the prepared crust and place the pie in the oven. Immediately decrease the heat to 350°F.

7. Bake the pie until the crust is baked through and the filling has set and taken on a deep golden color, 45 to 50 minutes.

8. Cool the pie on a rack and serve it on the day it's baked.

Makes one 9-inch pie, about 8 servings

One 9-inch piecrust made from Flaky Buttery Dough (page 14)

4 tablespoons/½ stick unsalted butter, softened

⅓ cup granulated sugar

⅓ cup turbinado or firmly packed light brown sugar

2 large eggs, separated

1 tablespoon lemon juice, strained before measuring

½ cup/2 ounces pecan pieces, coarsely chopped

½ cup/2 ounces raisins, coarsely chopped

¼ teaspoon fine sea salt

VARIATION

Though not traditional, chopped dried cranberries are wonderful in this pie; their tartness perfectly offsets the sweet filling.

COCONUT CREAM PIE

An old-fashioned American bakery and diner favorite, coconut cream pie has all but disappeared from retail bakeries and menus. This version intensifies the coconut flavor with Thai coconut cream added to the filling.

1. For the filling, whisk 1½ cups of the milk, the coconut cream, and sugar in a nonreactive saucepan and bring the mixture to a simmer over low heat.

2. Meanwhile, whisk the remaining ½ cup milk with the cornstarch and egg yolks. Sprinkle the gelatin on the water in a small bowl and set it aside.

3. When the milk mixture comes to a boil, whisk about a third of it into the yolk mixture. Return the remaining milk mixture to low heat and bring it back to a boil. When it starts to boil, begin whisking, then whisk in the yolk mixture. Continue whisking constantly until the cream thickens and returns to a boil, about 2 minutes.

4. Off the heat, whisk in the softened gelatin and the vanilla. Press plastic wrap directly against the surface of the filling and refrigerate for 30 minutes, then continue cooling it at room temperature (if left in the refrigerator, it will set solid before the whipped cream is added). Once the filling has cooled, rewhip the cream if it has become liquid, then quickly fold it into the filling. Scrape the filling into the cooled piecrust, doming it slightly in the center. Chill the pie to completely set the filling. After an hour or so, cover the pie with plastic wrap if you're not finishing it right away.

5. For the topping, whip the cream with the vanilla and sugar to a soft peak and spread it on the filling. Generously sprinkle the cream with the toasted coconut.

Makes one 9-inch pie, about 8 servings

One 9-inch piecrust made from Flaky Buttery Dough (page 14), fully baked

COCONUT CREAM FILLING

2 cups whole milk

1 cup unsweetened Thai coconut cream

½ cup sugar

2 tablespoons cornstarch

4 large egg yolks

1 envelope/7 grams unflavored granulated gelatin

¼ cup water

2 teaspoons vanilla extract

1 cup heavy whipping cream, whipped to a soft peak

TOPPING

1 cup heavy whipping cream

1 teaspoon vanilla extract

2 tablespoons sugar

1 cup sweetened, shredded coconut, lightly toasted

VARIATION

BANANA CREAM PIE: Replace the coconut cream with milk. When filling the pie, spread half the filling in the piecrust, then top it with a layer of sliced bananas—about 2 medium—and spread the rest of the filling over them. Top the pie with whipped cream but no coconut.

COTTAGE CHEESE PIE

A Pennsylvania Dutch standard, this cheese pie was popular because cottage cheese was easily made in farm kitchens and always available as an ingredient. Some more recent versions of this pie filling dress it up by adding cream cheese, but this one is a little more lean and uses a combination of milk and cream for slight added richness.

Makes one 9-inch pie, about 8 servings

One 9-inch piecrust made from Sweet Pastry Dough (page 19)

8 ounces/1 cup full-fat, small curd cottage cheese, drained in a fine strainer for 2 to 3 hours

½ cup sugar

2 tablespoons unbleached all-purpose flour

¼ teaspoon ground cinnamon, plus more for sprinkling

Large pinch of freshly grated nutmeg

Large pinch of fine sea salt

2 teaspoons finely grated lemon zest

3 large eggs

½ cup whole milk

½ cup light cream or half-and-half

VARIATION

Add 1 tablespoon lemon juice.

1. Set a rack at the lowest level in the oven and preheat to 350°F.

2. Pulse the cottage cheese in a food processor to make it smoother. Set aside.

3. Combine the sugar, flour, spices, and salt in a medium bowl and whisk them together.

4. Stir in the cottage cheese, then the lemon zest, eggs, milk, and cream.

5. Scrape the filling into the prepared piecrust and sprinkle with cinnamon.

6. Bake the pie until the crust is baked through and the filling is set and has turned a deep golden color, 45 to 50 minutes.

7. Cool the pie on a rack and serve it on the day it's baked.

MISSISSIPPI CHESS PIE

Chess pies are a classic dessert of the American South, though they have nothing to do with the board game that goes by the same name. Chess may be a corruption of "cheese," since in the distant past, any kind of a mixture that jelled or coagulated was considered a type of cheese. This version comes from my friend Ben Mims, formerly the baking expert of the *Saveur* magazine test kitchen. Recipes for chess pie often contain a little cornmeal. As it's not really enough to thicken the filling, nor is it detectable as a flavor, I've omitted it. This cries out for a little whipped cream, even though that's not traditional.

1. Set a rack at the lowest level in the oven and preheat to 350°F.

2. Whisk the eggs and yolks by hand in a large bowl, then whisk in the sugar, nutmeg, and salt just to blend. Avoid overwhipping, which will make the top of the filling crusty after baking.

3. Use a rubber spatula to stir in the butter, buttermilk, and lemon juice.

4. Pour the mixture into the prepared piecrust. Set the pan in the oven and decrease the temperature to 325°F. Bake until the crust is baked through and golden and the filling is set, 45 to 50 minutes. When you remove it from the oven, there should still be a soft area in the center about 1 inch in diameter.

5. Cool the pie on a rack and serve it on the day it's baked.

Makes one 9-inch pie, about 8 servings

One 9-inch piecrust made from Sweet Pastry Dough (page 19)

3 large eggs

2 large egg yolks

1 cups sugar

½ teaspoon freshly grated nutmeg

¼ teaspoon fine sea salt

4 tablespoons/½ stick unsalted butter, melted

1 cup buttermilk

2 tablespoons lemon juice, strained before measuring

BUTTERSCOTCH CUSTARD PIE

Makes one 9-inch pie, about 8 servings

One 9-inch piecrust made from Sweet Pastry Dough (page 19)

BUTTERSCOTCH FILLING

8 tablespoons/1 stick best-quality salted butter

2 cups whole milk

½ cup turbinado sugar

1 vanilla bean, split lengthwise

⅓ cup unbleached all-purpose flour (spoon into dry-measure cup and level)

4 large eggs

FINISHING

1 cup heavy whipping cream

2 tablespoons granulated sugar

1 teaspoon vanilla extract

1 teaspoon turbinado sugar

That elusive flavor butterscotch is a combination of equal parts butter and caramel coupled with a strong hint of salt. I decided to let some salted butter color until deep golden brown and to use turbinado sugar instead of standard brown sugar for this pie filling, and the results are as butterscotch as you can get.

1. For the filling, melt the butter over medium heat in a saucepan. Cook, watching the butter closely, until it turns a deep golden brown. Immediately pour the butter into a cool, dry stainless-steel bowl to stop the cooking and drop the temperature.

2. Set a rack at the lowest level in the oven and preheat to 375°F.

3. In the same saucepan, whisk the milk and half the turbinado sugar together. Add the split vanilla bean and bring the mixture to a simmer. Whisk well, then remove the vanilla bean.

4. Whisk the remaining sugar and the flour together, then whisk in the eggs until the mixture is smooth. Whisk in the milk mixture and finally the cooled brown butter.

5. Pour the filling into the prepared piecrust and set in the oven. Immediately decrease the temperature to 350°F and bake until the crust is baked through and the filling is set, about 45 minutes.

6. Cool the pie on a rack and chill it, loosely covered, before finishing.

7. To finish the pie, whip the cream with the sugar and vanilla to a soft peak. Spread the whipped cream on the chilled pie and sprinkle it with the turbinado sugar.

8. Keep at a cool room temperature until serving; cover and chill leftovers for up to 2 days.

RASPBERRY CREAM PIE

After a few experiments with an all-raspberry pie filling that turned into a watery mess, I decided to use these berries to their best advantage: some slightly cooked and thickened, with the remainder added uncooked. I then layered the fruit between a light pastry cream and a whipped cream topping. Blueberries and blackberries are just as good, and a combination of berries would work well too.

1. For the raspberry filling, combine a third of the berries and the sugar in a nonreactive saucepan and mash together. Place over low heat and bring to a simmer. Meanwhile, whisk the water and cornstarch together. When the raspberries begin to boil, stir a third of the hot juices into the cornstarch mixture. Return the raspberry mixture to a boil over low heat and quickly stir in the cornstarch mixture. Continue stirring until the juices thicken, return to a boil, and become clear. Stir in the lemon zest off the heat, then scrape the thickened raspberry mixture into a bowl. Press plastic directly against the surface and let the mixture cool.

2. For the pastry cream, combine the milk, cream, and half the sugar in a small saucepan and whisk to combine. Place over low heat and bring to a full boil. Meanwhile, in a bowl, whisk the yolks and then add the remaining sugar. Sift the flour over the mixture and whisk it in.

3. When the milk mixture boils, whisk it into the yolk mixture. Strain the pastry cream back into the pan and place it over medium heat. Use a small, pointed-end whisk to stir constantly, being sure to reach into the corners of the pan, until the cream comes to a full boil and thickens. Continue to cook, whisking constantly, for 30 seconds. Off the heat, whisk in the vanilla.

4. Scrape the cream into a glass or stainless-steel bowl and press plastic wrap directly against the surface. Chill until cold.

5. To finish the pie, whip the cream with the sugar and vanilla to a soft peak.

6. Evenly spread the cooled pastry cream in the bottom of the piecrust. Fold the fresh raspberries into the cooled, thickened cooked berries and spread the fruit on top of the pastry cream. Rewhip the cream if necessary and spread it, swirling it with a metal spatula or the back of a large spoon, over the raspberries.

7. Keep the pie at a cool room temperature until serving time. Refrigerate leftovers.

Makes one 9-inch pie, about 8 servings

One 9-inch piecrust made from Flaky Buttery Dough (page 14), fully baked

RASPBERRY FILLING

3 half-pint baskets/18 ounces fresh raspberries, picked over but not rinsed, divided use

⅓ cup sugar

¼ cup water

2 tablespoons cornstarch

2 teaspoons finely grated lemon zest

PASTRY CREAM

¾ cup whole milk

¼ cup heavy whipping cream

¼ cup sugar, divided use

3 large egg yolks

2 tablespoons unbleached all-purpose flour

1 teaspoon vanilla extract

FINISHING

1 cup heavy whipping cream

2 tablespoons sugar

1 teaspoon vanilla extract

OLD-FASHIONED SWEET POTATO PIE

Makes one 9-inch pie, about 8 servings

One 9-inch piecrust made from Sweet Pastry Dough (page 19)

2 medium sweet potatoes

⅓ cup granulated sugar

¼ cup turbinado or light brown sugar

1 teaspoon ground cinnamon

½ teaspoon ground ginger

½ teaspoon freshly grated nutmeg

¼ teaspoon salt

3 large eggs

1⅓ cups half-and-half or ⅔ cup each milk and heavy whipping cream

VARIATION

Use acorn or butternut squash instead of sweet potatoes. To prepare the squash, halve it and scrape out the seeds and filaments. Loosely cover with aluminum foil to keep the flesh from drying out and bake, cut side up, as for the sweet potatoes. Cool, scrape the squash from the skin and mash. If the squash is very fibrous, puree it in the food processor.

Though I love pumpkin pie, I have to admit that lately I've just gotten tired of using tasteless canned pumpkin. A couple of years ago, I tried substituting baked, mashed sweet potatoes for the pumpkin in my favorite recipe, and I was more than happy with the results. Baked winter squash, such as butternut or acorn, works just as well. Serve with lightly sweetened whipped cream.

1. Set a rack at the middle level in the oven and preheat to 375°F. Place the sweet potatoes on a small ovenproof pan and bake until tender, 50 to 60 minutes. Cool, peel, and mash the potatoes. You should have about 1 pound or 1½ cups puree. Prepare the puree several days in advance if you wish and keep it covered in the refrigerator but bring to room temperature before using.

2. Move the rack to the lowest level in the oven and and preheat to 375°F.

3. Whisk together the sweet potatoes, sugars, spices, and salt. Whisk in the eggs, followed by the half-and-half.

4. Pour the filling into the prepared crust. Place in the oven and decrease the temperature to 350°F. Bake the pie until the crust is baked through and the filling is set, 50 to 60 minutes.

5. Cool the pie on a rack.

Two-Crust Pie Tips and Tricks

Adding a top crust to a pie protects the filling from becoming dry while the pie is baking and reveals the filling with a little flourish as the pie is cut. Each of the pies that follow has a specific top crust in the recipe, but you can pretty much interchange them as you wish. See the variety of pie tops described and illustrated in chapter 2. Another possibility for covering a pie is the crumb topping on page 85.

Thickening Fruit Pie Fillings

Most fruit pie fillings need some thickening. For simple ones like apple and peach pies, I'm happy to use a little flour. It thickens the juices slightly so they aren't watery but doesn't make the filling overly dense.

For juicier pies, I like to use cornstarch, but I always cook it out first with some of the juices in the filling so that it thickens efficiently and no chalky cornstarch texture remains (as it would if it were added uncooked to the filling ingredients).

Fruit Pies and Simmering Juices

Before preheating your oven, slide a large sheet of aluminum foil onto the bottom of the oven. When fruit pie fillings start to simmer toward the end of baking, they frequently leak. Having the bottom of your oven lined will help to prevent the overflowing juices from remaining there and burning over several hours.

Positioning in the Oven

For any pie or tart that has an unbaked crust, the paramount concern is to make sure that the bottom of the crust bakes through. That's why I always specify placing the pie or tart on the lowest rack in the oven. In the case of two-crust pies, though, we also have to make sure that the top crust colors to an appetizing finish. Watch the pie during the last 15 minutes or so of the suggested baking time. If the juices are beginning to simmer but the top crust is still too pale, then move it to the upper third of the oven so it will sufficiently darken while finishing baking.

BLUEBERRY & APPLE PIE

Makes one 9-inch pie, about 8 servings

One 9-inch piecrust made from Sweet Pastry Dough (page 19), plus dough for a top crust

BLUEBERRY AND APPLE FILLING

2 pints blueberries, rinsed, dried, and picked over

¾ cup sugar

4 tablespoons water or apple juice

3 tablespoons cornstarch

¼ teaspoon ground cinnamon

¼ teaspoon freshly grated nutmeg

1 pound/2 large Granny Smith apples, peeled, halved, cored, and cut into ⅜-inch dice

3 tablespoons unsalted butter

Milk for brushing

1 to 2 teaspoons sugar

VARIATIONS

Use the crumb topping on page 85, without the almonds, instead of the full top. For this pie there's no need to prebake the crumbs.
For an all-blueberry pie, use 3 pints of blueberries and omit the apples. Add 2 teaspoons grated lemon zest to the filling along with the spices.

For a raspberry or blackberry pie, use 6 cups berries, 1 cup sugar, and ¼ cup cornstarch. Use water with the cornstarch, 2 teaspoons finely grated lemon zest, and omit the spices.

Tart apples marry well with sweet, spicy blueberries, even though their seasons are fairly opposite. In early summer when blueberries come into season there are always imported apples available, and when apples come into season it's okay to use frozen blueberries. I find that dicing the apples quite small makes them cook through easily, and their tartness gives a better boost to the blueberry flavor than adding lemon juice or zest.

1. Combine 1½ cups blueberries, the sugar, and 2 tablespoons of the water in a medium saucepan. Set over low heat and cook, stirring often, until the blueberries have become very juicy and the sugar has dissolved. Mix the cornstarch with the remaining water, then stir in about a third of the blueberry juices. Stir the cornstarch mixture into the saucepan, return to the heat, and cook, stirring constantly, until thickened and clear, about 3 minutes.

2. Remove from the heat, scrape the filling into a medium bowl, and stir in the spices. Let cool.

3. Set a rack at the lowest level in the oven and preheat to 375°F.

4. Fold the remaining blueberries and the diced apples into the cooled filing.

5. Scrape into the piecrust and spread evenly. Dot with the butter and arrange the top crust. Attach, flute, and pierce the top crust as on page 32. Brush with milk and sprinkle with the sugar.

6. Place the pie in the oven and decrease the temperature to 350°F. Bake until the crust is baked through and the juices are actively simmering, about 45 minutes.

7. Cool the pie on a rack and serve warm or at room temperature.

SWEET CHERRY & RHUBARB PIE

Makes one 9-inch pie, about 8 servings

One 9-inch piecrust made from Flaky Buttery Dough (page 14), plus dough for a lattice top

CHERRY AND RHUBARB FILLING

¾ cup sugar

¼ cup water

1 pound pink, tender rhubarb, trimmed and rinsed, cut into 2-inch lengths

3 tablespoons cornstarch

Large pinch of ground cinnamon

Finely grated zest of 1 small orange, about 1 teaspoon

1½ pounds sweet black cherries, rinsed, stemmed, and pitted

2 tablespoons unsalted butter

Milk for brushing

1 to 2 teaspoons sugar

Lightly sweetened whipped cream for serving

VARIATION

Substitute 1 pound strawberries, rinsed, hulled, and halved, for the cherries.

While sweet cherries are both abundant and delicious during the summer, they can be a little dull when cooked in a pie filling. Punching up the flavor with some tart rhubarb makes a big difference and rescues the cherries from a bland fate.

1. For the filling, combine the sugar and water in a nonreactive saucepan with a cover. Stir over medium heat until boiling, then add the rhubarb. Cook until the mixture returns to a simmer, then remove the pan from the heat and cover it. Let the rhubarb remain in the syrup until it's tender, about 15 minutes. Transfer the rhubarb to a bowl and set it aside.

2. Whisk the cornstarch into the rhubarb syrup and return the pan to the heat. Cook, stirring constantly, until the syrup thickens, comes to a boil, and turns clear, about 3 minutes. Off the heat, stir in the cinnamon and orange zest. Scrape the thickened juices over the rhubarb without stirring them together and let the mixture cool.

3. Set a rack at the lowest level in the oven and preheat to 400°F.

4. Add the cherries to the cooled rhubarb mixture and gently fold the filling together. Scrape into the piecrust and dot with the butter.

5. Finish the top of the pie with a diagonal or perpendicular lattice (page 33). Brush the lattice strips with milk and sprinkle them with sugar.

6. Place the pie in the oven and decrease the temperature to 375°F. Bake until the crust is baked through and the filling is actively bubbling, about 45 minutes.

7. Cool the pie on a rack and serve it on the day it's baked with a little whipped cream.

PEACH & GINGER PIE

A tablespoon of grated fresh ginger enlivens the filling of this peach pie. Use only really ripe height-of-summer peaches to make this. Less ripe peaches lack the flavor necessary for a good filling and are also a nightmare to peel. This is a perfect pie for a crumb topping, especially when you use my improved method for applying it: I often noticed that the bottom of the crumbs added in the usual way had a layer of wet and unbaked flour where they had absorbed moisture from the filling. Now I bake the crumbs and the pie separately for a few minutes before bringing them together.

1. Set racks at the middle and lowest levels in the oven and preheat to 400°F. Line a jelly-roll pan with parchment paper or foil.

2. For the topping, combine the flour, sugar, and nutmeg in a mixing bowl; stir well to mix and stir in the sliced almonds if using. Stir in the butter evenly. Set the mixture aside for 5 minutes, then break it into ¼- to ½-inch crumbs. Scatter the crumbs on the prepared pan.

3. To make the filling, peel the peaches by cutting a cross in the blossom end of each and dropping them three at a time into a pan of boiling water. After 20 or 30 seconds, use a slotted spoon to transfer them to a bowl of ice water. If the peaches are ripe, the skin will slip off easily. If it does not, remove the skin with a sharp stainless-steel paring knife. Holding the peaches over a bowl to catch any juices, slice them into wedges by cutting in toward the pit with a paring knife and drop the wedges into the bowl.

4. Add the sugar, flour, and ginger to the peaches and stir gently with a rubber spatula to combine. Pour the filling into the prepared piecrust and dot it with the butter.

5. Place the pie on the bottom rack of the oven and the crumbs on the middle rack, decrease the temperature to 350°F, and bake for 15 minutes.

6. Remove the pie and crumbs from the oven, chop the crumbs with a bench scraper if necessary and scatter them on top of the pie. Replace the pie on the lowest level and bake for another 30 minutes, or until the crust and the crumb topping are a deep golden and the juices are actively bubbling. Cool the pie on a rack and serve warm or at room temperature.

Makes one 9-inch pie, about 8 servings

One 9-inch piecrust made from Sweet Pastry Dough (page 19)

CRUMB TOPPING

1 cup unbleached all-purpose flour (spoon flour into dry-measure cup and level)

3 tablespoons sugar

¼ teaspoon freshly grated nutmeg

½ cup sliced almonds, optional

6 tablespoons/¾ stick unsalted butter, melted

PEACH FILLING

2½ to 3 pounds firm, ripe yellow-fleshed peaches, see Note

½ cup sugar

3 tablespoons unbleached all-purpose flour

1 tablespoon finely grated peeled fresh ginger

2 tablespoons unsalted butter

NOTE

Ripe peaches can exude an enormous amount of juices into a pie filling. Don't mound the filling beyond an inch above the side of the crust or it will spill a flood of juice into the oven.

VARIATIONS

For a traditionally flavored pie, omit the ginger and flavor the filling with ¼ teaspoon each almond extract and freshly grated nutmeg. An open diagonal or perpendicular lattice top (page 33), would also be perfect on this pie. I don't recommend a full top crust or a closed woven lattice because of the rawness factor mentioned above.

DRIED APRICOT PIE

This pie is directly modeled on old-fashioned recipes for Pennsylvania Dutch raisin pie. To my taste, dried apricots are so much more appealing than raisins for an entire pie filling— their flavor has a welcome touch of tartness that raisins lack.

1. Combine the apricots and water in a nonreactive saucepan and bring the mixture to a full boil. Remove the pan from the heat and let the apricots stand until cooled, about 2 hours.

2. Transfer the apricots and liquid to a bowl. Set a strainer over the saucepan in which the apricots soaked and drain the apricots well, letting the liquid fall back into the pan. Return the apricots to the bowl.

3. Combine the sugar and flour and whisk the mixture into the apricot liquid. Place over low heat and, stirring constantly, bring the juices to a full boil; decrease the heat and simmer for 2 minutes, stirring often. Stir in the lemon zest , butter, and almond extract. Pour the juices over the plumped apricots in the bowl and let cool.

4. Set a rack at the lowest level in the oven and preheat to 375°F.

5. Pour the filling into the piecrust and arrange the lattice top over it (page 33). Brush the lattice with milk and sprinkle with sugar.

6. Place the pie in the oven and decrease the temperature to 350°F. Bake until the crust is baked through and the filling is actively simmering, about 45 minutes.

7. Cool the pie on a rack and serve slightly warm or at room temperature.

Makes one 9-inch pie, about 8 servings

One 9-inch piecrust made from Sweet Pastry Dough (page 19), plus dough for a lattice top

1 pound dried apricots, cut into ½-inch dice (see Note)

3 cups water

¾ cup sugar

3 tablespoons unbleached all-purpose flour

2 teaspoons finely grated lemon zest

2 tablespoons unsalted butter

¼ teaspoon almond extract

Milk for brushing

1 to 2 teaspoons sugar

NOTE

For ease in cutting the apricots, snip them with lightly oiled scissors or use an oiled knife.

VARIATIONS

Substitute a combination of equal amounts dried plums (prunes) and apricots in the filling. Or if you're a real raisin lover, try a combination of dark and golden raisins instead of the apricots. Omit the almond extract and substitute 1 teaspoon vanilla extract.

APPLE & CHEDDAR PIE

Makes one 9-inch pie, about 8 servings

One 9-inch piecrust made from Flaky Buttery Dough or Flaky Dough Using Lard (pages 14 and 15), plus dough for a full top

APPLE AND CHEDDAR FILLING

¾ cup sugar

3 tablespoons unbleached all-purpose flour

1 teaspoon ground cinnamon

2 pounds Northern Spy apples or 1½ pounds Golden Delicious plus ½ pound McIntosh apples, peeled, halved, cored, and cut into ½-inch dice

1⅓ cups/5 ounces coarsely grated sharp cheddar

2 teaspoons lemon juice, strained before measuring

2 tablespoons unsalted butter, chilled and cut into 10 pieces

Milk for brushing

1 to 2 teaspoons sugar

Apple pie served with cheddar is a New England classic, so why not combine them right in the pie filling? My favorite apples for a pie are Northern Spies, but they're available only in the fall and early winter, and mostly in the northeastern United States. Failing that, I think a combination of two thirds Golden Delicious and one third McIntosh perfectly combines sweet and tart with firm and juicy.

1. Set a rack at the lowest level in the oven and preheat to 400°F.

2. For the filling, mix the sugar, flour, and cinnamon in a large bowl. Add the apples and cheddar and fold together to evenly coat the apples with the sugar mixture. Scrape the filling into the piecrust, making sure the top is flat and even rather than mounded in the center.

3. Sprinkle the filling with the lemon juice and dot with the butter.

4. Attach, flute, and pierce the top crust as on page 32. Brush with milk and sprinkle with sugar.

5. Bake the pie for 15 minutes, then decrease the temperature to 350°F. Continue baking until the crust is baked through and the juices are actively simmering, up to 45 minutes longer.

6. Cool the pie on a rack and serve it on the day it's baked.

VARIATIONS

For an apple pie without the cheddar, increase the apples to 2 pounds Golden Delicious and 1 pound McIntosh.

For a change of pace, use half granulated sugar and half turbinado or light brown sugar.

For a maple flavor, use ½ cup sugar and ⅓ cup maple syrup, adding the syrup along with the lemon juice and butter before topping the pie. Grade B maple syrup is heartier and better for baking than Grade A.

PEAR & CURRANT PIE

Baking a pear pie requires a little advance planning. Sold hard and green in most stores, pears need to ripen in a paper bag at room temperature for a couple of days before you use them. For the best results, they need to be ripe but still firm—when you press your thumb into the bottom of the pear near the blossom end, it should be just slightly springy. Softer than that, and the pear is too ripe—it will turn into a mass of water when cooked. The best pear to use for a pie is a Bartlett, called a Williams outside North America.

1. Set a rack at the lowest level in the oven and preheat to 375°F.

2. For the filling, thoroughly mix the sugar, flour, and nutmeg in a large mixing bowl. Add the pears and half the currants and gently fold them together.

3. Scrape the filling into the piecrust, making sure the top is flat and even rather than mounded in the center. Sprinkle with the remaining currants and the lemon juice and dot with the butter.

4. Attach, flute, and pierce the top crust as on page 32. Brush the top crust with milk and sprinkle with the sugar.

5. Bake the pie for 10 minutes, then decrease the temperature to 350°F. Continue baking until the crust is baked through and the juices are actively simmering, up to 45 minutes longer.

6. Cool the pie on a rack and serve it on the day it's baked.

Makes one 9-inch pie, about 8 servings

One 9-inch piecrust made from Sweet Pastry Dough (page 19), plus dough for a full top

PEAR AND CURRANT FILLING

½ cup sugar

2 tablespoons all-purpose flour

Pinch of freshly grated nutmeg

2¾ pounds firm, ripe pears, peeled, halved, cored, and sliced ¼ inch thick

½ cup dried currants

2 tablespoons lemon juice, strained before measuring

2 tablespoons unsalted butter

Milk for brushing

1 teaspoon sugar

VARIATION

Substitute the crumb topping, with or without the almonds (page 85) for the top crust; bake the pie and crumb topping according to the instructions in that recipe.

"FRENCH" APPLE PIE

This was a mainstay of retail bakeries about fifty years ago and has all but disappeared from sight. A cooked apple filling with raisins is baked in a sweet crust in a straight-sided pan. After cooling, the top is spread with a simple confectioners' sugar icing. I have no idea how or why it acquired the name, but despite the fact that there is no equivalent in France, it has always been one of my favorite bakery treats.

1. For the apple filling, melt the butter in a wide saucepan or Dutch oven with a cover and add the apples, sugar, cinnamon, and raisins. Stir well and place over medium heat. Cook until the apples start to sizzle, then cover the pan and decrease the heat. Cook until the apples have exuded water, 5 to 10 minutes. Uncover the pan and stir occasionally while the water evaporates. Off the heat, stir in the rum. Spread the filling in a shallow bowl and refrigerate until cooled or up to 2 days before filling the pie.

2. When you are ready to assemble the pie, set a rack at the lowest level in the oven and preheat to 350°F. Butter an 8-inch round pan, 2 inches deep, and line with parchment.

3. Roll out a little more than half of the dough on a floured surface and line the prepared pan, cutting away excess dough at the rim of the pan. Spread the apple filling in the crust. Roll the remaining dough and cut an 8-inch disk. Set it atop the filling and fold the dough on the side of the pan onto the disk of dough to seal it.

4. Bake the pie until the crust is baked through, 35 to 40 minutes. Cool on a rack.

5. Unmold the pie onto a platter, keeping the bottom of the pie as the top.

6. For the icing, place the confectioners' sugar and water in a small saucepan and stir well. Heat to lukewarm and quickly spread on the pie. Let the icing set before serving.

Makes one 8-inch pie, about 8 servings

One batch Sweet Pastry Dough (page 19)

APPLE FILLING

2 tablespoons unsalted butter

2 pounds Golden Delicious apples, peeled, halved, cored, and cut into ½-inch dice

½ cup sugar

½ teaspoon ground cinnamon

¾ cup dark raisins

1 tablespoon dark rum

ICING

1 cup confectioners' sugar, sifted after measuring

1½ tablespoons water

Cobblers & Crisps

There are probably dozens of regional names for fruit baked in a shallow dish with only a top crust. I'm calling anything a cobbler if it has a full top crust of baking powder biscuit, pastry dough, or even a poured-on batter; if it has a crumb or other non-dough topping, I consider it a crisp. These are versatile preparations, and you can have fun adding and subtracting ingredients and flavorings at will. If you want more guidance in the way of fillings, any of the fruit pie fillings on pages 82 to 91 will also make a great cobbler or crisp.

DEEP-DISH BLUEBERRY PIE (WITH CREAM BISCUIT CRUST)

There isn't much difference between this pie and what we normally call a cobbler, except that this has much more fruit in relation to the crust. The blueberries have no thickeners added to mar their natural flavor and juiciness, so the filling is quite soupy.

1. For the crust, place the flour, baking powder, sugar, and salt in a bowl and rub in the butter until fine and mealy. Do not allow the mixture to become pasty. Use a fork to stir in the cream—the dough will be very soft. Press the dough together on a floured surface, turn it over on itself several times to make it slightly more elastic, and wrap in plastic. Set aside.

2. Preheat the oven to 400°F and set a rack in the lower third.

3. Place the blueberries in a bowl and add all the remaining filling ingredients, except the butter. Toss well and pour into a 10- to 12-cup gratin or other baking dish. Distribute pieces of the butter evenly on the filling.

4. Press the dough out on a floured surface until it is roughly the size of the baking dish. Lift the dough onto the filling using a thin, flexible cookie sheet and cut several vent holes in the top. Brush it with some cream and sprinkle it with the sugar.

5. Bake the pie until the crust is deep golden and the filling is bubbling, 25 to 30 minutes. Cool slightly on a rack and serve warm or at room temperature.

6. To serve the pie, use a large spoon to remove a portion of the biscuit crust onto a soup plate. Pour a couple of large spoonfuls of the filling next to it and add some whipped cream or vanilla ice cream.

Makes 1 large pie, about 8 servings

CREAM BISCUIT CRUST

3 cups/400 grams unbleached all-purpose flour (spoon into dry-measure cup and level)

1 tablespoon baking powder

1 tablespoon sugar

1 teaspoon salt

12 tablespoons/1½ sticks/170 grams unsalted butter, slightly softened

1⅓ cups/300 grams half-and-half or light cream

FILLING

4 pints blueberries, rinsed and picked over

¾ cup sugar

2 teaspoons finely grated lemon zest

½ teaspoon freshly grated nutmeg

½ teaspoon ground cinnamon

3 tablespoons unsalted butter

Light cream for brushing

1 to 2 teaspoons sugar

Whipped cream or vanilla ice cream for serving

PLUM & RASPBERRY CRISP

You could use almost any combination of summer fruits in this, but sweet-tart ripe plums are perfect with tart raspberries. Choose red or green plums; prune plums come into season later in the summer and work beautifully too. Peaches or apricots would stand in well for the plums, and earlier in the season, you could sneak in some rhubarb instead of the raspberries. Baking the topping for a few minutes while the fruit begins to cook makes it much more crisp.

1. Set a rack at the middle level in the oven and preheat to 375°F. Butter an 8- to 10-cup baking dish and cover a jelly-roll pan with foil.

2. For the crisp topping, stir the flour, sugar, baking powder, cinnamon, and nuts, if using, together in a medium mixing bowl. Add the butter and use a rubber spatula to fold it in evenly. Let the crumb mixture stand while preparing the fruit.

3. For the filling, mix the sugars and cinnamon in a bowl, then stir in the plums and lemon zest. Pour half the plum filling into the prepared baking dish and scatter on half of the raspberries. Repeat with the remaining plums and raspberries. Dot with the butter.

4. Break the crumb mixture into ¼- to ½-inch crumbs and scatter them on the prepared jelly-roll pan. Bake the crumbs until they are set and beginning to color, about 15 minutes.

5. Use a bench scraper or metal spatula to break up the crumb topping if it has clumped together. Scatter the pieces on top of the fruit, using a large spoon if the crumbs are still hot.

6. Bake until the fruit is tender and bubbling and the crumbs are a deep golden color, 45 to 50 minutes. Cool slightly and serve warm with whipped cream, crème fraîche, or vanilla ice cream.

Makes 1 large crisp, about 8 servings

CRISP TOPPING

1⅓ cups unbleached all-purpose flour (spoon into dry-measure cup and level)

⅓ cup sugar

½ teaspoon baking powder

¼ teaspoon ground cinnamon

½ cup chopped walnuts or almonds, optional

9 tablespoons unsalted butter, melted

FILLING

¼ cup granulated sugar

¼ cup turbinado or light brown sugar

¼ teaspoon ground cinnamon

2½ pounds ripe plums, rinsed, halved, pitted, and sliced ½ inch thick

2 teaspoons finely grated lemon zest

2 half-pint baskets raspberries, picked over but not washed

2 tablespoons unsalted butter

Whipped cream, crème fraîche, or vanilla ice cream for serving

APPLE & CRANBERRY GRANOLA CRISP

Makes 1 large crisp, about 8 servings

APPLE FILLING

⅓ cup turbinado or light brown sugar

¼ cup granulated sugar

2 tablespoons unbleached all-purpose flour

½ teaspoon ground cinnamon

3 pounds Golden Delicious apples, peeled, cored, and cut into thin wedges

1 cup fresh cranberries or ¾ cup dried

2 tablespoons unsalted butter, chilled and cut into 10 pieces

GRANOLA TOPPING

1½ cups rolled oats

½ cup coarsely chopped walnuts, pecans, or almonds

⅓ cup granulated sugar

¼ cup turbinado or light brown sugar

6 tablespoons/¾ stick unsalted butter, melted

Juicy and tart, with a sweet and crunchy granola-type topping, this is as easy to assemble and bake as it is to enjoy. Use old-fashioned rolled oats, not the quick or instant types. The standard crumb topping on page 85, if you bake it for a few minutes first, would also be perfect on this crisp. If you want to serve some cream with this crisp, I prefer liquid heavy cream or crème fraîche to whipped.

1. Set a rack in the middle of the oven and preheat to 400°F. Butter an 8- to 10-cup baking dish.

2. To make the apple filling, mix the sugars, flour, and cinnamon in a bowl and thoroughly fold in the apples and cranberries. Scrape into the prepared dish and level the top; dot with the butter.

3. To make the topping, mix the oats, nuts, and sugars together and thoroughly fold in the butter. Scatter the granola mixture on the fruit in the baking dish.

4. Set the pan in the oven and immediately decrease the temperature to 375°F. Bake until the fruit is tender and bubbling and the topping has become a deep golden color, 45 to 55 minutes.

5. Cool the crisp slightly and serve warm or reheat at 350°F for about 10 minutes before serving.

MIXED BERRY COBBLER (WITH REVERSIBLE TOPPING)

This has been a popular recipe since my childhood. It's usually made with prepared baking powder biscuit mix, but that's easy enough to duplicate with fresh ingredients. Feel free to mix up the assortment of berries any way you like; only blueberries or blackberries have enough flavor and texture once baked to be used on their own, though. Don't try to crowd in extra berries or there might not be enough batter to cover them; and please use only an 8-cup baking dish or the layer of batter might be too thin or thick to magically rise up and cover the berries.

1. Set a rack at the middle level in the oven and preheat to 400°F. Grease an 8-cup baking dish with vegetable spray.

2. For the topping, stir the flour, sugar, salt, baking powder, and spices together in a bowl. Add the milk, 3 tablespoons of the butter, and the lemon zest; whisk smooth.

3. Pour the last tablespoon of butter into the baking dish and tilt the dish to evenly coat the bottom. Pour in the batter.

4. Evenly spoon the berries on top of the batter. Sprinkle with the ¼ cup sugar.

5. Place in the oven and decrease the temperature to 375°F. Bake until the topping has risen to cover the berries and has turned a deep golden color, about 45 minutes.

6. Cool the cobbler on a rack and serve warm or at room temperature with some liquid cream.

Makes 1 large cobbler, 8 to 10 servings

TOPPING

¾ cup unbleached all-purpose flour (spoon into dry-measure cup and level)

⅔ cup sugar

¼ teaspoon salt

2 teaspoons baking powder

Large pinch of ground cinnamon

Large pinch of freshly grated nutmeg

1 cup whole milk

4 tablespoons/½ stick unsalted butter, melted

Finely grated zest of 1 small lemon

BERRIES

2 to 3 cups assorted rinsed berries (blackberries, blueberries, raspberries, and hulled and sliced strawberries)

¼ cup sugar for sprinkling on the berries

Light or heavy cream for serving

CHAPTER 5

SAVORY TARTS & PIES

Savory baking has always appealed to me—at home my grandmother baked pizza rustica filled with dried sausage, prosciutto, and mozzarella every year for Carnival and then again for Easter, and we had the occasional side dish of rice seasoned with ricotta, eggs, and cheese.

Whenever I invite guests for lunch, I panic a few days before, because I haven't decided what to cook. A savory tart, quiche, or pie is often the solution. Add a salad and a fruit dessert, and you have a meal. A savory pie can also be a perfect part of an assortment of hors d'oeuvres for a large party or a first course to be served at the table, especially if the main course is a light dish.

Many nationalities have traditional savory pies. In France a quiche was pretty much always a quiche Lorraine until the "quiche revolution" of the 1960s and 70s added every imaginable savory ingredient to the filling. Now that the craze is over I think of a quiche as a savory tart that has a cream and egg custard poured over the solid ingredients before baking. In Italy a pizza rustica or a torta salata (salted pie) may be made with a single or double crust containing any type of savory filling, though when I think of pizza rustica it's mostly the meat and cheese–filled Easter version. There are quite a few vegetable fillings here, a great choice if you, as I often do, tire of meat and fish-based meals. Aside from pies, there are also some Argentine empanadas and British pasties here. And in chapter 6 you'll find some delicious savory strudels and other savory pastries made from Turkish yufka dough. Try a few of these, and I'm sure you'll add savory tarts and pies to your favorite list of recipes.

Quiches & Other Savory Tarts

These are usually baked in French removable-bottom tart pans with fluted sides about an inch deep. If you have a similar but deeper pan, bear in mind that you're going to have excess dough at the top of your quiche or tart. Once the filling is added, there will be no danger of the side collapsing.

REAL QUICHE LORRAINE Overleaf, page 102

Makes one 10-inch tart, about 8 servings

One 10-inch tart crust made from Flaky Buttery Dough (page 14)

8 ounces slab bacon without skin, sliced ¼ inch thick and cut into ½-inch strips, or thick-cut sliced bacon, cut into ½-inch strips

1¾ cups crème fraîche or 1¼ cups heavy whipping cream plus ½ cup sour cream, at room temperature

5 large eggs, at room temperature

¼ teaspoon fine sea salt

¼ teaspoon freshly ground black pepper

Large pinch of freshly grated nutmeg

Perfect for a fancy breakfast or for brunch, today's quiche Lorraine has its roots in the rustic baking traditions of northeastern France and southern Germany; due to changes in the political breezes, the area known as the Lorraine has several times been a part of both countries. The word *quiche* is derived from the German *Kuchen*, which can refer to both what we call a pie or tart as well as a simple cake. The crust used to be made from a thinly rolled bread dough, and the mixture of cream and eggs, known as *la migaine* in the Lorraine, has always been part of the preparation, but many authorities say the bacon was added later. No cheese, period. Yes, you can make an excellent quiche, tart, or pie with bacon, custard, and cheese—it's just not quiche Lorraine. (See the next recipe, and we can break the rules together.) A quiche Lorraine should be served immediately after it's baked, before the puffy crown of custard has time to sink, so plan accordingly.

1. Set a rack at the lowest level in the oven and preheat to 400°F.

2. Half fill a large saucepan with water and bring it to a boil over medium heat; add the bacon. Once the water returns to a boil, cook the bacon for 3 minutes. Drain.

3. Heat a nonstick sauté pan and add the bacon. Cook over medium heat until the bacon takes on a little color, 3 to 4 minutes. Set it aside to cool, then scatter it over the tart crust.

4. Whisk the crème fraîche and eggs together and season with the salt, pepper, and nutmeg.

5. Place the tart pan on the stovetop or close to the oven to avoid spills when moving it and pour the custard into the crust, filling it to within about ¼ inch of the top.

6. Bake the quiche until the crust is baked through and the filling is set, about 30 minutes.

7. Unmold the quiche and serve it immediately.

LEEK & MUSHROOM QUICHE Overleaf, page 103

The sweet flavor of slow-cooked leeks complements the woodsy scent of mushrooms especially well in the creamy custard of this quiche. Although it might be delicious to use some fancy wild mushrooms in this, I've crafted the recipe with the white cultivated mushrooms available everywhere. I would definitely prepare the leeks and mushrooms the day before to cut down on the last-minute rush. Since they both need to cook slowly for maximum flavor, cooking them simultaneously actually saves you time. This is a perfect appetizer for an elegant dinner.

1. Melt half the butter in a medium saucepan and add the leeks. Stir to coat them and cook over medium heat until they start to sizzle. Lower the heat and cook, stirring often, until the leeks are reduced and starting to color, about 30 minutes.

2. As soon as you have started the leeks, use a separate pan and the remaining butter to start cooking the mushrooms. Season them with salt and pepper, and once they start to exude their juices, cook them slowly until the juices evaporate and the mushrooms begin to color, about 30 minutes. Mix the mushrooms into the leeks, taste for seasoning, and scrape them into a bowl to cool. For advance preparation, cover and refrigerate them for up to a couple of days.

3. When you're ready to bake the quiche, set a rack at the lowest level in the oven and preheat to 400°F.

4. Whisk the eggs in a large bowl and season them lightly with salt and pepper. Whisk in the cream, cheese if using, and parsley.

5. Spread the leek and mushroom mixture on the tart crust. Pour in the custard mixture, filling only to within ¼ inch of the top of the crust.

6. Carefully set the pan in the oven and immediately lower the temperature to 375°F. Bake until the crust is baked through and the filling is set and puffed, 35 to 40 minutes.

7. Cool the quiche briefly on a rack, then unmold and serve it either hot or warm.

Makes one 10-inch tart, 8 to 10 servings

One 10-inch tart crust made from Flaky Buttery Dough or Olive Oil Dough (page 14)

4 tablespoons unsalted butter

1 pound leeks (about 2 medium), white part and 1 to 2 inches of the green part, sliced ¼-inch thick and washed repeatedly to remove all sand

12 ounces white mushrooms, rinsed and thinly sliced (see Note)

Fine sea salt and freshly ground black pepper

3 large eggs

1 cup half-and-half or light cream

½ cup finely grated Parmigiano-Reggiano, optional

2 tablespoons finely chopped fresh flat-leaf parsley

NOTE

If you want to boost the woodsy flavor, soak ¼ cup dried porcini in 1 cup boiling water for 10 minutes; lift them from the soaking water (they might be sandy), chop them finely, and add them to the mushrooms when you start to cook them.

APPLE, BACON & GRUYÈRE QUICHE

Makes one 10-inch tart, 8 to 10 servings

One 10-inch tart crust made from Flaky Buttery Dough (page 14)

4 ounces bacon, cut into ½-inch strips

2 Golden Delicious apples, peeled, cored, and cut into ½-inch dice

2 cups/6 ounces coarsely grated Swiss Gruyère

1 tablespoon unbleached all-purpose flour

2 cups half-and-half

3 large eggs

¼ teaspoon salt

2 pinches ground white pepper

The interplay of tart apples with the salty cheese and bacon filling make for a delicious and easy brunch dish.

1. Set a rack at the lowest level in the oven and preheat to 400°F.

2. Cook the bacon in a nonstick sauté pan slowly over medium heat until it is browned but not too crisp. Lift it from the fat with a slotted spoon and drain it on paper towels. Cool and scatter it over the tart crust.

3. Drain most of the bacon fat from the pan and add the apples. Cook over medium heat, stirring often, until tender. Cool and scatter them in the crust on top of the bacon.

4. Toss the cheese with the flour and evenly distribute it over the apples. Whisk the remaining ingredients together and pour the mixture over the cheese.

5. Set the tart in the oven and immediately lower the temperature to 375°F. Bake until the crust is baked through and the filling is set and well colored, about 30 minutes.

6. Cool the quiche in the pan on a rack for a few minutes before serving.

POTATO & CHEDDAR QUICHE

I know this sounds starchy, but give it a try. It is my attempt to combine the goodness of home-fried potatoes with the cheesy richness of a cheddar custard. It's a great breakfast or brunch dish and is so easy to get ready in advance. If possible, boil the potatoes the day before and let them dry at room temperature.

1. The day before preparing the quiche, place the potatoes in a saucepan and cover them with water. Place them over medium heat and bring them to a boil for 10 minutes, then cover the pan, remove it from the heat, and let the potatoes sit until they have cooled. Drain the potatoes for a few minutes, then keep them at a cool room temperature until the next day—this helps to evaporate some of the excess moisture the potatoes have absorbed.

2. Peel and trim any blemished areas and cut the potatoes into ⅜-inch dice—you don't need to use a ruler but the texture of the filling is better when the pieces aren't too large. Melt the butter in a nonstick sauté pan and add the onion. Cook over low heat until soft and translucent, about 10 minutes. Add the potatoes, season generously with salt and pepper, add the thyme (if you're substituting parsley, stir it in after the potatoes have cooled), and toss well. Increase the heat slightly so that the potatoes start to color. Cook, stirring often, until the potatoes are nicely flecked with brown, 10 to 15 minutes. Scrape the potatoes onto a plate and let cool.

3. Set a rack at the lowest level in the oven and preheat to 400°F.

4. Arrange the potato mixture in the tart crust without pressing it down, then toss the cheese and flour together and scatter on the potatoes. Whisk the eggs in a bowl, season lightly with salt, pepper, and nutmeg, and whisk in the half-and-half.

5. Pour the custard into the quiche, filling only to within ¼ inch of the top of the crust.

6. Set the pan in the oven and immediately lower the temperature to 375°F. Bake until the crust is baked through and the filling is set and puffed, 35 to 40 minutes.

7. Cool the quiche briefly on a rack, then unmold and serve either hot or warm. This doesn't make a great leftover as the filling becomes heavy after the potatoes have cooled. Reheat leftovers at 350°F for 15 minutes before serving.

Makes one 10-inch tart, 8 to 10 servings

One 10-inch tart crust made from Flaky Buttery Dough (page 14)

1 pound Yukon Gold or other flavorful yellow potatoes

3 tablespoons unsalted butter

½ cup minced white onion

Fine sea salt and freshly ground black pepper

1 teaspoon finely chopped fresh thyme leaves (substitute 1 tablespoon chopped fresh parsley rather than dried thyme)

1 cup/4 ounces coarsely grated sharp cheddar

1 tablespoon unbleached all-purpose flour

3 large eggs

Large pinch of freshly grated nutmeg

1 cup half-and-half or light cream

QUICHE OF SALMON & PEAS

Makes one 10-inch tart, 8 to 10 servings

One 10-inch tart crust made from Flaky Buttery Dough (page 14)

12 ounces skinless and boneless salmon fillet

Fine sea salt and freshly ground black pepper

1¼ cups/6 ounces shelled tiny peas, fresh or frozen

1 tablespoon unsalted butter

Pinch of sugar

1 tablespoon finely chopped fresh flat-leaf parsley

1 tablespoon finely chopped fresh dill

4 large eggs

⅔ cup light cream or half-and-half

1 teaspoon finely grated lemon zest

Long the traditional July Fourth meal in the state of Maine, early peas and salmon have not been in season so far north at the beginning of July for over a hundred years, according to culinary historians. Oh, well, they still taste great together, especially in a creamy quiche. All the elements of the dish are quite at home in a tart crust, and it's also an easy way to serve them all hot at the same time. A great way to use leftover cooked salmon or other firm-fleshed fish, this is also good with diced cooked shrimp or even crabmeat.

1. Set one rack at the middle level in the oven and another at the lowest level and preheat to 375°F. Butter a small baking dish.

2. Season the salmon with salt and pepper and place it in the prepared pan; bake the salmon on the middle oven rack until it just begins to flake easily, 15 to 20 minutes, depending on its thickness. Undercooked a little is preferable to the alternative. Transfer the salmon to a plate to cool. Raise the oven temperature to 400°F.

3. Meanwhile, fill the bottom of a small saucepan with water and add the peas, butter, and sugar. Bring to a boil and cook over low heat at a slow simmer until tender, about 5 minutes. Cool the peas.

4. Flake the salmon with a fork and scatter evenly on the tart crust. Top with the parsley and dill, then the peas.

5. Whisk the eggs well, season them lightly with salt and pepper, then whisk in the cream and the lemon zest.

6. Pour the custard mixture into the crust, filling only to within ¼ inch of the top.

7. Set the pan on the bottom rack in the oven and immediately lower the temperature to 375°F. Bake until the crust is baked through and the filling is set and puffed, 25 to 30 minutes.

8. Cool the quiche briefly on a rack, then unmold and serve it either hot or warm.

CURRIED CRABMEAT TART

Makes one 10-inch tart, about 8 servings

One 10-inch tart crust made from Flaky Buttery Dough (page 14), fully baked

2 tablespoons safflower or other mild vegetable oil

1 small bunch scallions, rinsed, trimmed, white part and half the green, cut into ½-inch pieces, about ½ cup

12 ounces lump crabmeat

2 tablespoons unsalted butter

1 tablespoon best-quality curry powder

1 teaspoon sugar

1 tablespoon nam prik pao (Thai chile oil condiment)

2 teaspoons oyster sauce

½ cup chicken stock or broth

2 to 4 green, red, or a combination of Thai chiles, stemmed, rinsed, and sliced (see Note)

¼ cup coarsely chopped Asian celery leaves (Western celery leaves can do in a pinch)

4 large eggs

½ teaspoon salt

½ teaspoon freshly ground white pepper

NOTE

If you don't want a lot of heat from the chiles, stem and halve them, then scrape out the seeds with a sharp pointed spoon or measuring spoon. Mexican serrano chiles are a decent substitute for the Thai ones.

A popular dish at seafood restaurants in Bangkok, curried crab is usually served in the shell, leaving diners in need of an immediate shower after the meal. My friend Chef Somsak, who used to have a restaurant in the northern part of the city before the 2011 fall floods destroyed it, made his version, using crabmeat, several times when I visited him there. I was surprised at the use of butter in a Thai dish but Chef Somsak assured me that it's an important part of the preparation. Since the dish already calls for several eggs, I knew it would make an excellent tart filling. This is also a great choice as an appetizer for an important dinner.

Since this only needs to bake long enough to set the eggs in the filling, I'm starting with a completely baked crust.

1. Heat the oil in a wok or sauté pan until medium hot, then add the scallions. Toss for half a minute, then add the crabmeat and butter. Stir-fry quickly, sprinkling on the curry powder and sugar after a few seconds. Stir-fry again very briefly, then pull the wok off the heat.

2. Quickly mix the nam prik pao, oyster sauce, and stock. Return the wok to high heat, add the liquid, and quickly stir-fry. Off the heat, fold in the chiles and celery leaves. Scrape the mixture to a bowl to cool briefly.

3. When you're ready to bake the tart, set a rack at the middle level in the oven and preheat to 400°F.

4. Whisk the eggs well in a bowl with the salt and white pepper and gently fold in the cooled crab mixture. Scrape the mixture into the prepared crust (still in its pan) and use a fork to evenly distribute the crabmeat.

5. Place the tart in the oven, lower the temperature to 375°F, and bake until the eggs are set, 15 to 20 minutes.

6. Cool the tart slightly on a rack, unmold it onto a platter, and serve it warm from the oven but not red hot.

ZUCCHINI & RED PEPPER TART

Zucchini's mild flavor reminds me of Brillat-Savarin's comment that chicken is to cooking what a canvas is to painting. In this case we're painting the zucchini with some red bell pepper and a touch of mildly spicy Turkish urfa chile flakes, both of which enhance but don't drown the mild squash. Less like a quiche and more like a frittata, this tart has no cream or soft cheese to dilute the eggs in the filling.

1. In a bowl toss the zucchini slices with a teaspoon or two of salt. Scrape into a nonreactive colander and set a small plate on the zucchini. Set the colander back in the bowl and place a weight such as a can of tomatoes on the plate. Let the water drain from the zucchini for an hour.

2. Rinse the salt from the zucchini and repeat the weighting and draining to remove the water.

3. While the zucchini is draining, pour the oil into a wide sauté pan and add the onion and bell pepper. Cook over high heat until the vegetables start to sizzle, then lower the heat and sauté gently until they are tender, about 20 minutes.

4. Raise the heat again and add the zucchini. Cook, tossing or stirring, until the zucchini is very tender and reduced in volume, lowering the heat to prevent burning if necessary.

5. Taste for seasoning and adjust with salt. Stir in the chile flakes and the marjoram. Let cool.

6. Set a rack at the lowest level in the oven and preheat to 400°F.

7. Whisk the eggs in a bowl and add the cheese and black pepper. Stir in the cooked zucchini mixture and pour the filling into the tart crust. Use a fork to make sure the vegetables are evenly distributed throughout the filing.

8. Place the tart in the oven and lower the temperature to 375°F. Bake until the crust is baked through and the filling has set, 35 to 40 minutes.

9. Cool the tart on a rack and unmold it to a platter. Serve it warm or at room temperature.

Makes one 10-inch tart, about 8 servings

One 10-inch tart crust made from Flaky Buttery Dough (page 14)

1 pound young, tender zucchini, rinsed, tipped, halved lengthwise, and cut into ¼-inch half moons

Fine sea salt

3 tablespoons olive oil

1 cup sliced white onion

1 large red bell pepper or fresh pimiento, about 8 ounces, cut into ½-inch dice

1 teaspoon urfa chile flakes or another crushed dried chile of your choice

1 tablespoon chopped fresh marjoram or oregano leaves

5 large eggs

½ cup finely grated pecorino Romano

Freshly ground black pepper

SUMMERY TOMATO TARTS

Makes eight 4 ½-inch tarts

Eight 4½-inch tart crusts made from Flaky Buttery Dough or Olive Oil Dough (page 14)

8 ounces fresh goat cheese such as Montrachet or a domestic brand, at room temperature

1 tablespoon finely snipped fresh chives

1 tablespoon chopped fresh flat-leaf parsley

Freshly ground black pepper

1 teaspoon plus 2 tablespoons best olive oil

2 pints/about 1¼ pounds grape tomatoes, rinsed, dried, and quartered

Fine sea salt to taste (see Note)

A handful of tiny top leaves of basil, or 6 large leaves, stacked and cut into thin ribbons

NOTE

Don't salt the tomatoes before baking, as it draws moisture from them and might make the tarts soggy.

Perfectly ripe tomatoes, cheese, and herbs are a great combination, so much so that I think I've done at least three recipes featuring them before. This time around, though, I decided that the combo needed revamping, because I wanted to be able to serve the tart completely cooled as well as fresh from the oven and during seasons when the sweetest field-ripened tomatoes might not be available. That ruled out cheeses I've used in the past, like Gruyère, Cantal, or mozzarella, all of which get rubbery on cooling. Fresh cow's or goat's milk cheese is perfect—but because I don't like how goat cheese dries out when exposed to the oven's heat, I hid it under the tomatoes.

1. Set a rack at the lowest level in the oven and preheat to 400°F.

2. Use a rubber spatula to mash the cheese in a bowl, then stir in the herbs and a few grindings of pepper. Spread the cheese mixture in the bottom of the tart crusts. Drizzle the cheese in each crust with about ½ teaspoon of the olive oil.

3. Divide the tomatoes equally among the tart crusts. Drizzle on a tablespoon of the oil, dividing it equally among the tarts. Grind some pepper over each.

4. Bake until the crusts are deep golden and the tomatoes have softened, 30 to 40 minutes.

5. If you're serving the tarts hot, unmold to a platter, sprinkle with salt, and scatter the basil on each. To serve them cooled, wait to add the salt and basil until you're ready to serve the tarts.

Savory Pies

These are meatier and more substantial than the tarts in this chapter and are served as a main course or on a buffet of savory dishes. The double-crusted ones are also perfect picnic food, because they can easily be eaten out of hand. Just unmold the pie to a cardboard cake round and wrap for transport. All you'll need is a knife to cut and some napkins for serving.

MEXICAN CHICKEN PIE (TARTA DE POLLO Y CHILTOMATE)

My friend Roberto Santibañez, chef/owner of Fonda restaurants in New York City, suggested this combination when I asked him about a chicken pie with Mexican flair. Chicken and vegetables are cooked in a chile salsa from the Yucatan called *chiltomate*, then topped with cornmeal dough before baking. Though the habanero is classic for this, serrano or jalapeño could be substituted. Sour cream harmonizes well served alongside.

1. For the *chiltomate*, preheat the broiler and set a rack about 8 inches from the flame. Cover a pie pan or other small pan with foil. Place the chiles and tomatoes stem sides up on the pan and broil until the tops begin to blacken and the tomatoes start to soften, about 20 minutes. Turn the chiles once or twice—it should take less than 10 minutes for them to soften and for the skin to blacken in spots. By the time the chiles are cooked, the tomatoes should be starting to collapse; let cool for a few minutes. If necessary, remove the chiles and let the tomatoes finish cooking.

2. Once the tomatoes and chiles have cooled, slip the skins from the tomatoes and pull the stems from the chiles. Pour the tomato pulp, chiles, garlic, onion, and salt into a blender and blend to a fine puree.

3. Sprinkle the chicken pieces all over with salt. Heat the oil in a Dutch oven and brown the chicken on both sides in batches, making sure not to overcrowd it. Once all the chicken has been seared and set aside, pour the excess fat from the pan and add the *chiltomate*. Bring the salsa to a boil, scraping up any brown bits clinging to the bottom of the pan. Add the chicken, potatoes, and carrots and return to a boil. Lower to a simmer, set the cover ajar on the pan, and cook until the chicken and vegetables are tender, about 30 minutes.

4. Set a rack at the middle level in the oven and preheat to 375°F. Lightly oil an 8- to 10-cup baking dish.

5. Stir the peas, cilantro, mint, sugar, and vinegar into the chicken and vegetables. Taste and adjust with salt if necessary. Scrape into the prepared dish.

6. Roll the cornmeal dough out on a floured surface until roughly the size of the baking dish. Lift the dough onto the filling using a flexible cookie sheet, and cut several vent holes in the top. Or cut the dough into 2½- to 3-inch disks and overlap on the filling to cover.

7. Bake until the crust is deep golden and the filling is bubbling, 25 to 30 minutes. Cool the pie for a few minutes before serving.

8. To serve, use a large spoon to remove a portion of the crust onto a soup plate. Pour a couple of large spoonfuls of the filling next to it.

Makes 1 large pie, 6 to 8 servings

1 batch Cornmeal Dough with or without cheese (page 18)

CHILTOMATE

2 green habanero chiles

5 large tomatoes, about 2 pounds, stem ends removed and a cross cut into the blossom end

2 to 3 small cloves garlic, crushed and peeled

½ cup coarsely chopped white onion

½ teaspoon fine sea salt

2 pounds skinless and boneless chicken thighs, trimmed of fat and cartilage and cut into bite-sized pieces

Fine sea salt

2 tablespoons olive or safflower oil

2 medium Yukon Gold potatoes, about 8 ounces, peeled and cut into ½-inch dice

2 medium carrots, about 6 ounces, peeled and cut into ¼-inch-thick rounds

1 cup frozen tiny peas

⅓ cup coarsely chopped fresh cilantro

2 tablespoons coarsely chopped fresh mint

½ teaspoon sugar

1 teaspoon sherry vinegar

PIZZA RUSTICA ALLA PARMIGIANA

Makes one 9-inch pie, about 12 appetizer servings

One 9-inch cake pan, 2 inches deep, lined with 1 batch Olive Oil Dough (page 14), using two-thirds for the bottom crust and the remainder for the top crust

1½ cups/12 ounces whole milk ricotta

Fine sea salt and freshly ground black pepper

¼ cup finely chopped fresh flat-leaf parsley

½ cup finely grated Parmigiano-Reggiano

2 large eggs, well beaten

6 ounces boiled ham, thinly sliced

6 ounces fresh mozzarella, thinly sliced

4 large Hard-Boiled Eggs (recipe follows), sliced

I call this Italianate savory pie by this name because I use Parmigiano-Reggiano as opposed to the more typical pecorino Romano in the filling. Cooked ham, thinly sliced mozzarella, parsley-flecked ricotta filling, and hard-cooked eggs make for a lighter pizza rustica than the traditional prosciutto, dried sausage, and soppressata. Serve this as part of a selection of antipasti or as the main course of a light meal.

1. Set a rack at the lowest level in the oven and preheat to 375°F.

2. Use a rubber spatula to mash the ricotta smooth in a mixing bowl and beat in the pepper, parsley, and Parmigiano. Taste for seasoning and add a pinch or two of salt if necessary. Stir in the beaten eggs.

3. Spread a third of the filling in the pastry crust and top it with a layer of half the ham, half the mozzarella, and half the sliced eggs.

4. Spread another third of the filling on the eggs and repeat the layering with the remaining ham, mozzarella, and eggs. Spread on the last third of the filling.

5. Put the top crust in place and seal the edges.

6. Bake the pie for 15 minutes, then lower the temperature to 350°F and continue baking until the filling puffs slightly and the crust is baked through, another 20 to 30 minutes. Avoid overbaking, as this will cause the whey to drain from the ricotta and make the crust soggy.

7. Cool the pie on a rack, unmold it to a platter, and serve it at room temperature. Wrap and refrigerate leftovers.

Hard-Boiled Eggs

1. Put as many large eggs as you need in a saucepan to fit in a single layer and cover by several inches with cold water. Place the pan over medium heat and bring to a full rolling boil. Set a timer and cook the eggs for exactly 6 minutes; the yolks will be set but not overcooked.

2. Put a large bowl in the sink and use a slotted spoon to transfer the eggs to the bowl. Let cold water run over the eggs as you use the back of the spoon to gently smash the shell of each one in several places, then add a couple of cups of ice cubes and enough water to cover the eggs.

3. Peel, then rinse each egg under running water and return to the bowl of ice. Once fully cold, place the eggs in a bowl, cover it with plastic, and refrigerate until needed.

BIANCO FAMILY PIZZA CHIENA

While pizza rustica and pizza chiena are similar, the latter started out with a yeast dough crust and was made like a Neapolitan calzone. Today in southern Italy and among many Italian American families, either sweet or unsweetened pastry dough is used and the pie is baked in a pan. I always use sweet dough for the simple reason that that's the way my family did it. The fresh basket cheese used in the filling of this pie is all but impossible to obtain, even in New York City, except at Easter—you will probably need to substitute ricotta. Try to get the freshly made type; it's much more firm than the supermarket variety.

Thanks to my longtime friend and colleague Andrea Tutunjian for sharing the recipe she learned from her mother, Barbara Bianco Tutunjian.

Makes one 9-inch pie, about 12 appetizer servings

One 9-inch cake pan, 2 inches deep, lined with 1 batch Olive Oil Dough (page 14), using two thirds of the dough for the bottom crust and the remainder for the top

4 large eggs

4 ounces Genoa salami, sliced ⅛ inch thick and cut into ½-inch squares

4 ounces sweet dried sausage, peeled, sliced ⅛ inch thick, and cut into ½-inch squares

3 ounces soppressata, peeled, sliced ⅛ inch thick, and cut into ½-inch squares

5 ounces fresh mozzarella, cut into ½-inch dice

2 ounces provolone, cut into ½-inch dice

6 ounces fresh basket cheese, cut into ½-inch dice, or firm ricotta

5 large Hard-Boiled Eggs (page 114), coarsely chopped

1. Set a rack at the lowest level in the oven and preheat to 375°F.

2. Whisk the eggs in a large bowl, then add the meats, cheeses, and hard-boiled eggs, and thoroughly fold everything together.

3. Scrape the filling into the pastry crust and smooth the top.

4. Put the top crust in place and seal the edges.

5. Bake the pie for 15 minutes, then lower the temperature to 350°F and continue baking until the filling puffs slightly and the crust is baked through, another 20 to 30 minutes. Avoid overbaking, as this will cause whey to drain from the cheese and make the crust soggy.

6. Cool the pie on a rack, unmold to a platter, and serve at room temperature.

ITALIAN KALE PIE (TORTA DI CAVOLO NERO)

In Italy, where they make savory pies from almost every vegetable imaginable, kale is a popular choice, especially in Tuscany, where it's known as *cavolo nero* or black cabbage. Teamed up with pancetta, onion, garlic, ricotta, eggs, and grated pecorino, its slightly bitter flavor is complemented rather than hidden. This is another great solo dish or delicious accompaniment to plain grilled meat or fish.

1. Bring a large pan of salted water to a boil. Add the kale and return to a boil. Cook until tender, about 5 minutes. Drain well, pressing the kale against the colander, cool, and coarsely chop.

2. Combine the pancetta and oil in a large pan and cook over medium heat, stirring often, until the pancetta has colored but is still soft, about 2 or 3 minutes. Using a slotted spoon, transfer the pancetta to a plate covered with paper towels to drain.

3. Add the onion to the pan and cook over medium-low heat until softened, about 10 minutes, stir in the garlic, cook for a few seconds, and then stir in the kale. Heat through and taste for seasoning, adding salt and pepper if necessary. Let cool.

4. Set a rack at the lowest level in the oven and preheat to 400°F.

5. To finish the filling, whisk the ricotta and eggs in a large bowl and whisk in the parsley and pecorino. Fold in the kale mixture and the pancetta.

6. Scrape the filling into the prepared crust and spread evenly. Roll the remaining dough for the top crust and use a pattern to cut it to a 9-inch disk. Fold the dough at the side of the pan down over the filling and place the disk of dough on the filling and folded dough. Cut several vent holes in the top of the pie and brush with oil.

7. Set the pie in the oven and lower the temperature to 375°F. Bake until the crust is deep golden and the filling is set, 35 to 40 minutes.

8. Cool the pie on a rack and serve at room temperature.

Makes one 9-inch pie, about 8 servings

One 9-inch cake pan, 2 inches deep, lined with Olive Oil Dough (page 14), using two thirds of the dough for the bottom crust and the remaining dough for the top

Fine sea salt

1 ½ pounds kale, leaves separated from the lower and interior stems, washed, and drained, see Note

2 ounces pancetta, cut into ¼-inch dice

1 tablespoon olive oil, plus more for brushing

1 cup, about 4 ounces, finely chopped white or yellow onion

1 clove garlic, grated on a Microplane

Freshly ground black pepper

1½ pounds whole milk ricotta

4 large eggs

2 tablespoons finely chopped flat-leaf parsley

½ cup finely grated pecorino Romano

NOTE

If you find kale that has long, thick stems, start with 2 pounds.

SUMMER VEGETABLE PIE

Makes one 9-inch pie, about 8 servings

One 9-inch piecrust made from Flaky Buttery Dough (page 14), plus dough for an open-lattice top crust

3 tablespoons unsalted butter

1 medium white onion, cut into ¼-inch dice, about ¾ cup

1 pound young, tender zucchini, cut into ½-inch dice

1 pound young, tender yellow summer squash, cut into ½-inch dice

Fine sea salt and freshly ground black pepper

Kernels cut from 2 large ears sweet corn

1 cup half-and-half or light cream

⅓ cup finely grated Parmigiano-Reggiano

¼ cup finely cut fresh chives

½ teaspoon fresh marjoram leaves, finely chopped, or ¼ teaspoon dried

3 large eggs

This pie came about when my friend Nancy Nicholas shared some of the produce from her Long Island garden with me. I had a couple of several kinds of vegetables, and not having enough to make a full dish from just one type, I combined them. You can add and subtract at will as long as you keep to the same weight of vegetables so you'll have the right amount of filling for the pie. This pie is excellent on its own, but it's also a handy side dish for simple grilled meats or fish.

1. Melt the butter in a Dutch oven that has a cover and stir in the onion. Cook over medium heat until the onion starts to sizzle. Stirring often, cook until the onion starts to color a little, 3 to 4 minutes. Stir in the zucchini and yellow squash, let them start to sizzle, then lower the heat, season the mixture lightly with salt and pepper, and stir in the corn kernels. Cover and cook until the vegetables are tender, stirring occasionally, 10 to 15 minutes.

2. Remove the cover, increase the heat, and let any accumulated water evaporate. Stir in the half-and-half and cheese. Cook, stirring often, until the mixture comes to a boil.

3. Taste for seasoning (the filling should be slightly overseasoned before the final step of adding the eggs) and stir in the herbs. Cool the filling to room temperature.

4. Set a rack at the lowest level in the oven and preheat to 400°F.

5. Whisk the eggs in a medium bowl and gently fold them into the cooled filling. Pour the filling into the piecrust and set the lattice top on the pie (page 33).

6. Bake the pie for 15 minutes, then lower the temperature to 350°F. Continue baking until the crust is deep golden and the filling is set, about 30 minutes longer.

7. Cool the pie on a rack and serve at room temperature.

PROVENÇAL SPINACH PIE (TOURTE D'ÉPINARDS)

Makes one 10-inch pie, about 10 servings

One 10-inch tart crust made from Olive Oil Dough (page 14), using two thirds of the dough for the bottom crust and the remaining dough for the top

2 pounds baby spinach, rinsed and drained

2 tablespoons olive oil, plus more for brushing

1 large white onion, finely chopped

1 large clove garlic, grated

Fine sea salt and freshly ground black pepper

2 large eggs

1 cup finely grated Parmigiano-Reggiano

½ cup pine nuts, lightly toasted

VARIATION

Sometimes a pie like this has a little soft cheese added to the filling. The closest we can come to that type of cheese is ricotta; if you want to try it, use ½ cup whole milk ricotta, pressed through a fine strainer.

While the official leafy green vegetable of Provence is Swiss chard, I've substituted spinach here for a variety of reasons. First, chard is not a vegetable you can get everywhere, and in the United States we never get the young, tender leaves with entirely undeveloped stems that are required for this pie. On the other hand, baby spinach is only as far away as the nearest supermarket. All sorts of elaborate versions of this pie exist; I gave one of those in a previous book. This time, I've made it simple, straightforward, and easy to prepare. Great alone, it's also an excellent vegetable accompaniment to plain grilled meat or fish. Unlike the other savory pies here, this one is made in a 1-inch-deep French tart pan.

1. Place the spinach, with the rinse water still clinging to it, in a large Dutch oven with a cover and place over high heat. Cover, lower the heat to medium, and steam the spinach for 1 to 2 minutes, stirring once or twice, until wilted and reduced. Drain, let cool, then coarsely chop.

2. Set a rack at the lowest level in the oven and preheat to 400°F.

3. Rinse the pan and cook the oil and onion slowly until the onion is soft, about 10 minutes. Stir in the garlic, cook for a few seconds, then stir in the spinach. Generously salt the spinach and taste to make sure you've added enough. Add pepper, then remove the pan from the heat.

4. Whisk the eggs in a medium bowl, then whisk in the cheese. Fold in the cooled spinach mixture along with the pine nuts.

5. Scrape the filling into the prepared crust and spread evenly. Roll the remaining dough for the top crust and use a pattern to cut it to a 9-inch disk. Fold the dough at the side of the pan down over the filling and place the disk of dough on the filling and folded dough. Cut several vent holes in the top of the pie and brush with oil.

6. Set the pie in the oven and lower the temperature to 375°F. Bake until the crust is deep golden, 35 to 40 minutes.

7. Cool the pie on a rack and serve at room temperature.

FRENCH CANADIAN MEAT PIE (TOURTIÈRE)

Rich, hearty, and perfect for a winter lunch, a tourtière is one of the most beloved and argued over French Canadian dishes. What with slight regional variations, familial preferences, and other influences that have crept in over the years, no one agrees about exactly what's in the filling besides ground meat. This version is adapted from my friend Rhonda Caplan, the recipe developer at Robin Hood Flour, Canada's largest miller.

1. Heat the oil in a large sauté pan and add the celery, onion, and mushrooms and cook on medium heat until the mixture starts to sizzle. Cook, stirring occasionally, until the water from the mushrooms has evaporated and the celery and onion are softened, about 10 minutes.

2. Stir in the garlic and cook for a few seconds, then add the ground meat. Use a wooden spoon to mash the meat and vegetables together so that the meat doesn't cook into large clumps. Continue cooking and mashing until the meat is separated into fine crumbs and starting to color.

3. Stir in the grated potato, salt, pepper, thyme, and spices. Cook, stirring, until the filling is well mixed and very aromatic, about 5 minutes.

4. Scrape the filling into a bowl and cover loosely; refrigerate until completely cooled.

5. Set a rack at the lowest level in the oven and preheat to 400°F.

6. Stir up the filling and taste for seasoning, adding more salt and pepper if necessary. Scrape it into the piecrust and set the top crust in place. Cut vent holes in the top of the pie and brush with the egg wash.

7. Place the pie in the oven and lower the temperature to 375°F. Bake until the crust has turned deep golden, 45 to 50 minutes.

8. Cool the tourtière slightly on a rack and serve warm.

Makes one 9-inch pie, about 8 servings

One 9-inch piecrust made from Flaky Buttery Dough or Flaky Dough Using Lard (page 14 or 15), plus dough for the top crust

2 tablespoons safflower oil or lard

1 outer stalk celery, finely chopped

1 medium yellow onion, finely chopped

3 ounces cultivated mushrooms, rinsed, trimmed, and thinly sliced, about 1 cup

2 cloves garlic, grated

1½ pounds ground pork, beef, veal, or a combination

1 small baking potato (6 to 8 ounces), peeled and grated on the largest holes of a box grater, about 1 cup

2 teaspoons fine sea salt

½ teaspoon freshly ground black pepper

2 teaspoons fresh thyme leaves, finely chopped, or 1 teaspoon dried

Pinch of ground cinnamon

Pinch of ground cloves

Pinch of freshly grated nutmeg

Egg wash: 1 egg whisked with a pinch of salt

Empanadas & Pasties

While the word *empanada* merely means "in bread," empanadas are a popular casual snack in all Spanish-speaking parts of the world. The term refers to the familiar turnover-shaped pastry in the following recipes but may also be used for a large round or rectangular pie.

Doughs for empanadas can vary: In Mexico and Argentina they often use dough that's similar to puff pastry. I've substituted extra-flaky Sour Cream Dough (page 16) for that one. For nonflaky empanadas, I like to use the yeasted dough on page 17—it always bakes to a tender and moist texture.

From Cornwall on the south coast of England come the famous pasties, turnovers of flaky pastry with a meat and vegetable filling. They're easy to make and have a simple, homey flavor. Though the vegetables may be blanched first, the meat, usually beef, is entirely cooked inside the pasty while it's baking. Today's pasties, especially the ones made by chain shops, have all sorts of fillings—even eggs and cheese for breakfast.

ARGENTINE CHICKEN EMPANADAS (EMPANADAS DE FAMAILLÁ)

A city in northern Argentina, Famaillá is also referred to as that country's empanada capital, a well-deserved title, since an annual empanada festival is held there. Don't be put off by the long ingredient list for the filling; it's an easy recipe.

1. Put the chicken in a medium saucepan and cover with water. Add the salt and bouquet garni and bring to a simmer. Cook at an active simmer for 20 minutes, skimming the foam as it rises to the surface, then let the chicken cool in the broth. If you like, cook the chicken in advance, then refrigerate it in the strained broth, covered, for a couple of days.

2. Drain and cut the chicken into ½-inch dice. Reserve ½ cup of the broth.

3. Put the oil and onion in a sauté pan and cook over medium heat until the onion starts to sizzle. Stir once, decrease the heat, and cook until the onion is soft, about 10 minutes.

4. Off the heat, stir in the chicken, potato, and reserved broth, then scrape the mixture into a bowl. Sprinkle on the cumin, paprika, oregano, olives, raisins, and eggs.

5. While the filling is cooling, divide the dough into 80-gram pieces and shape each into a flat disk. Roll each piece of dough into an 8-inch disk and chill if you're not going to assemble the empanadas immediately.

6. Arrange the disks of dough on the work surface and brush the edges with water. Divide the filling equally among the dough rounds, mounding it in the center of each one. Fold the dough over to make a fat half-moon-shaped pastry. >>

Makes twelve 7-inch empanadas

1 pound skinless, boneless chicken thighs, trimmed of fat and cartilage

½ teaspoon fine sea salt

Bouquet garni: 2 small stalks celery, 2 sprigs flat-leaf parsley, 1 large bay leaf, 2 sprigs fresh thyme, tied together

2 tablespoons olive oil

⅓ cup finely chopped onion

1 Yukon Gold potato, boiled until tender and cooled

½ teaspoon ground cumin

½ teaspoon hot Spanish paprika (pimentón)

2 teaspoons chopped fresh oregano leaves or 1 teaspoon crumbled dried leaves

½ cup coarsely chopped green Spanish olives

½ cup raisins

2 large Hard-Boiled Eggs (page 114), coarsely chopped

1 batch Empanada Dough (page 17)

Egg wash: 1 egg whisked with a pinch of salt

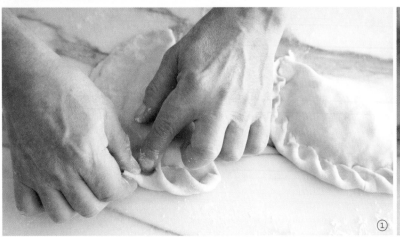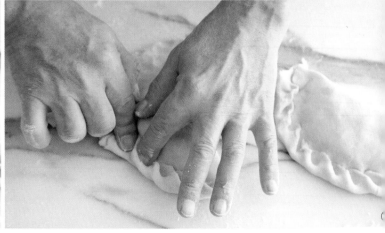

VARIATION

EMPANADAS WITH SAUSAGE FILLING (EMPANADAS DE SALCICA): Omit the chicken and begin with step 3. Remove the casings from 1 pound Italian sausage without fennel and crumble the meat. Add the meat after the onion has begun to soften and cook, breaking the meat up so that it doesn't set in clumps, until any juices have evaporated and the meat is starting to color. Resume with step 4, adding broth if you have it; if not, skip it.

Makes eight 7-inch empanadas

2 pounds baby spinach, rinsed and drained, or 2 10-ounce packages frozen chopped spinach, thawed, squeezed dry, and chopped

3 tablespoons olive oil

1 cup finely sliced scallions (the white part and half the green)

2 cloves garlic, grated

1 ounce anchovy fillets packed in olive oil, finely chopped

Fine sea salt and freshly ground black pepper

2 tablespoons chopped fresh flat-leaf parsley

1½ teaspoons hot Spanish paprika (pimentón)

1 batch Sour Cream Dough (page 16), chilled

Egg wash: 1 egg well whisked with a pinch of salt

7. Press the edges of the pastry together with a fingertip ①, then fold and overlap the edge of the dough ② to seal the empanadas, as in the photographs above.

8. Chill the empanadas, loosely covered with plastic wrap, until you're ready to bake them, up to 24 hours. When you're ready to bake, set a rack in the lower third of the oven and preheat to 400°F.

9. Arrange the empanadas on a cookie sheet lined with parchment and brush them with the egg wash, making sure not to let puddles accumulate on or under the empanadas. Place the pan in the oven, lower the temperature to 375°F, and bake until deep golden, 20 to 25 minutes.

10. Cool the empanadas briefly on the pan on a rack and serve warm.

ARGENTINE CHRISTMAS EVE EMPANADAS
(EMPANADAS DE VIGILIA)

These spinach empanadas make a delicious alternative to the typical meat-laden ones and are traditionally eaten on Christmas Eve, a day of abstinence from meat in Catholic countries. These are usually deep-fried, but I decided to bake them—it's easier, and they turn out much less rich.

1. Put the fresh spinach with the rinse water still clinging to it in a large Dutch oven with a lid. Place over medium heat, cover, and steam for a few minutes until it reduces in volume. Uncover and, stirring occasionally, cook for 1 to 2 minutes longer. Drain, cool, and chop the spinach.

2. Put the oil and scallions into a large saucepan over medium heat. Once the scallions start to sizzle, lower the heat and cook slowly, stirring often, until tender, about 5 minutes. Stir in the garlic and cook for a few seconds. Stir in the chopped spinach and anchovies; cook for a minute or two. If using frozen spinach, cook a couple of minutes longer at this point.

3. Taste the spinach and season with salt and pepper. Stir in the parsley and paprika. Cool the filling.

4. Roll the dough, finish, and bake the empanadas according to steps 5 through 10 on page 122 and above.

CORNISH-STYLE PASTIES

The recipe below is for the steak-filled classic, with a few Variations for taking off on your own. Many thanks to my London friends Rachel Fletcher and her husband, Stephen Fagg, for devoting part of a Cornwall vacation to tasting and photographing pasties for me.

1. Put the potatoes and rutabaga in a saucepan and fill with enough water to cover. Bring to a boil over medium heat and cook for 2 minutes. Drain and cool.

2. Combine the potatoes, rutabaga, and onion in a bowl and sprinkle with the salt and pepper. Use a rubber spatula to fold the vegetables together and then fold in the meat.

3. To form the pasties, divide the dough into 6 equal pieces (or 12 for smaller pasties) and form each into a fat disk. Flatten one and roll to form a 10-inch round (or a 7-inch round for the smaller pasties). Use a pattern such as a cake cardboard to trim the pasty evenly all around. Repeat with the remaining pieces of dough and line them up on your work surface.

4. Divide the filling among the disks of dough, arranging it in a pile in the center. Top each with a piece of butter.

5. Slide your hands, palms up, under opposite sides of a disk; fold your hands to bring the sides of the pasty together. Holding the pasty in one hand, pinch the edges of the dough together to seal them. Place the pasty on the work surface with the fold facing you and pleat and seal the open edge of the dough. As you finish each pasty, set it on a cookie sheet lined with parchment.

6. Let the pasties rest at room temperature for an hour or so before baking. When you're ready to bake, set a rack at the middle level in the oven and preheat to 400°F.

7. Carefully brush the pasties with the egg wash. For darker color and sheen, let the pasties dry for 10 minutes and then egg wash again. Bake for 20 minutes, then lower the temperature to 350°F. Continue baking until the dough turns a deep golden color, at least 20 minutes longer.

8. Cool the pasties on a rack and serve warm. Or let cool completely and reheat at 375°F for 10 minutes before serving.

Makes 6 large pasties or 12 smaller ones

16 ounces Yukon Gold potatoes, peeled and cut into ½-inch dice, about 1½ cups

8 ounces rutabaga, peeled and cut into ½-inch dice, about 1½ cups

7 ounces white onion, cut into ½-inch dice, about 1½ cups

1 teaspoon fine sea salt

½ teaspoon freshly ground black pepper

1½ pounds beef skirt steak, trimmed of excess fat and cut into ½-inch chunks

1 batch Pasty Dough (page 16)

3 tablespoons unsalted butter, cold, cut into 6 or 12 pieces

Egg wash: 1 egg whisked with a pinch of salt

VARIATIONS

Substitute an equal amount of diced skinless, boneless chicken thigh meat for the steak. A tender cut of lamb from the butt end of the leg also works well. Or mix the vegetables and seasonings with a pound of lean ground beef and evenly divide the mixture among the pieces of dough.

If you want a little more seasoning, try a sprinkling of finely chopped fresh thyme leaves or flat-leaf parsley, curry powder, or some hot Spanish paprika.

CHAPTER 6

STRUDEL & OTHER THIN DOUGHS & PASTRIES

If you've never tried making strudel from scratch, you'll be amazed at how easy it is. All you need to do is knead the dough well (or let a stand mixer do the work for you), and you've already taken the necessary steps to make sure that the dough will stretch to the required transparent thinness.

Before completing this book, I had an opportunity to visit Turkey and find out about traditional Turkish pastry doughs firsthand. In both Istanbul and Gaziantep, I visited bakeries and gained some experience in preparing doughs for both savory and sweet specialties.

While I understand that it's faster and easier to purchase a package of phyllo dough at the supermarket, I urge you to try the Turkish yufka dough (it's rolled, not stretched). Both homemade and packaged versions are far superior to any packaged phyllo dough in flavor and performance. Hand-rolled and partially baked yufka leaves are available from Turkish and Middle Eastern stores.

For some sweet Turkish baklava specialties, I've given a dough recipe for those who wish to try it. It's neither difficult to prepare nor tricky to roll, but it is a slow, exacting process that not everyone will have time to attempt. If you decide to resort to using packaged dough, try to find the absolute thinnest dough available, and your results will be as similar as possible to homemade.

STRUDEL DOUGH

Strudel has been made in Austria and Hungary for hundreds of years. My own history with this pastry is a long one. I first tried a strudel recipe in one of my mother's cookbooks as a teenager and was amazed that the dough was so easy to stretch paper thin, especially since I had absolutely no pastry skills at the time. This recipe is straightforward and easy to follow, and outlines the basic method for pulling the dough to the required transparent thinness. When you make a strudel, it is best to prepare the dough up to the point described here, then prepare the filling while the dough is resting. Once the filling has cooled, you can go ahead and stretch the dough, as instructed opposite. Don't try to get away with putting a warm filling in the dough—the strudel will disintegrate when you try to move it to the baking pan. Using an egg in the dough makes it easier to stretch, but a little less fragile after it's baked.

Makes about 12 ounces dough, enough for one 15-to 18-inch strudel

1½ cups/200 grams unbleached bread flour (spoon into dry-measure cup and level)

¼ teaspoon fine sea salt

1 tablespoon vegetable oil or melted butter

1 large egg, optional

Warm water

STRETCHING THE STRUDEL DOUGH

A square or rectangular table 24 x 36 inches or larger

A cloth to cover the table, either an old tablecloth or a clean bedsheet

Flour for dusting

Vegetable oil and a brush

1. Stir the flour and salt together in the bowl of an electric mixer.

2. If you're using the egg, beat the oil and egg together with a fork in a 1-cup liquid measure; if not, just add the oil. Either way, add enough warm water to make ⅔ cup.

3. Use a rubber spatula to mix the liquid into the flour; make sure no flour remains on the side of the bowl and clean off the spatula.

4. Attach the dough hook and mix the dough on the lowest speed until it begins to hold together, about 1 minute. Increase the speed a couple of notches to just below medium and mix until the dough is smooth and elastic, another 2 minutes.

5. Scrape the dough onto a lightly floured work surface and knead for 1 minute. Coat a small bowl with a very thin layer of oil and invert the dough into it; turn the dough over so that the top is oiled, and cover with plastic wrap. Let rest for 1 hour.

Stretching the Strudel Dough

1. Before beginning to stretch the strudel dough, be sure that your filling is ready to go. If a cooked filling needs to cool, the dough can wait in the bowl where it's resting. Once the dough is fully stretched, you have only 10 minutes before you need to fill and bake the strudel.

2. Cover the table with the cloth and dust flour all over it, especially in the center.

3. Take the rested strudel dough out of the bowl without folding it over on itself and set it in the center of the table. Use the palms of your hands to flatten the dough ①.

4. Dust a little flour on the dough and roll it in all directions, going over the edges of the dough too. Make it as thin as you can ②.

5. Brush the top of the dough with oil ③, then begin to stretch it: Place both hands under the center of the dough, make fists, and stretch from the center outward over the backs of your hands ④. Don't worry about the rest of the dough at this point, but keep stretching from the center outward. The dough will lighten in color as it becomes thinner.

6. Again place your fists under the dough; this time, work them hand over hand to stretch the outer thicker part of the dough, going all around the piece of dough.

7. Eventually, the dough will become thin and large enough that you can secure one of the corners over a corner of the table ⑤. Continue stretching from all directions, pulling on the thick ends of the dough, until you cover the table ⑥ or until the dough is at least 24 by 30 inches. Be careful not to pull too hard or too fast—this is what tears the dough.

8. Once the dough has been stretched, let it dry for 10 minutes. While the dough is drying, use scissors to trim away the thick edges and discard them. The following strudel recipes pick up the process from this point.

POPPY SEED STRUDEL

Makes one 15- to 18-inch strudel, 10 to 12 servings

1 batch Strudel Dough (page 128), stretched and ready to be filled

POPPY SEED FILLING

½ cup whole milk

4 tablespoons/½ stick unsalted butter

1 tablespoon honey

Large pinch of ground cinnamon

1 teaspoon finely grated lemon zest

1½ cups ground poppy seeds

¼ cup dark raisins or currants

¾ cup fine dry bread crumbs

1 large egg yolk

¼ cup orange juice, strained before measuring

¼ cup dark rum

2 large egg whites

⅓ cup sugar

4 tablespoons unsalted butter, melted

Confectioners' sugar for finishing

Crème Anglaise (page 180) for serving

NOTE

The correct size *Rehrücken* pan is available at bakingpans.kaiserbakeware.com. It's listed with the loaf pans and is called "classic half-round loaf pan, 12 inches." In a pinch, you can substitute a 12-inch-long loaf pan.

This is adapted from the recipe used at Demel, Vienna's most famous pastry shop, which I visited for an article that appeared in *Saveur* magazine in 2009. I remember testing this recipe at the time, but it never appeared in the article. I like it because it's baked in a *Rehrücken* pan (see Note), and if the strudel bursts while it's in the oven, once it's unmolded, the unsightly part is safely concealed underneath. Viennese deception at its most sophisticated . . .

1. For the filling, bring the milk, butter, and honey to a boil in a small pan and remove from the heat. Stir in the cinnamon, lemon zest, ground poppy seeds, raisins, and bread crumbs; scrape into a bowl and let cool.

2. Once the mixture has cooled, stir in the egg yolk, orange juice, and rum, one at a time.

3. Whip the egg whites in a stand mixer on medium-high speed using the whisk attachment. Once white, opaque, and beginning to hold their shape, increase the speed to high and add the sugar in a slow stream; continue whipping until the egg whites hold a soft peak—don't overwhip.

4. Use a rubber spatula to fold the egg whites into the filling.

5. Set a rack at the middle of the oven and preheat to 375°F. Butter a 12-inch Rehrücken pan.

6. Trim the dough to a 24 x 30-inch rectangle. Spread the filling on a 10 x 12-inch rectangle with the 10-inch side centered about 3 inches in from the edge of the 24-inch side.

7. Use a brush to drizzle the melted butter over the unfilled portions of the dough, reserving a little to brush onto the outside of the strudel.

8. Begin rolling the strudel: Fold the 3 inches of dough over the filling, then fold the unfilled dough in from each side. Lift the cloth and roll the strudel ①, stopping and folding the edges inward as you go ②. End with the edge of the dough on the bottom of the strudel ③.

9. Fold back the excess cloth so that the strudel is right side up at the cloth's edge, then invert it into the pan seam side up ④. Brush the top with butter and snip vent holes with scissors.

10. Place the strudel in the oven and lower the heat to 350°F. Bake until golden, about 30 minutes, then lower the temperature to 325°F and bake until the internal temperature reaches 180°F, about 20 minutes longer.

11. Unmold the strudel to a rack to cool. Dust lightly with confectioners' sugar and slide onto a platter; serve it with Crème Anglaise.

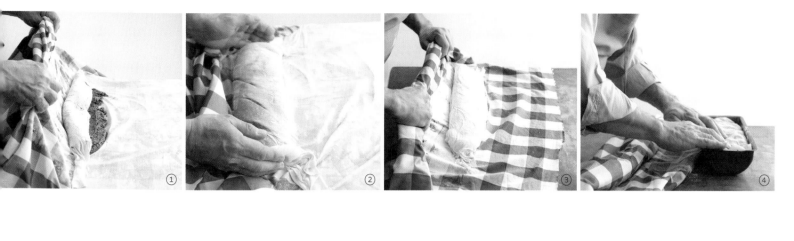

OLD VIENNA APPLE STRUDEL

Makes one 15- to 18-inch strudel, 10 to 12 servings

1 batch Strudel Dough (page 128), stretched and ready to be filled

APPLE FILLING

2 pounds Golden Delicious apples, peeled, halved, cored, and thinly sliced

½ cup sugar

½ teaspoon cinnamon

½ cup raisins

¼ cup water

8 tablespoons/1 stick unsalted butter

¾ cup dry bread crumbs

¾ cup coarsely chopped walnut pieces

1 cup sour cream

Confectioners' sugar for finishing

Lightly sweetened whipped cream for serving

VARIATION

For a simpler filling, omit the sour cream and walnuts.

This is justifiably the most popular strudel in Vienna, whether homemade, enjoyed at a coffeehouse, or bought from a pastry shop. In Vienna it's common to use very tart raw apples in the filling; all the steam and juices generated by the apples result in a strudel where the dough is soft and moist rather than crisp. I like cooking the apples for the filling so that the strudel bakes crisp. Spooning some sour cream in with the apples is a classic old-fashioned Viennese way with strudel. See the Variation for a plain apple strudel.

1. For the filling, combine the apples, sugar, cinnamon, and raisins in a nonreactive pan with a cover. Add the water and bring to a boil over medium heat, stirring occasionally. Cover and steam for 5 minutes. Uncover the pan, increase the heat to high, and let the juices concentrate for a couple of minutes. Pour the filling onto a shallow platter and let cool to room temperature.

2. Melt 5 tablespoons of the butter in a small sauté pan and add the bread crumbs. Cook over medium-low heat, stirring often, until toasted and golden, about 5 minutes. Set aside to cool. Wipe the pan and melt the remaining 3 tablespoons butter.

3. Set a rack at the middle level in the oven and preheat to 400°F. Cover a large jelly-roll pan with heavy-duty aluminum foil or a double thickness of parchment.

4. Trim the dough to a 24 x 30-inch rectangle and arrange it with the 24-inch edge facing you. Scatter the bread crumbs on a 12 x 16-inch rectangle of dough centered about 3 inches in from the 24-inch side so the 16-inch side of filling is parallel to the 24-inch side of dough. Scatter the cooled filling on the same space, followed by the walnuts. Use a teaspoon to drop the sour cream all over.

5. Use a brush to drizzle the remaining butter all over the unfilled portions of the dough, reserving a little to brush on the outside of the rolled strudel.

6. Roll the strudel and transfer to the pan (see the photos on page 131). If your pan is short, position the strudel diagonally.

7. Brush the outside of the strudel with the remaining butter and use sharp scissors to snip some vent holes in the top.

8. Place the strudel in the oven and lower the heat to 375°F. Bake until deep golden and crisp, 30 to 40 minutes. Cool on a rack. If you are going to serve the strudel soon after it's baked, cut into portions and transfer one at a time to a serving platter, reassembling the strudel. (In Vienna, strudel is almost always cut on the pan.) Dust lightly with confectioners' sugar and serve with lightly sweetened whipped cream.

APRICOT & CHEESE STRUDEL

Both this and the plainer cheese strudel with raisins described in the Variation are Viennese classics. This cheese filling is equally good with sour cherries, prune plums, or blueberries, though in Vienna soft fruits and berries are usually used with a nut-based filling that bakes somewhat dry to accommodate the juices from the fruit.

1. For the filling, bring the milk to a simmer in a small saucepan and stir in the cubed bread off the heat. Leave the mixture to soak for 1 minute, then force the bread through a strainer into a bowl, followed by the cheese.

2. In another bowl, use a rubber spatula to beat the butter and sugar together, then beat in the yolks, lemon zest, and vanilla. Beat in the bread and cheese, then stir in the cream.

3. Set a rack at the middle level in the oven and preheat to 400°F. Cover a large jelly-roll pan with heavy-duty aluminum foil or a double thickness of parchment.

4. Trim your piece of dough to a 24 x 30-inch rectangle and arrange it with the 24-inch edge facing you. Spread the cheese filling on a 12 x 16-inch rectangle of dough centered about 3 inches in from the 24-inch edge so the 16-inch side of filling is parallel to the 24-inch side of dough. Scatter the sliced apricots all over the filling.

5. Use a brush to drizzle the melted butter over the unfilled portions of the dough, leaving a little to brush onto the outside of the rolled strudel.

6. Roll the strudel and transfer to the pan (see the photos on page 131). If your pan is short, position the strudel diagonally.

7. Brush the outside of the strudel with the remaining butter and use sharp scissors to snip some vent holes in the top.

8. Place the strudel in the oven and lower the heat to 375°F. Bake the strudel until it is deep golden and crisp, 30 to 40 minutes. Cool it on a rack. If you are going to serve the strudel soon after it's baked, cut it into portions and transfer them one at a time to a serving platter, reassembling the strudel. (In Vienna, strudel is almost always cut on the pan on which it was baked.) Dust it lightly with confectioners' sugar.

Makes one 15- to 18-inch strudel, 10 to 12 servings

1 batch Strudel Dough (page 128), stretched and ready to be filled

APRICOT AND CHEESE FILLING

⅓ cup whole milk

3 ounces good-quality white bread, trimmed of crusts before measuring, diced

1½ pounds salted farmer cheese or part-skim ricotta

3 tablespoons unsalted butter, softened

½ cup sugar

3 large egg yolks

2 teaspoons finely grated lemon zest

1½ teaspoons vanilla extract

½ cup heavy whipping cream

1 pound fresh apricots, rinsed, stemmed, halved, pitted, and sliced

4 tablespoons/½ stick unsalted butter, melted

Confectioners' sugar for finishing

VARIATION

Omit the apricots and use 1 cup golden raisins, soaked in a tablespoon of rum for 1 hour.

TYROLEAN STRUDEL See page 134

Makes one 15- to 18-inch strudel, 10 to 12 servings

1 batch Strudel Dough (page 128), stretched and ready to be filled

DRIED FRUIT AND NUT FILLING

1½ cups milk

⅓ cup sugar

2 tablespoons unbleached all-purpose flour

4 large eggs, separated

Finely grated zest of 1 small lemon

¼ teaspoon ground cinnamon

1 cup currants

1 cup diced pitted dates

1 cup stemmed and diced dried figs

1 cup coarsely chopped walnut pieces

4 tablespoons/½ stick unsalted butter, melted

Confectioners' sugar for finishing

VARIATION

The classic Viennese recipe for this also calls for dried pears. If you wish to add them, reduce the other dried fruits to ¾ cup each and add ¾ cup diced dried pears.

This rich strudel, studded with dried fruit and nuts, is a perfect dessert for winter, when fresh fruit is not as plentiful. This strudel is particularly beloved in Austria; anything referred to as coming from the Tyrol makes the Austrians recall the pleasure of vacationing in the mountains and donning *Lederhosen* or *Dirndln*. This is adapted from *Wiener Susspeisen/Viennese Sweet Foods* by Eduard Mayer, the bible of Viennese baking.

1. For the filling, bring the milk to a boil with a third of the sugar over low heat. Meanwhile, mix another third of the sugar with the flour and whisk in the egg yolks smoothly. Once the milk boils, whisk half into the yolk mixture. Return the remaining milk to a boil and pour in the yolk mixture, whisking constantly, until the cream thickens and comes to a full boil. Whisk in the lemon zest and cinnamon. Scrape the cream into a bowl, press plastic against the surface, and chill until cold.

2. Stir in the dried fruits and walnuts.

3. Whip the egg whites in a stand mixer on medium-high speed using the whisk attachment. Once the egg whites are opaque and beginning to hold their shape, increase the speed to high and add the remaining third of the sugar in a slow stream; continue whipping until the egg whites hold a soft peak—don't overwhip.

4. Use a rubber spatula to fold the egg whites into the filling.

5. Set a rack at the middle level in the oven and preheat to 400°F. Cover a large jellyroll pan with heavy-duty aluminum foil or a double thickness of parchment.

6. Trim your piece of dough to a 24 x 30-inch rectangle arranged with the 24-inch edge facing you. Spread the filling on a 12 x 16-inch rectangle of dough centered about 3 inches in from the 24-inch side so the 16-inch side of filling is parallel to the 24-inch side of dough. Use a brush to drizzle the melted butter all over the unfilled portions of the dough, reserving a little to brush onto the outside of the strudel.

7. Roll the strudel and transfer to the pan (see the photos on page 131). If your pan is short, position the strudel diagonally.

8. Brush the outside of the strudel with the remaining butter and use sharp scissors to snip some vent holes in the top.

9. Place the strudel in the oven and lower the heat to 375°F. Bake until deep golden and crisp, 30 to 40 minutes. Cool the strudel on a rack. If you are going to serve the strudel soon after it's baked, cut into portions and transfer to a serving platter one at a time, reassembling the strudel. (In Vienna, strudel is almost always cut on the pan.) Dust lightly with confectioners' sugar.

STRUDEL OF GREENS, BACON & GOAT CHEESE See page 135

Savory strudels are home-style fare in Vienna, and cabbage strudel is the most popular by far. I like cabbage, but for a strudel, I like the idea of using darker greens. When buying the greens, make sure the leafy, tender parts will add up to a pound after you've removed any tough stems. Feel free to substitute another cheese like feta, Gruyère, or a blue-veined cheese like Roquefort.

1. For the filling, bring a large pan of salted water to a boil. Add the greens and bring back to a boil. For spinach and other tender greens, drain immediately. For tougher ones like kale, let the greens cook until tender, then drain. Cool, coarsely chop, and place the greens in a large bowl.

2. Cook the bacon until nicely colored but not too crisp; transfer to the bowl of greens.

3. Bring the milk and butter to a boil over low heat; remove the pan from the heat, stir in the flour until the mixture is smooth, and cool slightly. Stir in the eggs, one at a time; fold the mixture into the greens and bacon. Season well with salt and pepper.

4. Set a rack at the middle level in the oven and preheat to 400°F. Cover a large jellyroll pan with heavy-duty aluminum foil or a double thickness of parchment.

5. Trim your piece of dough to a 24 x 30-inch rectangle and arrange it with the 24-inch edge facing you. Spread the filling on a 12 x 16-inch rectangle of dough centered about 3 inches in from the 24-inch side so the 16-inch side of filling is parallel to the 24-inch side of dough. Scatter the cheese, walnuts, and chives on the filling.

6. Use a brush to drizzle the melted butter over the unfilled portions of the dough, reserving a little to brush onto the outside of the rolled strudel.

7. Roll the strudel and transfer to the pan (see the photos on page 131). If your pan is short, position the strudel diagonally.

8. Brush the outside of the strudel with the remaining butter and use sharp scissors to snip some vent holes in the top.

9. Place the strudel in the oven and lower the heat to 375°F. Bake until deep golden and crisp, 30 to 40 minutes. Cool on a rack. If you are going to serve it soon after it's baked, cut into portions and transfer to a serving platter one at a time, reassembling the strudel. (In Vienna, strudel is almost always cut on the pan.) If you are making the strudel ahead of time and would like to serve it warm, leave it whole; when you are ready to serve, reheat it at 350°F for 10 minutes, then cut and place on plates or a platter.

Makes one 15- to 18-inch strudel, 10 to 12 servings

1 batch Strudel Dough (page 128), stretched and ready to be filled

GREENS, BACON & GOAT CHEESE FILLING

Fine sea salt

1¼ pounds assorted greens, such as baby spinach, Swiss chard, kale, watercress, or a combination, tough stems removed, rinsed and drained

4 ounces slab bacon or thick-cut bacon, cut into ¼-inch dice

½ cup whole milk

3 tablespoons unsalted butter

½ cup unbleached all-purpose flour (spoon into dry-measure cup and level)

2 large eggs

Freshly ground black pepper

8 ounces crumbled fresh goat cheese, such as Montrachet

1 cup coarsely chopped walnut pieces, lightly toasted

½ cup finely snipped fresh chives

4 tablespoons/½ stick unsalted butter, melted

TURKISH PISTACHIO PASTRY (KATMER)

Makes two 9-inch square katmer,
about 6 servings

KATMER DOUGH

1½ cups/200 grams unbleached all-purpose
flour (spoon into dry-measure cup and level)

¼ teaspoon fine sea salt

1 large egg

1 tablespoon vegetable or light olive oil,
plus more for rolling the dough

Warm water

2 ounces kaymak (Turkish clotted cream;
see Note)

6 ounces unsalted very green pistachios,
finely chopped

¼ cup sugar

NOTE

Kaymak, made from the cream that solidifies
on the surface when milk is boiled to make
yogurt, is available both fresh and frozen in
Middle Eastern grocery stores.

My friend Cenk Sönmeszoy first told me about katmer—a square pastry containing several layers of dough as well as Turkish clotted cream, sugar, and finely chopped pistachios—and sent me links to videos of some very skilled bakers who throw the dough around like a bedsheet to make it larger and thinner. I even had a chance to try my hand at it when I visited Mustafa Özgüler's Orkide pastry shop in Gaziantep and had a lesson from katmer master Murat Güney. The method here is simplified but gives excellent results.

1. For the dough, stir the flour and salt together in the bowl of an electric mixer.

2. Use a fork to beat the egg and oil in a 1-cup liquid measure, then add enough warm water to make ⅔ cup. (Or place a bowl on the scale, set it to zero, and add the eggs, oil, and enough water to make 150 grams.) Use a rubber spatula to stir the liquid and the flour together. Scrape the bowl and spatula, then beat the dough on the lowest speed using the dough hook, until it begins to turn smooth, about 3 minutes. Stop the mixer and let the dough rest for 15 minutes.

3. Beat the dough on medium speed until smooth and elastic, about 1 minute. Then scrape the dough onto an oiled surface, and repeatedly smack it against the table ①, folding and kneading it between smacks. After smacking the dough against the work surface 100 times, knead it together and divide into 2 pieces, each about 225 grams.

4. Round, then oil the pieces of dough. Place them close together on a plate and cover them with plastic wrap. Let the dough rest for at least 1 hour and up to 8 hours; longer is better.

5. Set a rack at the middle level in the oven and preheat to 450°F. Lightly oil 2 jelly-roll pans.

6. Oil a smooth work surface and the dough and roll it as thinly as possible ②. Once the dough is rolled, oil the top of it again. Starting at the edge of the dough closest to you, lift the edge of the dough and pull it thinner toward you ③. Continue around each side of the dough, lifting and pulling thinner as you do, until the dough is approximately an 18-inch square ④.

7. Tear or cut the thick edges from the dough, then fold it inward on 4 sides to make a 12-inch square ⑤. Dot the surface of the dough with half of the kaymak, followed with half each of pistachios and sugar ⑥.

8. Fold the corners of the square in toward the center, overlapping them slightly—you'll have an approximate 9-inch square ⑦. Slide the katmer onto one of the prepared pans, then repeat the process with the remaining piece of dough. Bake until deep golden and crisp, 10 to 15 minutes.

9. Slide each katmer to a cutting board and cut into 2-inch squares. Slide the squares onto a platter and serve immediately.

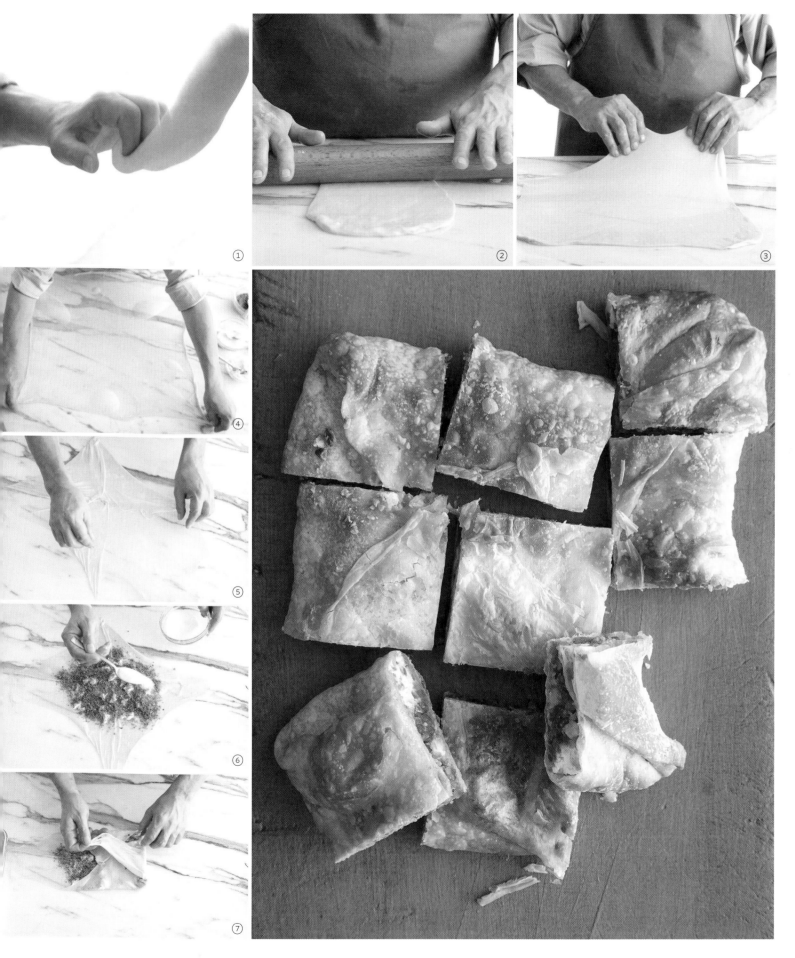

Thin Doughs

Though once a dough is pulled, stretched, or rolled to paper thinness, it might look exactly like other doughs in this category, there are subtle differences in ingredients, thickness, and even storage. Here are some of the principal types, with a short explanation of how each one is made:

Packaged phyllo (or filo) dough: Made from a combination of bread or other strong flour, water, a little oil or vegetable shortening, and salt, most Greek-style phyllo is sold refrigerated and often loaded with preservatives and/or vegetable shortening; unfortunately, it remains the best choice available for making baklava if you don't prepare the dough yourself.

Yufka: A thin Turkish dough made from flour, water, and a little salt, it is stretched over a thin dowel. Yufka is mostly used for savory Turkish pastries.

Baklava: A generic term for sweet pastries made from thin dough in Turkey. The dough is made from high-gluten flour, eggs, water, and salt. While most of us think of baklava as many layers of pastry stacked with a nut filling between, in Turkey, baklava takes on many different shapes. Nuts, most often pistachios, are always used for the filling and may be accompanied by an unsweetened "cream" made from reduced milk thickened with semolina.

TURKISH BAKLAVA DOUGH

Unlike dough for strudel, baklava dough is entirely rolled, and the end result is much thinner. Professional baklava makers roll a stack of eight layers of dough simultaneously, a feat you don't need to duplicate. Using a pasta machine at the beginning of the process is helpful, letting you start with pieces of dough that are evenly squared off. Try rolling four pieces of dough at a time; if that's too difficult, then try with two, and it will go much more quickly. You will need a 7/8-inch diameter dowel, 24 inches long, preferably hardwood, for rolling the dough. Also, have everything ready to assemble your baklava before you start rolling. The dough has to be used immediately after it's rolled, or it will dry out and shatter.

Makes sixteen 12 x 18-inch sheets of dough

2 large eggs

Warm water

1 teaspoon lemon juice, strained before measuring

½ teaspoon fine sea salt

3¾ cups/500 grams high-gluten flour (spoon into dry-measure cup and level)

Wheat starch for rolling

MIXING THE DOUGH

1. Place the bowl of an electric mixer on your scale and set it to zero. Crack the eggs into the bowl and break them up with a fork. Add enough warm water to bring the total weight to 300 grams and whisk the eggs and water together. Whisk in the lemon juice and salt.

2. Use a rubber spatula to stir in the flour, making sure that none sticks to the side of the bowl.

3. Place the bowl on the mixer with the dough hook and mix on the lowest speed until it pulls cleanly away from the side of the bowl, about 5 minutes. Let rest for 15 minutes.

4. Start the mixer again on low-medium speed and mix until smooth and elastic, 3 to 5 minutes more ①. Cover the bowl and let the dough rest for 1 hour.

INITIAL ROLLING

1. Scrape the dough onto a floured surface and divide it into 4 pieces, each 200 grams.

2. Dust the surface and one piece of dough with wheat starch and roll to an even 4-inch square. Set aside covered with a towel and repeat with the remaining pieces.

3. Start running the pieces of dough, one at a time, through the widest setting on the pasta machine ②. If a piece of dough comes through with a narrow strip on either end, fold the narrower area back onto the dough so that the ends of the piece are straight and even. Remember to dust the dough often with starch while rolling it through the machine.

4. Once the sheets of dough are smooth and even, start running them through every other setting, stopping when the dough is a little less than ⅛ inch thick, 4 inches wide, and about 24 inches long ③ (this is usually the third setting before the thinnest, depending on the machine).

5. Cut each of the strips of dough crosswise into 4 pieces, so that you have 16 that are approximately 4 x 6 inches. Stack the sheets of dough on a starch-dusted work surface, sprinkling starch between each one. Cover with plastic wrap and a towel. >>

①

②

③

ROLLING THE DOUGH

1. Dust the work surface with starch and place a sheet of dough on it. Dust the top with more starch and place another sheet of dough on it; repeat until you have stacked 4 layers of dough. Turn the stack of dough so that the narrower end is facing you and dust the top with starch. It's also possible to roll only 2 pieces of dough at a time according to all the instructions below, or even a single piece—see step 10.

2. Roll over the stack of dough from the end closest to you toward the far end and back 2 or 3 times ①. Roll over the width of the dough, without rolling over the ends, to make the sheets of dough wider ②.

3. Place the rolling pin about 1½ inches onto the dough and begin wrapping the whole stack of dough around the rolling pin, rolling it away from you.

4. Place both hands on the dough while it's wrapped on the pin and roll it back and forth, also stretching horizontally with your hands to widen it. Roll and stretch the stack 4 or 5 times, then unfurl from the pin.

5. Dust the top piece of dough with starch and roll it up onto the rolling pin. Repeat with the remaining pieces of dough so that you add another piece right up against the end of the previous one ③; the four sheets of dough are now rolled consecutively around the rolling pin.

6. Wrap both hands around the dough on the rolling pin and hold the rolling pin out in front of you. Gently pull on the dough to widen it ④.

7. Repeat step 4.

8. Unfurl the outside sheet of dough onto the work surface and dust with starch. One by one, unfurl the remaining dough pieces and stack them on top, dusting the surface of each with starch.

9. Repeat steps 2 through 7.

10. Alternatively, follow steps 2, 3, 4, 6 and 7 with a single piece of dough ⑤ and ⑥. Cover the dough stack with plastic wrap and a towel.

11. Repeat steps 1 through 11 with the remaining 12 pieces of dough, rolling them 4 or 1 at a time.

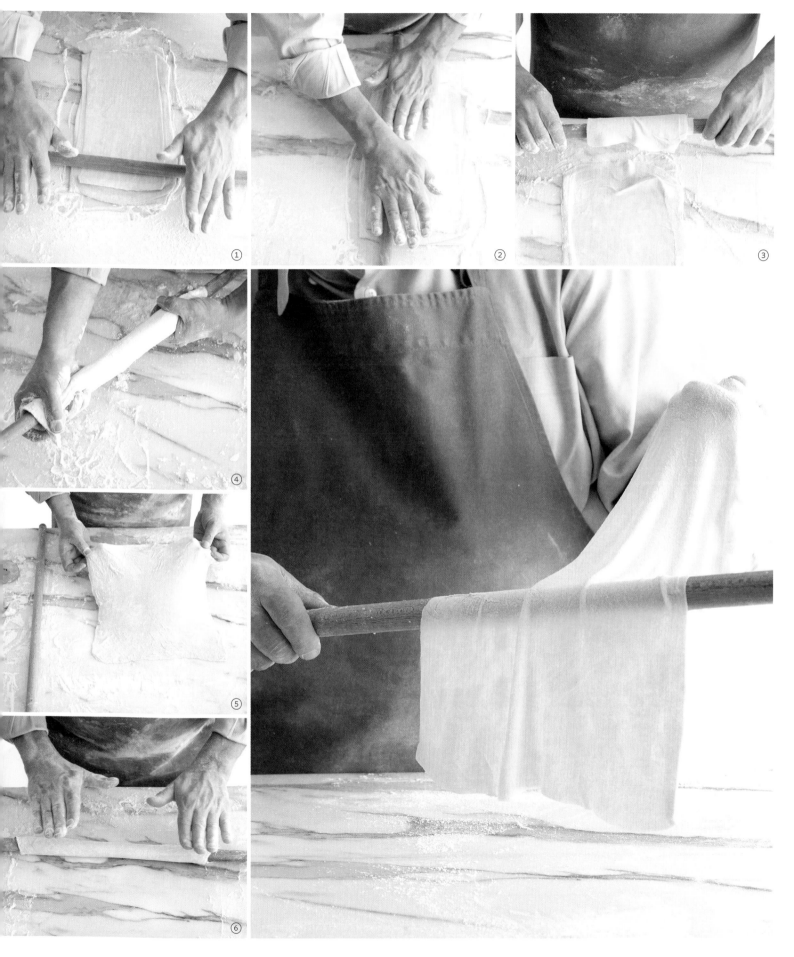

TURKISH "CARROT SLICE" BAKLAVA (HAVUÇ DİLİMİ BAKLAVA)

Makes one 10-inch-diameter baklava, about 16 servings

1 batch Turkish Baklava Dough (page 140)

FILLING CREAM

1 cup whole milk

½ cup light or heavy cream

3 tablespoons fine semolina

SYRUP

1½ cups water

1½ cups sugar

2 teaspoons lemon juice, strained before measuring

1 pound/4 sticks unsalted butter, clarified (see Note)

1 pound very green pistachios, finely ground, plus more for serving, optional

Kaymak (Turkish clotted cream); see Note, page 138, optional

NOTE

To clarify butter, melt slowly over low heat in a medium saucepan. Let stand for 10 minutes, then use a spoon to skim off the foamy solids on top. Pour off the clarified butter, leaving the watery residue in the pan. Cool, then put the butter into a plastic container, cover, and refrigerate for up to a month.

VARIATION

To substitute packaged phyllo dough, use about one and a half 1-pound packages of phyllo. Packaged phyllo is available in several thicknesses; look for the thinnest type, usually labeled as #4.

This traditional baklava derives its name from the shape of its cut wedges—it's baked in a round pan and filled with a generous amount of chopped pistachios and a creamy, unsweetened mixture of milk and cream thickened with fine semolina. All the sweetening arrives when hot sugar syrup is poured over the freshly baked pastry.

1. Prepare the cream right before assembling the baklava: Bring the milk and cream to a simmer in a nonstick saucepan. Skim any skin from the surface and sift the semolina in, whisking constantly to avoid lumps. Place on medium-low heat and cook, stirring constantly, until the cream thickens and comes to a boil; it will do so very quickly. Scrape the cream into a bowl, press plastic wrap directly against the surface, and set aside at room temperature.

2. For the syrup, bring the water and sugar to a boil, stirring occasionally, over medium heat. Once it boils, lower the heat and simmer for 10 minutes. Remove from the heat and set aside.

3. Set a rack at the middle level in the oven and preheat to 400°F.

4. Line a buttered 10-inch round, 2-inch deep pan with one of the dough sheets, letting it cover the sides of the pan and hang over the edges. Sprinkle with butter. Lay another sheet of dough into the pan, placing it perpendicular to the first, and sprinkle with butter.

5. Stack the remaining sheets of dough on a work surface and, using the pan as a pattern, use a sharp knife to cut the stack into 14 round layers. Save the dough scraps.

6. Place 6 of the round layers in the pan, one at a time, sprinkling butter between them. Set the remaining round layers and half of the scraps aside, covered.

7. Use the other half of the dough scraps to build more layers in the pan, assembling them next to each other without overlapping too much. It's not necessary to sprinkle butter between these layers of dough.

8. Use an offset spatula to spread the filling cream on the dough. Sprinkle the pistachios on top.

9. Make more unbuttered layers of dough using the remaining scraps as in step 7. Fold the overhanging dough inward to cover the scraps, and sprinkle butter on top.

10. Cover with the remaining 8 round layers, sprinkling butter between them but not on top of the last layer.

11. Use a 3-inch cutter to mark a circle in the center and then use a small, sharp knife to cut along the circle, slicing almost through to the bottom. Cut the outer ring of the baklava into 16 even wedges, again slicing almost to the bottom.

12. Reheat the remaining clarified butter slightly if it has started to solidify and pour half of it onto the baklava, tilting the pan in all directions to evenly distribute. Let the pastry stand for a minute or two, then pour on the remaining butter.

13. Bake the baklava until the top layers are deep golden and crisp, about 30 minutes. Use a small knife to lift the layers of dough from the bottom upward to check that they are baked through. If they are still white and soft, bake for 10 to 15 minutes and check again.

14. About 10 minutes before the baklava is ready, reheat the syrup to boiling, remove from the heat, and stir in the lemon juice.

15. Place the pan of baked baklava in your kitchen sink. Evenly pour the hot syrup over the baklava, averting your face, as the syrup will bubble up and steam. Let the baklava stand in the sink for a minute, then set it on a rack to cool completely.

16. Finish cutting through the baklava, this time slicing down to the bottom of the pan. Sprinkle the very center with the reserved chopped pistachios. Serve at room temperature with some kaymak and more chopped pistachios if you wish.

TURKISH PISTACHIO ROLLS (FISTIKLI SARI BURMA)

1 batch Turkish Baklava Dough (page 140)

1 cup water

1 cup sugar

8 ounces very green fragrant pistachios, finely ground

8 ounces/2 sticks unsalted butter, clarified (see Note, page 144)

2 teaspoons lemon juice, strained before measuring

VARIATION

To substitute packaged phyllo dough, use a little more than half (16 sheets) of a 1-pound package of phyllo. Packaged phyllo is available in several thicknesses; look for the thinnest type, usually labeled #4.

You will need a ⅜-inch wooden dowel, about 24 inches long, to make this simple and beautiful baklava variation, in which dough and chopped pistachios are rolled around the dowel and the outside layer of dough wrinkles as the roll is removed. A hint of lemon that emphasizes the pistachio flavor is added to the syrup used to moisten these after baking.

1. For the syrup, bring the water and sugar to a boil, stirring occasionally, over medium heat. Once the syrup boils, remove the pan from the heat and set it aside.

2. Set a rack at the middle level in the oven and preheat to 450°F. Fill a clean spray bottle with cool water. Butter a 9 x 13 x 2-inch metal pan.

3. To form the pastries, place a sheet of dough on the work surface. If using packaged phyllo dough, spray it lightly with water.

4. Fold over 2 inches of the 12-inch side of the dough; place the dowel at the narrow end of the dough closest to you and roll the dough around it once. Sprinkle about 2 tablespoons of the pistachios directly in front of the rolled area, then begin rolling so that the pistachios roll into the dough. Some will fall out the side; just scrape them back onto the dough as you go.

5. When you reach the end of the dough, push the roll to the end of the dowel and ease it off, leaving the dough wrinkled and about 6 inches long. Set the roll lengthwise into the prepared pan, placing it to one side of the pan. Repeat the rolling process with the remaining pieces of dough, placing them side by side in the pan as you go.

6. Once the pan is filled with the pastries, use a small sharp knife to cut down the center of each row to make 32 pastries in all.

7. Pour on the clarified butter, then place the pan in the oven. Lower the heat to 400°F and bake until the tops of the rolls are very light golden, 20 to 25 minutes.

8. Ten minutes before the rolls are ready, reheat the syrup to boiling. Stir in the lemon juice.

9. Place the pan in your kitchen sink and pour the hot syrup over the rolls, averting your face, as the syrup will bubble up and steam. Let the pastry stand in the sink for a minute, then set it on a rack to finish cooling. Use a narrow spatula to remove the rolls from the pan and slice each one into 16 pieces. Serve the pastries at room temperature.

YUFKA

Originally used as a griddle-baked flatbread by Turkic nomads, in today's Turkey, yufka leaves are the principal dough for preparing savory pastries. Most Turkish cooks buy yufka from a shop called a *yufkacı* (YOOF-ka-juh) that specializes in the preparation. Like the dough for baklava, yufka is rolled substantially by hand, and you'll need a 20- to 24-inch-long dowel, 1 inch in diameter, preferably made of hardwood.

1. Whisk the water and salt together in the bowl of a stand mixer; use a rubber spatula to stir in the flour, being careful that none sticks to the side of the bowl.

2. Place the bowl on the mixer with the dough hook and mix on low speed until the dough pulls cleanly away from the side of the bowl, about 5 minutes. Let the dough rest for 15 minutes.

3. Mix on low-medium speed until the dough is smooth and elastic, 3 to 5 minutes more.

4. Scrape the dough onto a floured work surface and divide it into 9 pieces, each 75 grams. Round each piece of dough and place it, rounded side downward, on a floured work surface. Cover with plastic wrap and a towel and let rest for 1 hour.

5. Place a piece of parchment paper on a large tray or board near the rolling surface.

6. Flour the work surface and place a piece of dough on it, rounded side upward. Press it to a flat pancake using the palm of your hand. Flour underneath and on top of the dough again and roll it as for a tart crust, rolling away and back toward yourself, from 6 o'clock to 12 o'clock and back, never rolling over the edges closest and farthest from you, then turning the disk of dough 60 degrees to the right (to 2 o'clock) and repeating until the dough is 10 to 12 inches in diameter.

7. Flour the work surface and the dough and place the rolling pin an inch or so away from the edge closest to you; roll the dough around the pin. Place your hands in the middle of the pin and begin rolling, and at the same time, pressing and moving your hands away from each other to widen the sheet of dough. Unfurl it from the pin and rotate it 120 degrees.

8. Repeat step 7 twice. If the dough isn't yet fully 16 to 18 inches in diameter at that point, repeat the process one more time.

9. Slide the rolling pin under the dough across the diameter of the round, lift the dough from the work surface, and unfurl it onto the parchment. Place another piece of parchment on top. Continue rolling and stacking the remaining pieces of dough.

10. Cover the last piece of dough with parchment and fold the entire stack into quarters. Slide into a large plastic bag and refrigerate until you're ready to use. Homemade yufka of this type stays fresh for a week. It can't be frozen or it will become brittle.

Makes nine 16- to 18-inch-diameter leaves of dough

1⅓ cups/300 grams water

2½ teaspoons fine sea salt

3¾ cups/500 grams high-gluten or bread flour (spoon into dry-measure cup and level)

NOTE

When yufka leaves are prepared at a yufkacı, they're baked on one side on a round griddle, then cooled, dampened to prevent cracking, and blotted between cloths to absorb excess moisture. The partially baked leaves are wrapped airtight and will keep refrigerated for a couple of weeks. Turkish import stores sell hand-rolled yufka made in Turkey in packages of three round sheets for pan-baked börek or twenty-four or more triangular wedges to make fried "cigarette" börek (see the recipes that follow).

Rolling yufka is good practice for attempting the hand-rolled dough for baklava. In one yufkacı I visited in Istanbul, the twenty-two-year-old son of the owner told me he'd mastered the rolling in two months—not quite the seven years it takes for baklava dough.

FETA AND MINT BÖREK (PEYNİRLİ BÖREK)

This savory pie made from thin yufka dough was shared by my friend Cenk Sönmeszoy, an accomplished cookbook author, food stylist, and blogger in Istanbul. This is a typical Turkish savory pie, with crisp, flaky layers on the outside and moist, creamy ones within. In Turkey, yufka is used to make many types of savory pies, up to 16 inches in diameter, some of which are eaten for breakfast. To make this for family or guests, I would suggest using a slope-sided pie pan or a porcelain quiche pan.

1. Set a rack in the lower third of the oven and preheat to 375°F. Butter a 9-inch pie pan.

2. Melt 4 tablespoons of the butter; cube the remaining butter and set aside.

3. Whisk the milk and eggs together and whisk in the melted butter.

4. Center one of the yufka leaves on the prepared pan and ease it in so that it's wrinkled rather than stretched. Pour in ⅓ cup of the egg and milk mixture.

5. Take the second yufka leaf, tear it into large pieces, and stack them in the pan; pour in another ⅓ cup of the milk mixture.

6. Mix the feta and mint together and evenly distribute half in the lined pan. Sprinkle on a third of the butter cubes.

7. Top with another torn layer of yufka, as in step 5 above. Pour in another ⅓ cup of the milk mixture, followed by the remaining feta and mint and another third of the butter cubes.

8. Top with another whole layer of yufka, centering it on the filling. Fold in any overhanging yufka over the top of the pie and use a sharp knife to cut the pastry into 8 wedges, cutting almost but not quite through the dough on the bottom of the pan, then pour the remaining milk mixture over all. Scatter on the remaining butter cubes and sprinkle with sesame seeds.

9. Bake the börek until the top layer is crisp and the filling is hot, 30 to 40 minutes.

10. Cool slightly on a rack and serve warm.

VARIATIONS

GROUND MEAT FILLING: Coat a sauté pan with 2 tablespoons olive oil and add ½ cup finely minced white onion. Cook slowly over low heat until soft and translucent, stirring occasionally, 15 to 20 minutes. Increase the heat to medium and add 1 pound ground beef or lamb; use a wooden spoon to stir and break up the meat for a few minutes, until it starts to color and separate into fine granules. Season with salt, pepper, and a large pinch of ground allspice. Pour into a strainer set over a bowl to allow excess fat to drain; let cool. Right before assembling the börek, stir in ½ cup each chopped mint and flat-leaf parsley. Fill the pastry as above, using the meat filling in place of the mint and feta mixture and omitting the cubed butter in steps 6 and 7. Top the pie with 2 tablespoons butter cubes and the sesame seeds as in step 8 and bake.

Makes one 9- or 10-inch börek, 8 to 10 servings

4 leaves homemade Yufka (page 147). To use packaged yufka, see Note

8 tablespoons/1 stick unsalted butter

1 cup whole milk

3 large eggs

2 cups crumbled feta cheese

1½ cups chopped fresh mint leaves

1 to 2 tablespoons sesame seeds for finishing

NOTE

To use packaged yufka, which has much larger leaves, in steps 5 and 7 use half of one of the large leaves, torn apart.

TURKISH FRIED "CIGARETTE" PASTRIES (SİGARA BÖREĞİ)

Makes 24 small hors d'oeuvre pastries

**3 sheets homemade Yufka (page 147) or
1 package triangular yufka leaves (to use
packaged phyllo dough, see Note)**

1 cup finely crumbled feta cheese

¼ cup chopped fresh mint leaves

¼ cup chopped fresh flat-leaf parsley or dill

3 cups safflower oil for frying

NOTE

To use packaged phyllo dough, you'll need 12
sheets of dough, 2 tablespoons olive oil, and a
brush. Place 1 phyllo sheet on the work surface.
Drizzle very lightly with oil and place another
sheet on top. Cut across widthwise into 2
smaller rectangles, then cut each rectangle
diagonally into 2 triangles. Repeat with the
remaining sheets and proceed as above.

These are so called because of their shape. Since cigarettes have fallen into such disgrace, though, there is even a movement afoot to change the name of this pastry to "pen," *böreği*. The G in *böreği* is silent.

1. Let the dough come to room temperature.

2. Stir the cheese and herbs together.

3. If you're using homemade yufka, stack the 3 leaves and use a small, sharp paring knife to cut 8 equal-size wedges, for a total of 24 pieces.

4. To form each roll, place 1 teaspoon of filling in a line ½ inch in from the base of a triangle, then fold the sides in. Roll up jelly-roll style. Use a brush to moisten the tip of the triangle with water to seal the pastry. Arrange the roll with the point underneath.

5. Line a jellyroll pan with paper towels. Heat the oil in a deep Dutch oven or wok to 350°F.

6. Fry several pastries at a time, taking care not to crowd them. Using a slotted spoon, transfer to the jelly-roll pan to drain. Serve while still warm and crisp.

CHAPTER 7

PUFF PASTRY, CROISSANTS & OTHER LAMINATED DOUGHS

Doughs like puff pastry that consist of alternating layers of dough and butter formed by repeated rolling and folding are known as "laminated." You start with a slightly elastic, lean dough that has only a small amount of butter in it and use that to enclose a large, flat piece of butter that has been mixed with a little flour to make for easier handling. The dough is rolled to press the layers of dough and butter thinner, then folded to increase the number of layers. On paper, the process is pretty easy to explain; it's not difficult to execute, either, but it requires close attention to detail. The following rules are important to follow for all laminated doughs:

• Give the base dough plenty of time to rest and chill before wrapping it around the butter.

• Always start with cold butter and soften it to a malleable consistency quickly—leaving the butter at room temperature too long will soften it too much. >>

• For maximum success in rolling the dough and butter together, both should be at approximately the same temperature and have a similar consistency. Butter that's too soft will make the layers of dough slide apart from each other, and butter that's too hard will pierce through the dough and resist forming even layers.

• Always make the dough very thin on the initial rolling. If the butter layer is too thick after the first couple of rollings, it will fragment into flakes when the chilled, rested dough is rolled again; fragments of butter melt and leak out of the dough instead of forming even layers.

• Take your time with the rolling and keep the dough even; you'll be rewarded with a beautiful result.

• Traditional puff pastry may be made in dozens of ways. The version here is one I've used for years and have taught thousands of students to prepare successfully. It's a slight twist on the classic formula that also helps to guarantee a good, even rise, the proof that the pastry is well made.

• Quick puff pastry is just that, a faster and easier way to get almost the same results as the traditional method. Perfect for thin pieces of dough, like a baked sheet to make Napoleons or a mille-feuille, quick puff pastry is also excellent for small puff pastries.

• Croissant dough is made in a manner similar to traditional puff pastry, but the base dough contains yeast, so that the croissants rise both from the puffing of the layers and from the action of the yeast.

• Plunderteig, or Viennese layered dough, is a sweeter version of croissant dough. It contains yeast, but also more sugar, as well as eggs. It's richer than the typical Danish pastry made in the United States, yet not as rich and flaky as that made in Scandinavia.

PUFF PASTRY

All the laminated doughs in this chapter are made the same way—with a square of butter at one end of a rectangle of dough so that a single fold of the dough over the butter encloses it. This method requires starting with a thin layer of butter, which makes it easier to get even layers of butter in your dough and consequently a better rise and a more delicate texture after baking. This recipe makes more than enough dough for any pastry in this chapter.

Makes about 2 pounds/900 grams dough

DOUGH

2⅓ cups/315 grams unbleached all-purpose flour (spoon into dry-measure cup and level)

6 tablespoons/¾ stick/85 grams unsalted butter, softened

⅔ cup/150 grams cold water, plus about 1 tablespoon more if necessary

1 teaspoon fine sea salt

BUTTER BLOCK

¼ cup/32 grams unbleached all-purpose flour (spoon into dry-measure cup and level)

11 ounces/2¾ sticks/312 grams unsalted butter, cold

1. For the dough, combine the flour and butter in a bowl and rub in the butter so that no visible pieces remain. Don't mix so much that it starts to become pasty. Stir the water and salt together and sprinkle all over the flour. Use a rubber spatula to dig to the bottom of the bowl and bring up the unmoistened flour, turning the bowl as you go. Don't exert pressure on the dough, just bring the spatula up from the bottom of the bowl. After 10 or 12 strokes, if there are any dry bits of flour remaining, sprinkle a few drops of water until they adhere to the main mass of dough.

2. Scrape the dough from the bowl to a lightly floured surface and dust the top with flour. Use your hands, the straight side of a bench scraper, and a ruler to shape the dough into an 8-inch square. Wrap the dough in plastic and chill for 1 hour.

3. Shortly before the hour is up, prepare the butter block: Scatter half the flour on the work surface and cut the butter into 5 or 6 pieces. Turn the pieces in the flour to coat them and use a rolling pin to gently pound each piece of butter to soften it. Once all the butter has been pounded, scatter on some of the remaining flour, dusting the work surface again if necessary; stack one piece of butter on another and use the rolling pin to hammer them together. Repeat, adding the remaining pieces of butter to the stack. Scatter on the last of the flour, then quickly knead the butter into a solid mass and use your hands, the straight side of a bench scraper, and a ruler to shape the butter into an 8-inch square ①.

4. Set the butter aside for a moment, scrape the surface free of any sticky bits of butter, and flour it. Unwrap the dough and place it on the work surface; flour the dough and roll it evenly to an 8 x 16-inch rectangle, with a short edge near you ②. Brush away any excess flour on the dough's surface and place the butter on the end closest to you. Fold the dough down to enclose the butter ③ and pinch the edges of the dough together ④. >>

5. Flour under and on top of the dough and use the rolling pin to start pressing the package of dough and butter in a succession of gentle and even strokes, moving from the closest edge to the farthest edge. Gently roll the dough in one direction, starting at the end nearest to you and without going over the opposite edge. Repeat, rolling from the far end back toward yourself. Repeat the rolling once more and make the dough an 8 x 16-inch rectangle.

6. Brush excess flour from the dough, then fold both narrow ends toward the middle, leaving about a ½-inch space between them ⑤⑥. Fold the dough in half along that center line to make 4 layers ⑦⑧.

7. Position the folded package of dough so that the closed fold, resembling the spine of a book, is on your left ⑨. Repeat step 5, this time rolling across as well as lengthwise, until the dough is as close to 8 x 16 inches as possible. Repeat step 6.

8. Wrap and chill the dough for an hour or so. If you wait longer, you will need to let the dough soften slightly at room temperature before completing the rolling and folding process.

9. When ready to resume rolling, repeat step 7 twice more.

10. You've now rolled and folded the dough 4 times, giving it 4 "turns." Wrap and chill the dough for at least half a day. After this, it's ready to be used in any recipe that calls for it.

MAKE AHEAD
Keep the dough refrigerated for up to 2 days. For longer storage, double wrap and freeze. Thaw in the refrigerator overnight before using.

QUICK PUFF PASTRY

Variously called rough, half, express, and even Scottish puff pastry, this quick method works especially well for thin or small pastries when you don't need the dough to rise to great heights. It's much faster to prepare because all the ingredients are mixed together from the outset with no separate rolling and layering of dough and butter. The ingredients are the same as the traditional dough; the assembly is completely different and the dough gets only three instead of four turns.

1. Combine the flour and 6 tablespoons/¾ stick/85 grams of the butter in a bowl and rub in the butter so that no visible pieces remain. Don't mix so much that it starts to become pasty.

2. Add the remaining butter to the bowl and toss it through the flour. Use your fingertips to slightly soften and flatten the pieces of butter, making sure they stay covered in flour.

3. Stir the water and salt together and sprinkle it all over the flour and butter mixture. Use a rubber spatula to dig to the bottom of the bowl and bring up the unmoistened flour, turning the bowl as you do. Don't exert pressure on the dough, just bring the spatula up from the bottom of the bowl. After 10 or 12 strokes, if there are any dry bits of flour remaining, sprinkle a few drops of water until they adhere to the main mass of dough.

4. Scrape the dough from the bowl onto a lightly floured surface and dust the top with flour. Squeeze the dough together, shaping it into a fat sausage shape. Flour under and on top of the dough again and press it into a rough rectangle. If the dough feels soft, wrap and chill it for half an hour to firm up the butter.

5. Flour under and on top of the dough and use the rolling pin to start pressing in a succession of gentle and even strokes, moving from the closest edge outward. Gently roll the dough in one direction, starting at the end nearest to you and without going over the opposite edge. Repeat, rolling from the far end back toward yourself. Repeat the rolling once more and make the dough an 8 x 16-inch rectangle.

6. Brush excess flour from the dough, then fold both narrow ends toward the middle, leaving about a ½-inch space between. Fold the dough in half along that center line to make 4 layers.

7. Position the folded package of dough so that the closed fold, resembling the spine of a book, is on your left. Repeat step 5, this time rolling across as well as lengthwise, until the dough is as close to 8 x 16 inches as possible.

8. If possible, give the dough a third turn by repeating steps 5 and 6. If the dough is too soft to handle, chill it for 1 hour and then perform the third turn.

9. After the third turn, wrap and chill the dough; it's ready for use once it has chilled and rested for a couple of hours.

Makes about 2 pounds/900 grams dough

2⅓ cups/315 grams unbleached all-purpose flour (spoon into dry-measure cup and level)

14 ounces/3½ sticks/400 grams unsalted butter, chilled and cut into ½-inch pieces

¾ cup/170 grams cold water, plus about 1 tablespoon more if necessary

1 teaspoon fine sea salt

MAKE AHEAD

Keep the dough refrigerated for up to 2 days. For longer storage, double wrap and freeze the dough. Thaw it in the refrigerator overnight before using.

VARIATION

You can use a food processor for steps 1 and 2 by adding in the first, smaller quantity of butter into the flour and pulsing it repeatedly at 1-second intervals until it has been completely absorbed. Add the second, larger quantity of butter and give two 1-second pulses, then use a long metal spatula to scrape the side of the bowl. Repeat the two pulses and invert the food processor bowl into a large mixing bowl, carefully remove the blade, and resume the recipe at step 3.

PROFESSOR CALVEL'S CROISSANT DOUGH

Makes 2½ pounds/1120 grams, enough for 30 to 40 pastries

DOUGH

½ cup/112 grams room-temperature tap water, about 75°F

3½ teaspoons fine granulated active dry or instant yeast

¾ cup/170 grams whole milk, scalded and cooled to room temperature

¼ cup/50 grams sugar

1 teaspoon organic malt syrup or honey

3¾ cups/500 grams unbleached bread flour (spoon into dry-measure cup and level)

2 teaspoons fine sea salt

1 tablespoon/15 grams unsalted butter, softened

BUTTER BLOCK

¼ cup/34 grams unbleached bread flour (spoon into dry-measure cup and level)

8 ounces/2 sticks/225 grams unsalted butter, cold

The late Raymond Calvel, the father of modern French bread making, wrote about croissants in his second book, *Le Goût du Pain (The Flavor of Bread)*. This recipe is modified from his in that I've used whole milk instead of dry milk because whole milk contributes a fresher taste to the croissants and I have not added ascorbic acid (vitamin C).

1. Whisk the water and yeast together in the bowl of a stand mixer, then whisk in the milk, sugar, and malt syrup. Use a large rubber spatula to stir in the flour; make sure there is no flour stuck to the sides or bottom of the bowl. Place the bowl on the mixer fitted with the dough hook and mix on lowest speed for 2 minutes. Let the dough rest for 15 minutes.

2. Mix the dough on medium speed, adding the salt and butter, until smooth and elastic, 2 to 3 minutes more. Cover the bowl with plastic wrap and let the dough ferment at room temperature until it starts to puff, 30 to 60 minutes. Without deflating the dough, place the bowl in the refrigerator for 2 hours.

3. Once the second hour is almost up, prepare the butter block: Scatter half the flour on the work surface and cut the butter into 5 or 6 pieces. Turn the pieces in the flour to coat them and use a rolling pin to gently pound each piece of butter to soften it. Once all the butter has been pounded, scatter on some of the remaining flour, dusting the work surface again if necessary; stack one piece of butter on another and use the rolling pin to hammer them together. Repeat, adding the remaining pieces of butter. Scatter on the last of the flour, then quickly knead the butter into a solid mass and shape into an 8-inch square. Set aside.

4. Scrape the work surface free of any sticky bits of butter and flour it. Unwrap the dough onto the surface, flour it and roll evenly to an 8 x 16-inch rectangle, with a short edge near you. Brush away any excess flour on the dough's surface and place the butter on the end closest to you. Fold the dough down to enclose the butter and pinch the edges together around it.

5. Flour under and on top of the dough and use the rolling pin to start pressing in a succession of gentle and even strokes, moving from the closest edge to the farthest. Gently roll the dough in one direction, starting at the end nearest to you and without going over the opposite edge. Repeat, rolling from the far end back toward yourself. Repeat the rolling once more and make the dough an 8 x 16-inch rectangle.

6. Brush excess flour from the dough, then fold both narrow ends toward the middle, leaving about a ½-inch space between. Fold the dough in half along that center line to make 4 layers.

7. Position the folded package of dough so that the closed fold, resembling the spine of a book, is on your left. Repeat step 5, this time rolling across as well as lengthwise, until the dough is as close to 8 x 16 inches as possible. Repeat step 6.

8. Wrap and chill the dough and be ready to form and bake the croissants within 2 to 4 hours.

VIENNESE DANISH DOUGH (PLUNDERTEIG)

The German word *Plunder* can refer to stacked planks or beams of wood, which is how the term came to be applied to a laminated pastry dough. Recently, I visited with my old friend Hans Diglas, proprietor of Café Diglas and Konditorei Diglas in Vienna. Herr Diglas gave me some pastries made with plunderteig, and I was an immediate convert. Over the following several days, I spent some time at his production facility and this recipe is the result.

1. Whisk the milk and yeast together in the bowl of a stand mixer, then whisk in the egg yolks, vanilla, and sugar. Use a large rubber spatula to stir in the flour, making sure there is none stuck to the sides or bottom of the bowl. Place the bowl on the mixer fitted with the dough hook and mix on the lowest speed for 2 minutes.

2. Increase the speed to medium, adding the salt and butter, and mix until smooth and elastic, 2 to 3 minutes more. Cover the bowl with plastic wrap and chill in the refrigerator for 2 hours.

3. Once the second hour is almost up, prepare the butter block: Scatter half the flour on the work surface and cut the butter into 5 or 6 pieces. Turn the pieces in the flour to coat them and use a rolling pin to gently pound each piece to soften it. Once all the butter has been pounded, scatter on some of the remaining flour, dusting the work surface again if necessary; stack one piece of butter on another and use the rolling pin to hammer them together. Repeat, adding the remaining pieces of butter. Scatter on the last of the flour, then quickly knead the butter into a solid mass and shape into an 8-inch square. Set aside.

4. Scrape the work surface free of any sticky bits of butter, and flour it. Unwrap the dough and place it on the surface, flour it and roll evenly to an 8 x 16-inch rectangle, with a short edge near you. Brush away any excess flour on the dough's surface and place the butter on the end closest to you. Fold the dough down to enclose the butter and pinch the edges together around it.

5. Flour under and on top of the dough and use the rolling pin to start pressing in a succession of gentle and even strokes, moving from the closest edge to the farthest edge. Gently roll the dough in one direction, starting at the end nearest to you and without going over the opposite edge. Repeat, rolling from the far end back toward yourself. Repeat the rolling once more and make the dough an 8 x 16-inch rectangle.

6. Brush any excess flour from the dough, then fold both narrow ends toward the middle, leaving about a ½-inch space between. Fold the dough in half along that center line to make 4 layers.

7. Position the folded package of dough so that the closed fold, resembling the spine of a book, is on your left. Repeat step 5, this time rolling across as well as lengthwise, until the dough is as close to 8 x 16 inches as possible. Repeat step 6.

8. Wrap and chill the dough; use it the same day or chill overnight and form and bake the pastries the next morning.

Makes 30 ounces/850 grams dough, enough for 18 to 24 finished pastries

DOUGH

¾ cup/170 grams whole milk, scalded and cooled to 100°F

4½ teaspoons fine granulated active dry or instant yeast

2 large egg yolks, at room temperature

1 teaspoon vanilla extract

3 tablespoons sugar

2¼ cups/300 grams unbleached bread flour (spoon into dry-measure cup and level)

½ teaspoon fine sea salt

2 tablespoons/30 grams unsalted butter, softened

BUTTER BLOCK

¼ cup/34 grams unbleached bread flour

8 ounces/2 sticks/225 grams unsalted butter, cold

CARAMELIZED PUFF PASTRY LAYERS

Makes one 10 x 15-inch layer

⅓ batch Puff Pastry or Quick Puff Pastry (page 155 or 157)

2 tablespoons granulated sugar

2 tablespoons confectioners' sugar

VARIATION

If you don't need the layer to be caramelized, omit both sugars. Bake the pastry at 375°F, and at the end of step 4, invert the stack of pans and dough and continue baking until the layer is crisp and golden, 10 to 15 minutes longer. Cut and store as in step 7.

Thin, fragile baked layers of puff pastry are a must for any kind of mille-feuille, large or individual, or classic Napoleons. Start with these instructions to prepare the pastry; further instructions for finished desserts using these layers are in the recipes that follow. This is loosely adapted from a recipe by Pierre Hermé that appears in his first book, *Secrets Gourmands*. See Variation for a plain puff pastry layer.

1. Lightly flour the work surface and the dough and roll it to a 10 x 15-inch rectangle. (It's helpful to roll the dough part of the way, then transfer one of the pieces of parchment for lining a pan to your work surface, flour it, and finish rolling the dough directly on the paper.)

2. Slide the paper and dough into one of the pans and use a fork to pierce it all over at ½-inch intervals. Cover the dough loosely with plastic wrap and let it rest for several hours.

3. When you're ready to bake the layer, set a rack in the upper third of the oven and preheat to 400°F. Line two 10 x 15-inch jellyroll pans with parchment paper.

4. Sprinkle the dough with the granulated sugar and place the second piece of parchment paper on top; stack the second pan on top of the parchment. Place in the oven and lower the temperature to 375°F. Bake until the layer is almost cooked through, about 15 minutes.

5. Remove the stack of pans and dough from the oven and invert them, grasping both sides to avoid having the dough slide out. Increase the oven temperature to 450°F.

6. The dough will now be resting on a piece of parchment on the back of a baking pan. Lift off the top pan, peel away the top paper, and slide the layer of dough, still on the second piece of paper, back into the original pan. Evenly sprinkle with the confectioners' sugar and bake, watching carefully, until the sugar melts and glazes, 7 to 10 minutes. Don't walk away, or it will definitely burn.

7. Slide the baked layer, still on its paper, to a cutting board and slice it into the desired pieces while it is still warm. To prevent the pastry from warping, once it has cooled, slide it or the pieces back between the papers and pans until you are ready to proceed.

TRADITIONAL VANILLA MILLE-FEUILLE

It's a mystery why this is referred to as a "Napoleon" in the United States, though the best explanation is that it has nothing to do with the French emperor but is a corruption of the word *Neapolitan*. In any case, this version of a mille-feuille combines the simple elements of crisp, buttery caramelized puff pastry layers and pastry cream perfumed with vanilla bean and lightened with whipped cream. It's definitely a case where the whole is much greater than the sum of the separate parts.

1. For the pastry cream, whisk together the milk, 2 tablespoons of the sugar, and the vanilla bean in a small saucepan; if you're using vanilla bean paste, add it in step 3, when you take the pastry cream off the heat. Bring the mixture to a full boil over low heat. Meanwhile, in a bowl, whisk the yolks and then whisk in 2 tablespoons sugar. Sift over and whisk in the flour.

2. When the milk mixture boils, whisk it into the yolk mixture. Strain the mixture back into the pan (leaving the vanilla bean in the strainer) and place over medium heat. Using a small, pointed-end whisk, whisk constantly, being sure to reach into the corners of the pan, until the cream comes to a full boil and thickens. Cook, whisking constantly, for 30 seconds more.

3. Scrape the cream into a glass bowl, stir in the vanilla paste, if using, and press plastic wrap directly against the surface. Chill until cold.

4. When you're ready to assemble the mille-feuille, no more than 3 to 4 hours before you intend to serve it, prepare the whipped cream: Whip the cream and remaining 2 tablespoons sugar to a firm peak, but not until dry or grainy. Fold into the chilled pastry cream.

5. Place one of the baked layers, glaze side up, on a platter or serving board, and spread it with half the cream. Add a second layer and the remaining pastry cream.

6. Use a sharp serrated knife to cut the last layer into 8 separate pieces, each 1½ x 3 inches. Dust half with confectioners' sugar. Alternate the dusted and plain glazed pieces of pastry on top of the pastry cream.

7. Use a sharp serrated knife to cut the mille-feuille all the way through; having the top layer already cut eliminates most of the squish factor during this process.

Makes 8 servings

1 batch Caramelized Puff Pastry Layers (opposite), cut into three 3 x 12-inch layers

VANILLA BEAN PASTRY CREAM

1 cup whole milk

6 tablespoons sugar

1 Madagascar Bourbon vanilla bean (see Note below), split, or 1 teaspoon vanilla bean paste

3 large egg yolks

2 tablespoons unbleached all-purpose flour

1 cup heavy whipping cream

Confectioners' sugar

NOTE

Rinse the vanilla bean and let it dry for a day at room temperature. Embed it in your sugar canister to lightly scent the sugar.

VARIATION

Fold a couple of tablespoons of Lemon Curd (page 48), into the pastry cream along with the whipped cream for a subtle lemon flavor.

STRAWBERRY RASPBERRY MILLE-FEUILLES

Makes 8 individual servings

1 batch Caramelized Puff Pastry Layers (page 160), cut into two 7 ½-inch square layers

VANILLA ORANGE PASTRY CREAM

¾ cup whole milk

¼ cup heavy whipping cream

¼ cup sugar

Zest of 1 small orange, removed in large strips with a vegetable peeler

3 large egg yolks

2 tablespoons unbleached all-purpose flour

1 teaspoon vanilla extract or vanilla bean paste

FINISHING

1 cup heavy whipping cream

2 tablespoons sugar

3 cups berries, a mixture of small strawberries, rinsed and hulled, and raspberries, picked over but not washed

VARIATIONS

Any ripe fruit that's sweet and not excessively juicy can be substituted for the berries. Try really ripe apricot halves, sliced pitted plums or prune plums, or even well-drained sliced poached pears.

In France it's popular during the summer to make tarts and other pastries like *mille-feuille aux fruits rouges* or "with red fruits," meaning basically whatever berries are available. We can't obtain the tiny, intensely flavored wild strawberries or *fraises des bois* as easily as they do in France, but small, perfectly sweet, height-of-the-season berries work very well in this dessert. It's fun and tasty to combine several types of berries, and if you have access to red currants, sprinkle in a few—not too many, or the fruit mix might be too tart.

1. For the pastry cream, combine the milk, cream, half the sugar, and the orange zest in a small saucepan and whisk to combine. Bring to a full boil over low heat. Meanwhile, in a bowl, whisk the yolks and then whisk in the remaining sugar. Sift over and whisk in the flour.

2. When the milk mixture boils, whisk it into the yolk mixture. Strain the mixture back into the pan (leaving the orange zest in the strainer) and place over medium heat. Use a small, pointed-end whisk to stir constantly, being sure to reach into the corners of the pan, until the cream comes to a full boil and thickens. Cook, whisking constantly, for another 30 seconds. Off the heat, whisk in the vanilla. Scrape the cream into a glass bowl and press plastic directly against the surface. Chill until cold.

3. A few hours before serving the mille-feuilles, use a sharp serrated knife to cut each of the layers into 8 rectangles, each about 1 ¾ x 3 ¾ inches.

4. Right before assembling, whip the cream with the sugar to a soft peak.

5. Arrange 8 of the cut layers, caramelized side up, on dessert plates. Top each with a heaping tablespoon of pastry cream. Arrange some of the strawberries and raspberries on the pastry cream, then top with a spoonful of whipped cream. Cover each with another puff pastry layer, caramelized side up, and gently press to adhere the layer to the whipped cream.

6. Serve immediately; these can wait an hour at a cool room temperature but not much longer.

PUFF PASTRY TART CRUST

Makes one 10-inch round crust (see Variation for the square shape)

⅓ batch Puff Pastry or Quick Puff Pastry (page 155 or 157)

Water for brushing the dough

VARIATION

For a square crust, place the dough on a floured surface and lightly flour it. Press with a rolling pin to soften and thin the dough, then roll to an 8 x 16-inch rectangle. Use a sharp pastry wheel to trim the long edges straight, then cut the dough lengthwise into two 1-inch strips, and one 6-inch strip. Fold the 6-inch strip in thirds and transfer to the prepared pan. Unfold and use a fork to pierce the dough all over at ½-inch intervals. Moisten the long edges of the 6-inch strip, then place one of the 1-inch strips on each moistened edge to form a lip (the narrow ends of the crust will be left open). Flour a fingertip and press the side strips down to adhere. Use the back of a paring knife to make indentations on the side strips to help them stay in place. Finally, pierce the top of the side strips down through the bottom with the point of a paring knife at ½-inch intervals. Then rest and bake, as described in steps 7 through 9.

These are versatile, easy to prepare, and a lifesaver when you want a simple tart with a layer of pastry cream and some fresh fruit but you don't have a special pan to bake it in. You can use any dimensions you like and make the tart crust round, square, or rectangular. When planning the size and shape of your tart if it's different from the ones below, remember to consider the size and shape of your serving platter.

1. Roll the dough into an 11-inch square, then cut three 1-inch-wide strips from one side ①②.

2. Roll the remaining large piece of dough back into an 11-inch square and place on a jellyroll pan lined with parchment ③.

3. Place a 10-inch round pattern, such as a cake cardboard, on the dough and use a sharp pastry wheel to cut around it ④. Remove the scraps of dough.

4. Pierce the large disk of dough with a fork at ½-inch intervals ⑤.

5. To make the sides of the crust, moisten the edge of the disk ⑥ and then apply one of the strips at the edge, letting the inch or so at each end of the strip stray off the edge onto the work surface. Moisten the ends of the strip and apply another one the same way. Repeat for the third strip. You'll now have 6 strip ends that need to be trimmed away. Use a fingertip to press the strips so they will adhere to the disk of dough beneath ⑦.

6. Then use a sharp pastry wheel to cut away the dangling ends and make the edge of the disk even ⑧. Indent and pierce the strips using a paring knife, as in photo 5 on page 166.

7. Loosely cover the crust with plastic wrap, and refrigerate for at least 2 hours or overnight.

8. When you're ready to bake, set a rack at the middle level in the oven and preheat to 400°F.

9. Place the pan in the oven, lower the temperature to 375°F, and bake until golden and dry, 20 to 25 minutes. Cool the crust on a rack and fill and serve that same day.

INDIVIDUAL HAZELNUT PITHIVIERS

A large gâteau Pithiviers is one of France's most famous pastries. Named for a town outside Paris, the puff pastry cake usually has an almond filling. Here, I've recast it as an individual dessert with a hazelnut filling and a creamy caramel sauce to offset the richness of the buttery dough. Using traditional puff pastry is preferable, since you want plenty of rise from even layering.

1. For the filling, pulse the hazelnuts and sugar in a food processor until finely ground. Add the butter, rum, vanilla, cinnamon, and yolks and pulse again to mix. You might need to use a metal spatula to scrape down the bowl. Add the flour, pulse again, then invert the filling into a bowl; carefully remove the blade and use a rubber spatula to scrape any remaining filling into the bowl. Cover loosely and set aside.

2. Roll the dough on a floured surface to an 8 x 12-inch rectangle; cut in half. Roll one half to 8 x 12 inches, and the other half to 10 x 15 inches. If the dough begins to get soft, slide the pieces onto a cookie sheet and chill for a few minutes.

3. Place the smaller sheet of dough on the work surface and use a ruler and bench scraper to mark it into 4-inch squares. Use a sharp pastry wheel or knife to cut them apart. Line the squares up on a jellyroll pan lined with parchment and divide the filling equally among them, making a 2-inch-diameter mound in the center ①.

4. Mark, then cut the remaining, large piece of dough into 5-inch squares. Carefully brush egg wash around each pastry's filling and place a 5-inch square of dough on top ②. Cup your hand over the center and press the dough around the filling, leaving no air pockets, then line up the sides of the dough. As long as the top square covers the bottom one, it's okay.

5. Invert a 2-inch round cutter over the filling and press just enough to seal the layers of dough together ③. Then use a 4-inch round cutter to cut each of the pastries, saving the scraps for another use ④.

6. Indent the side of the pastries at ½-inch intervals using the back of a paring knife ⑤. Make several arc-shaped slashes in the top of the pastry over the filling, only cutting about halfway through the dough. Cover and chill the pastries for at least 4 hours or overnight.

Makes 6 individual (4-inch) cakes

⅔ batch Puff Pastry or Quick Puff Pastry (page 155 or 157)

HAZELNUT FILLING

1 cup whole hazelnuts

½ cup sugar

6 tablespoons/¾ stick unsalted butter, softened

1 tablespoon dark rum

1 teaspoon vanilla extract

Large pinch of ground cinnamon

3 large egg yolks

⅓ cup unbleached all-purpose flour (spoon into dry-measure cup and level)

Egg wash: 1 egg whisked with a pinch of salt

CARAMEL SAUCE

1 cup sugar

2 tablespoons light corn syrup or golden syrup

¼ cup water

⅔ cup heavy whipping cream

Pinch of fine sea salt or fleur de sel

7. Set a rack in the lower third of the oven and preheat to 400°F.

8. Brush the pastries with egg wash using a fairly dry brush to avoid puddles. Bake until well risen and deeply golden, 45 to 55 minutes. Cool on a rack.

9. Meanwhile, for the caramel sauce, stir the sugar, corn syrup, and water together in a medium saucepan and melt over low heat undisturbed. Meanwhile, heat the cream in another small pan until scalded; turn off the heat. Stir the sugar occasionally but only until completely liquefied. Then cook, still over low heat, until the syrup is a deep caramel color. Holding the pan at arm's length and averting your face, pour the cream into the caramel in 3 additions, letting it boil up and recede before adding more. Once all the cream has been added, give the caramel sauce a good stir and bring to a full boil. Season with salt.

10. To serve, reheat the sauce to lukewarm and the pastries briefly at 350°F. Place the pastries on dessert plates and pass the caramel sauce separately.

VARIATIONS

Substitute almonds for the hazelnuts and omit the cinnamon in the filling. You could press a small apricot or plum half onto the filling before placing the top layer of dough, but avoid overfilling the pastries, or they will burst open while baking.

MAKE AHEAD

Make the filling ahead of time, cover and chill it. It will keep for several days.

① ② ③

PEAR & ALMOND DUMPLINGS

Most fruit dumplings are constructed by wrapping a piece of fruit in a square of dough. This one is a little different—the fruit and a dab of almond filling are sandwiched between two layers of puff pastry, and the dough never shrinks, falls away, or does anything but rise to flaky perfection around the fruit.

1. For the poached pears, half-fill a 4- to 5-quart Dutch oven with a cover with ice water and the lemon juice. Peel, halve, and core the pears, dropping them in one piece at a time. Skim out the ice, add the sugar, vanilla bean, and cinnamon and bring to a boil over medium heat. Boil for 1 minute, cover the pan, remove from the heat, and let the pears cool in the syrup. Remove the vanilla bean and cinnamon stick and refrigerate for up to several days.

2. For the almond filling, beat the almond paste and sugar together at medium speed in a stand mixer using the paddle attachment. Beat in 1 yolk and continue beating until smooth and free of lumps. Beat in the remaining yolk and the butter, followed by the flour. Set aside.

3. Drain the pears and trim the stem ends off, to make them round. Line a jellyroll pan with parchment paper.

4. Roll the dough on a floured surface to an 8 x 16-inch rectangle. Cut it half and roll each half to 8 x 16 inches. If the dough begins to get soft, slide the pieces onto a cookie sheet and chill for a few minutes.

5. Place one sheet of dough on the work surface and use a ruler and bench scraper to mark it into 4-inch squares. Cut them apart, line them up on the prepared pan and spoon a dab of almond filling into the center of each ①. Cover the filling with a pear half ②.

6. Mark and cut the second piece of dough as above, then use a sharp pastry wheel to cut a 2-inch cross in the center of each piece, ends pointing toward the corners of the square. Lightly brush egg wash around each pastry's pear, then lay one of the dough squares over it, lining up the edges of the pastry so that the top of the dumpling opens at the cut cross ③. Press with a fingertip all around the perimeter of the square ④. Repeat with the remaining pastry squares, then cover the dumplings loosely with plastic wrap and chill for at least 4 hours.

7. Set a rack in the lower third of the oven and preheat to 400°F. Use a dry brush to dab egg wash on the pastries, then bake until well risen and baked through, 45 to 55 minutes.

8. Cool the dumplings on a rack and serve warm. Dust lightly with confectioners' sugar right before serving.

Makes 8 pastries

⅔ batch Puff Pastry or Quick Puff Pastry (page 155 or 157)

POACHED PEARS

Ice water

2 tablespoons lemon juice, strained before measuring

4 firm-ripe Bartlett pears, about 2 pounds

1 cup sugar

1 vanilla bean, left whole

3-inch piece of cinnamon stick

ALMOND FILLING

¼ cup almond paste

2 tablespoons sugar

2 large egg yolks

2 tablespoons unsalted butter, softened

2 tablespoons unbleached all-purpose flour

Egg wash: 1 egg whisked with a pinch of salt

Confectioners' sugar for finishing

VARIATIONS

Substitute firm-ripe peaches, apricots, or prune plums for the pears. The apricots and plums don't need to be poached. For the peaches, just halve and pit them before poaching them—the skins will easily slip off.

CROISSANTS

Once your dough is made and well chilled, you can use it for croissants or for a variant such as the two recipes that follow, pains au chocolat or chocolate twists. Here, I'm giving the dimensions and instructions for using half the dough for croissants. See the Note for dimensions and instructions for using a third in case you'd like to make all three pastries at once.

Makes 16 large croissants

½ batch Professor Calvel's Croissant Dough
(page 158), chilled

Egg wash: 1 egg whisked with a pinch of salt

1. Place the dough on a floured surface and roll to a 16-inch square, then cut into 2 strips, each 16 x 8 inches. Patch the strips together by overlapping them by ¼ inch ① so you have a 32 x 8-inch rectangle.

2. Mark one long side every 4 inches. On the other long side, start marking at 2 inches in from the left, then mark every 4 inches—you'll have one 2-inch section at the end. Use your bench scraper to mark triangles ②, then use a sharp pastry wheel to cut them ③. You'll have 15 triangles and a half triangle at each end. Patch the halves together.

3. Form the croissants by positioning the base of the triangle so it faces you. Pull the corners of the base to widen it. With one hand, start rolling upward ④ from the base while gently pulling on the apex of the triangle to lengthen it ⑤. Roll toward the point, and leave the point on top. Curve the pastries slightly as you put them on two large jelly-roll pans lined with parchment ⑥.

4. Cover the croissants with a lightweight, flat-weave towel and let proof until almost doubled in size, about 1 hour, depending on the temperature of the room.

5. Once the croissants have started to puff, set racks in the upper and lower thirds of the oven and preheat to 450°F.

6. Gently brush the croissants with the egg wash. Place in the oven and decrease the temperature to 400°F. Bake until well risen and starting to color, about 10 minutes.

7. Switch the positions of the pans, swapping from one oven rack to the other and turning from front to back. Bake for about 10 minutes more, until baked through.

8. Cool on a rack and serve the day they are baked, or bag and freeze. Reheat frozen croissants at 350°F for 10 minutes, then cool slightly before serving.

NOTE

To use a third of the dough, roll a 12 x 16-inch rectangle, then cut it into two 12 x 8-inch rectangles, patching them together as above and cutting them the same way. This will yield 11 full croissants and 2 patched ones.

④ ⑤ ⑥

PUFF PASTRY BOW TIES

This beautiful variation on caramelized puff pastry can be a little challenging to prepare. If the dough gets sticky, just refrigerate it for 10 minutes or so and continue.

Makes about 24 cookie-sized pastries

1 cup sugar

⅓ batch Puff Pastry or Quick Puff Pastry (page 155 or 157)

1. Scatter about a third of the sugar on the work surface and place the dough on it. Turn the dough over to coat the other side with sugar and begin to press and roll into a 12-inch square. Move the dough frequently while rolling and add sugar under and on top.

2. Slide the dough onto a cookie sheet lined with parchment and refrigerate until firm, 10 to 15 minutes.

3. Trim the side edges even and cut the dough into six approximately 2-inch strips. Stack 3 strips together, making 2 separate stacks.

4. Use the handle of a wooden spoon to press a narrow trough lengthwise into the center of each stack, turn the stacks over, and repeat on the other side.

5. Carefully cut each stack of dough lengthwise into long slices ⅓ inch thick. One at a time, take the slices and twist them at the indentation, making a bow-tie shape.

6. Put a pile of the remaining sugar on the work surface and dip one side of each pastry into it. Arrange the bow ties, sugared sides down, on a parchment-lined cookie sheet (you may need two), leaving a couple of inches around each one.

7. Let rest at room temperature while you set a rack at the middle level in the oven and preheat to 375°F.

8. Bake one pan at a time until the bow ties expand and the sugar on the bottom caramelizes, about 20 minutes.

9. Cool the bow ties on a rack and turn the caramelized side upward to serve. They're great on their own or to accompany any plain fruit, custardy, or frozen dessert. They can be stored for a couple of days between sheets of wax paper in a tin or plastic container with a tight-fitting cover, but they're best on the day they're baked.

MAKE AHEAD
Cut and bake one of the stacks of sugared dough, then double wrap and freeze the other. Thaw in the refrigerator for several hours or overnight, then proceed from step 6. Much of the sugar will melt, but they'll bake very well.

PAINS AU CHOCOLAT

Makes 16 large pastries

½ batch Professor Calvel's Croissant Dough (page 158), chilled

32 small ¼-ounce chocolate bars, or two 3- to 4-ounce bars semisweet or bittersweet chocolate cut into 16 pieces measuring ¾ x 4 inches

Egg wash: 1 egg whisked with a pinch of salt

VARIATIONS

To use a third of the croissant dough, roll it to a 12 x 16-inch rectangle, then cut it into twelve 4-inch squares. Resume at step 2, above.

These "chocolate loaves" are usually filled with tiny specially made bars of semisweet chocolate called *batons boulangers* (bakers' sticks). You can order those online, or you can buy two 3- to 4-ounce bars of premium semisweet or bittersweet chocolate, let it soften at room temperature, and cut it into ¾-inch strips using a thin sharp knife run under hot water and wiped between cuts.

1. Place the dough on a floured surface and roll to a 16-inch square. Mark, then cut the dough into sixteen 4-inch squares. Line 2 large jellyroll pans with parchment paper.

2. Place 2 small bars or 1 larger piece of chocolate about 1½ inches in from one side of the dough square, then fold the dough over to enclose it. Fold the dough over once more and place the pastry, seam side down, on one of the prepared pans. Repeat until all the dough squares have been filled with chocolate, leaving as much space as possible between them on the pans.

3. Cover with a lightweight flat-weave towel and let proof until almost doubled in size, about 1 hour or a little longer, depending on the temperature of the room.

4. Once the pastries have started to puff, set racks in the upper and lower thirds of the oven and preheat to 450°F.

5. Gently brush the pains au chocolat with the egg wash. Place in the oven and decrease the temperature to 400°F. Bake until well risen and starting to color, about 10 minutes.

6. Switch the positions of the pans, swapping from one oven rack to the other and turning from front to back. Bake about 10 minutes more, until the pastries are baked through.

7. Cool on a rack and serve the day they are baked, or bag and freeze them. Reheat frozen pains au chocolat at 350°F for 10 minutes, then cool slightly before serving.

VIENNESE CHEESE-FILLED SQUARES (TOPFENTASCHERL)

Viennese pot cheese, or *Topfen*, isn't unlike our part-skim-milk ricotta, but it's a little firmer. In this recipe, I've combined the ricotta with some cream cheese, and it works perfectly. This is another wonderful recipe shared by Hans Diglas in Vienna.

Makes 12 pastries

½ batch Viennese Danish Dough (page 159)

½ cup dried currants or golden raisins

1 teaspoon dark rum

4 ounces cream cheese, at room temperature

¼ cup sugar

2 large egg yolks

1 teaspoon vanilla extract

1 cup part-skim-milk ricotta

Confectioners' sugar for finishing

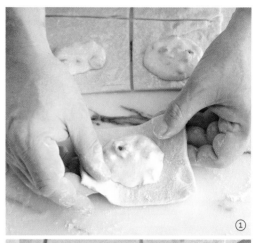

1. Toss the currants with the rum and set aside. Line a cookie sheet with parchment paper.

2. Use a rubber spatula to beat together the cream cheese, sugar, yolks, and vanilla. Gently fold in the ricotta.

3. Roll the dough on a floured surface to a 12 x 16-inch rectangle. Mark, then cut the dough into twelve 4-inch squares.

4. Carefully fold the currants and rum into the cheese filling and distribute evenly among the squares of dough, spooning into the center of each.

5. Pick up opposite corners of the dough ①, stretching slightly ②. Overlap the corners, then pinch together ③; repeat with the two other corners ④. Repeat with the rest of the dough.

6. Arrange the pastries on the prepared pan, leaving a couple of inches all around each one.

7. Cover with a lightweight flat-weave towel and proof until almost doubled in size, about 1 hour, depending on the temperature of the room.

8. Once they have started to puff, set racks in middle level in the oven and preheat to 400°F.

9. Place the pastries in the oven and decrease the temperature to 375°F. Bake until well risen and starting to color, about 15 minutes.

10. Turn the pan from back to front and continue baking until the pastries are baked through, about 10 minutes longer.

11. Cool on a rack and serve the day they are baked; dust with confectioners' sugar right before serving. Because the filling is delicate, these don't freeze well.

CHOCOLATE CINNAMON TWISTS (TORSADES AU CHOCOLAT)

Makes 16 pastries

½ batch Professor Calvel's Croissant Dough
(page 158), chilled

ALMOND FILLING

¼ cup almond paste

2 tablespoons sugar

2 large egg yolks

2 tablespoons unsalted butter, softened

2 tablespoons unbleached all-purpose flour

6 ounces semisweet mini chips, or semisweet
chocolate cut into small pieces

1 teaspoon ground cinnamon

Egg wash: 1 egg whisked with a pinch of salt

NOTE

To use a third of the dough, roll it to a 16-inch
square, then cut it into two 8-inch strips. Fill and
finish the pastry as described, but cut only ten
1½-inch pieces in step 4.

These aren't a classic croissant variation but a French way of having croissant dough
stand in for Danish pastry. The dough is spread with almond filling, then sprinkled with
chocolate and cinnamon. You could easily substitute or add raisins or currants.

1. For the almond filling, beat the almond paste and sugar together at medium speed in a stand
mixer using the paddle attachment. Beat in 1 yolk and continue beating until smooth and free of
lumps. Beat in the remaining yolk and the butter, followed by the flour.

2. Place the dough on a floured surface and roll it to a 16 x 24-inch rectangle. Mark, then cut the
dough into 2 strips, each 8 x 24 inches. Line 2 large jelly-roll pans with parchment paper.

3. Spread the almond filling on one of the strips, then evenly sprinkle the chocolate and
cinnamon over it. Cover with the second piece of dough, gently pressing them together.

4. Use a sharp pastry wheel to cut the dough crosswise into 16 strips, each 1½ inches wide.

5. Give each strip a couple of twists as you put it on one of the prepared pans, arranging the
pastries about 2 inches apart in all directions.

6. Cover with a lightweight, flat-weave towel and let proof until almost doubled in size, about
1 hour or a little longer, depending on the temperature of the room.

7. Once they have started to puff, set racks in the upper and lower thirds of the oven and
preheat to 450°F.

8. Gently brush the torsades with the egg wash. Place in the oven and decrease the temperature
to 400°F. Bake until well risen and starting to color, about 10 minutes.

9. Switch the positions of the pans, swapping from one oven rack to the other and turning from
front to back. Continue baking until the torsades are baked through, about 10 minutes longer.

10. Cool on a rack and serve the day they are baked, or bag and freeze. Reheat frozen torsades
at 350°F for 10 minutes, then cool them slightly before serving.

VIENNESE WALNUT CINNAMON CRESCENTS
(ISCHLER KIPFERL)

Bad Ischl, not far from Salzburg, was a favorite watering place among nineteenth-century Viennese aristocracy, including Emperor Franz Josef. These sweet and indulgent crescents are a specialty of a pastry shop in Bad Ischl, but they've been widely copied all over Austria. This version comes from Café Diglas in Vienna.

1. Roll the dough on a floured surface to a 12-inch square. Cut it into 2 strips, each 6 x 12 inches, then join them together into a long strip that's 6 x 24 inches. Following the instructions for cutting croissant dough in step 2 on page 170, mark, then cut the strip into triangles with a 4-inch base. You will get 11 full triangles, along with 2 half-triangles on the ends, which you can patch together to make a twelfth pastry.

2. Stir the granulated sugar and cinnamon together in a small bowl. Generously brush the dough with the butter, then evenly sprinkle with the cinnamon sugar and walnuts. Use the palm of your hand to press the sugar and nuts against the dough to adhere.

3. Invert one pastry so that the sugar and nuts are underneath. Roll from the base of the triangle toward the point, pulling gently on the point to lengthen it. If some of the sugar and nuts fall off, just sprinkle them back on as you roll. Finish with the point at the top of the roll, then curve the pastry slightly and arrange it on one of the prepared pans. Repeat with the remaining pastries.

4. Cover with a lightweight flat-weave towel and proof until almost doubled in size, about 1 hour, depending on the temperature of the room.

5. Once they have started to puff, set racks in the upper and lower thirds of the oven and preheat to 400°F.

6. Place the pans in the oven and decrease the temperature to 375°F. Bake until well risen and starting to color, about 10 minutes.

7. Switch the positions of the pans, swapping from one oven rack to the other and turning from front to back. Continue baking until the pastries are baked through, about 10 minutes longer.

8. Cool on a rack and serve the day they are baked; dust with confectioners' sugar right before serving. Because the topping is delicate, these don't freeze well.

Makes 12 pastries

½ batch Viennese Danish Dough (page 159)

TOPPINGS

⅓ cup granulated sugar

½ teaspoon ground cinnamon

4 tablespoons/½ stick unsalted butter, melted and cooled

1 cup walnut pieces, finely chopped

Confectioners' sugar for finishing

2 jelly-roll pans covered with parchment

DANISH DOUGH COFFEECAKE (PLUNDERKRANZKUCHEN)

Baking this filled, split, and twisted cake in a ring or tube pan is a perfect way to get a symmetrical and moist result. The original recipe calls for candied orange peel, but I've substituted dried apricots to offset the sweetness of the currants and the almond filling.

1. Butter a 10-inch ring or tube pan. For the filling, combine the milk and almond paste in a medium saucepan and set over low heat. Whisk often to avoid lumps.

2. Thoroughly mix the sugar and flour in a small bowl, then whisk in the yolks all at once. When the milk mixture comes to a boil, whisk a third of it into the yolk mixture, then return the milk to medium heat. Once the milk boils again, begin whisk in the yolk mixture, continuing to whisk until the filling thickens and comes to a boil. Cook, whisking constantly, for 30 seconds more.

3. Off the heat, whisk in the lemon zest and vanilla; scrape the filling into a bowl, press plastic directly against the surface, and chill thoroughly.

4. Place the dough on a floured work surface and lightly dust the top with flour. Roll to a 12 x 16-inch rectangle. Use an offset metal spatula to spread the chilled filling on the dough—it will be a thin layer. Set aside 2 tablespoons each of the currants and apricots for finishing the cake, then sprinkle the rest on top of the filling.

5. Tightly roll up the dough, starting from one of the long sides, then use a sharp knife to split the roll lengthwise. Leave the halves, cut sides up, next to each other.

6. Without stretching the filled and split pieces of dough, gently twist the halves together and arrange in the prepared pan so that some of the split areas are facing upward.

7. Cover the pan and proof the cake for several hours, until it puffs to double its original volume.

8. Set a rack in the lower third of the oven and preheat to 375°F.

9. Set the pan in the oven and decrease the temperature to 350°F. Bake until well risen and golden with an internal temperature of 200°F, about 1 hour.

10. Cool the cake on a rack and unmold onto the rack or a cardboard. Replace the pan with another rack or cardboard and turn the cake right side up.

11. For the icing, stir the confectioners' sugar, milk, and vanilla together in a small saucepan and heat, stirring constantly, until just lukewarm. Use a spoon to generously drizzle the icing on the cake. Quickly sprinkle with the reserved currants and apricots, then the sliced almonds.

12. Slide the cake to a platter and serve on the day it is baked. Store loosely covered at room temperature.

Makes one 10-inch ring, about 12 servings

½ batch Viennese Danish Dough (page 159)

ALMOND CREAM FILLING

1½ cups whole milk

½ cup almond paste, cut into ¼-inch pieces

⅓ cup sugar

¼ cup unbleached all-purpose flour (spoon into dry-measure cup and level)

5 large egg yolks

Finely grated zest of 1 small lemon

2 teaspoons vanilla extract

1 cup currants

1 cup snipped dried apricots

VANILLA ICING

1½ cups confectioners' sugar, sifted after measuring

3 tablespoons milk

1 teaspoon vanilla extract

½ cup lightly toasted sliced almonds

VARIATIONS

To substitute almonds or other nuts for the almond paste, combine ½ cup shelled nuts and ¼ cup sugar and grind until fine and beginning to become pasty. When using almonds, add ¼ teaspoon almond extract.

VIENNESE APRICOT POCKETS (MARILLENTASCHERL)

Makes about 16 small pastries, or 8 servings

½ batch Viennese Danish Dough (page 159)

16 very small whole apricots (see Note)

⅓ cup almond paste

Egg wash: 1 egg whisked with a pinch or salt

1 tablespoon dark rum

½ cup sliced almonds

Confectioners' sugar for finishing

Crème Anglaise (recipe follows)

NOTE

Out of season, canned apricot halves in light syrup, well drained, work well for this recipe.

CRÈME ANGLAISE

1½ cups whole milk

¾ cup heavy whipping cream

⅓ cup sugar

1 vanilla bean, split

4 large egg yolks

Ice water for cooling

Plunderteig is a perfect sweet and tender covering for small individual fruits like apricots, prune plums, and tiny apples or pears. Here, the dough is wrapped *around* the fruit, unlike the puff pastry version on page 169, where the fruit is sandwiched between two layers of dough. This is excellent served with the crème Anglaise that follows the recipe.

1. Rinse, stem, and pit the apricots without fully cutting them in half. Stuff each with a small piece of almond paste and set aside.

2. Set a rack at the middle level in the oven and preheat to 400°F. Line a large cookie sheet with parchment paper.

3. Roll the dough to a 12 x 14-inch rectangle. Cut away a 2-inch strip to make the dough a 12-inch square. Slide the extra strip of dough onto a cookie sheet and chill.

4. Mark, then cut the dough square into sixteen 3-inch squares. Lightly brush the egg wash onto the edges of the squares, then position an apricot in the center of each. Sprinkle each apricot with a drop or two of the rum.

5. Bring 2 opposite corners of the dough together over the apricot, pinching them together; repeat with the other corners. Repeat with the remaining pastries and arrange on the prepared cookie sheet, seam side up.

6. Use a small fluted cutter or a serrated pastry wheel to cut the reserved strip of dough into 1-inch disks or squares. Egg wash the pastries and press a piece of dough onto each one, placing it over the juncture of the corners of dough. Brush the added pieces of dough with egg wash and sprinkle with the sliced almonds.

7. Without proofing them beforehand, place the pastries in the oven and decrease the temperature to 375°F. Bake until well risen and starting to color, about 15 minutes.

8. Turn the pan from back to front and bake until the pastries are fully baked through, about 10 minutes more.

9. Cool the pastries on a rack and plan on serving warm. Dust with confectioners' sugar right before serving with the crème Anglaise.

Crème Anglaise

Bring the milk, cream, and sugar to a boil with the vanilla bean. Whisk the egg yolks in a bowl, then whisk them into the boiling liquid; remove the vanilla bean. Strain the mixture back into the pan and cook it over low heat, stirring constantly, until it is slightly thickened. Be careful not to let the sauce boil, or it will scramble. Pour the thickened sauce into a bowl set over ice water. Use it the same day or on the following day; if necessary, store it in the refrigerator.

VIENNESE ALMOND CRESCENTS (KLOSTERKIPFERL)

These aren't anything like croissants or the Viennese Ischler Kipferl on page 177, but they are a traditional pastry nonetheless. Here the Viennese Danish Dough is spread with an almond filling, folded, creased into a vague crescent shape, then strewn with sliced almonds. It's creamy, crunchy, and sweet all at the same time—and thoroughly delicious.

1. Roll the dough on a floured surface to a 12 x 18-inch rectangle. Mark, then cut the dough into four 3 x 18-inch rectangles and line them up in a row.

2. Spread the almond filling in a 1½-inch strip at the closer end of each rectangle, then fold the tops of the rectangles over the filling so that the long edges meet. Cut each rectangle into 1½ x 6-inch strips.

3. Ease each strip into a crescent shape and transfer to a cookie sheet lined with parchment.

4. Cover the pastries with a lightweight flat-weave towel and proof until almost doubled in size, about 1 hour, depending on the temperature of the room.

5. Set a rack at the middle level in the oven and preheat to 400°F.

6. Carefully brush the pastries with the egg wash and sprinkle with the almonds.

7. Place in the oven and decrease the temperature to 375°F. Bake until well risen and starting to color, about 15 minutes.

8. Turn the pan from back to front and continue baking the crescents until baked through, about 10 minutes longer.

9. Cool on a rack and serve them the day they are baked; dust with confectioners' sugar right before serving.

Makes 12 pastries

½ batch Viennese Danish Dough (page 159)

1 batch Almond Filling as in Chocolate Cinnamon Twists (page 176)

Egg wash: 1 egg whisked with a pinch of salt

½ cup sliced almonds, lightly crushed

Confectioners' sugar for finishing

CHAPTER 8

BRIOCHE & OTHER YEAST-RISEN PASTRIES

Most of the recipes in this chapter are best as breakfast, brunch, or tea pastries, though there are a couple like the brioche tart and shortcake that can be varied with different fruit and served as a dessert. The advantage to using brioche dough as a tart crust, aside from its tender sweetness, is its ability to absorb any juices the fruit generates while baking. Unlike a thinner pastry dough, which would become soggy, the thicker and slightly drier brioche dough welcomes the additional flavor and moisture. Both the tart and the shortcake are light and elegant enough to serve in the evening, too.

Of course, there are a few Viennese pastries here. It's not for no reason that brioches, croissants, Danish, and the whole assortment of breakfast baking is referred to as *Viennoiserie* in French. I've included some personal favorites, like Beugelteig, which is a sweet but not especially rich yeast dough that can be used to make poppy seed or walnut-filled bows or strudels.

BRIOCHE MOUSSELINE DOUGH

Makes 2 pounds/900 grams, enough for 15 to 18 individual brioches depending on the size of the molds used or 1 large or 2 smaller loaves baked in loaf or round pans

2 tablespoons/25 grams sugar

2¼ teaspoons/1 envelope/7 grams fine granulated active dry or instant yeast

⅓ cup/75 grams whole milk, scalded and cooled to 100°F

4 large eggs, at room temperature

3 cups/400 grams unbleached bread flour (spoon into dry-measure cup and level)

1 teaspoon/6 grams fine sea salt

8 ounces/2 sticks/225 grams unsalted butter, softened

This is a richer, softer, and in some ways lighter dough than the brioche in *BAKE!* and *BREAD.* Use it for a standard or round loaf baked in a pan or for any of the brioche roll variations on page 186. Softer and stickier than a leaner brioche dough, it's a little difficult to handle but don't let that stop you from trying it. Flour the palms of your hands rather than the work surface or the dough and you'll have no problems forming the dough. No matter what size or shape pan you choose, it will look appealing and taste even better.

1. Stir the sugar and yeast together in the bowl for a stand mixer, then whisk in the cooled milk. Let sit for 1 minute, then whisk again. Whisk in the eggs.

2. Use a large rubber spatula to stir in the flour, making sure not to leave any in the bottom of the bowl or stuck to its sides.

3. Using the dough hook, beat the dough on the lowest speed until it comes together but isn't completely smooth, 2 to 3 minutes. Let the dough rest for 15 minutes.

4. Mix again on low-medium speed and sprinkle in the salt. Add the butter in 8 or 10 separate pieces, then let the dough mix until it completely absorbs the butter and becomes smooth, shiny, and elastic, about 5 minutes. If the dough doesn't absorb the butter easily, stop and scrape down the bowl and dough hook every couple of minutes. Once you see that the butter is on its way to being completely absorbed, increase the speed to medium for about 1 minute.

5. Scrape the dough into a buttered bowl, turn it over so that the top is buttered, and cover with plastic wrap. Let ferment until it doubles in bulk, 1 to 2 hours, depending on the temperature.

6. Once the dough has fermented, scrape onto a floured surface and give it a turn: Press the dough into a fat disk and fold one side over the center, then fold the other side over both. Roll the dough down from the top to form an uneven sphere. Place the dough back in the bowl (butter the top again if necessary) seam side down and cover again.

7. Refrigerate the dough for a couple of hours or until it rises again and then chills down. It's now ready to use. You can leave the dough in the refrigerator overnight, but you should bake it within 18 hours of beginning to mix it.

VIENNESE SWEET YEAST-RISEN DOUGH (BEUGELTEIG)

This versatile dough is tender and buttery, but is always meant to surround a filling, whether as individual pastries like the walnut and poppy seed bows or a large strudel, all of which appear later in this chapter. *Beugel* is the German word for bow, as in bow and arrow. The poppy seed bows resemble the wood handle of the bow, while the walnut bows are made to somewhat resemble the bowstring after it's pulled to shooting position.

1. Stir the sugar and yeast together in the bowl for a stand mixer, then whisk in the cooled milk. Let sit for 1 minute, then whisk again. Whisk in the egg.

2. Use a large rubber spatula to stir in the flour, making sure not to leave any in the bottom of the bowl or stuck to its sides.

3. Sprinkle on the salt and distribute the butter in 8 or 10 pieces on the dough. Using the dough hook, beat on low-medium speed until the butter is absorbed, about 5 minutes. Stop and scrape down the sides of the bowl and the dough hook several times, more often if the butter is staying stuck to the sides of the bowl instead of being incorporated.

4. Once the butter is incorporated, increase the speed to medium and beat the dough until it is no longer stuck to the sides of the bowl and is more elastic, 2 to 3 minutes.

5. Scrape the dough into a buttered bowl, turn it over so that the top is buttered, and cover with plastic wrap. Let ferment until it doubles in bulk, 1 to 2 hours, depending on the temperature.

6. Once the dough has fermented, scrape to a floured surface and deflate it. Use immediately or place the dough back in the bowl, cover, and refrigerate. Chill for an hour or two or overnight, but be sure to use within 18 hours of beginning to mix it.

Makes about 1 pound/450 grams, enough for any recipe in this chapter that calls for it

¼ cup/30 grams confectioners' sugar, sifted after measuring

3 teaspoons/10 grams fine granulated active dry or instant yeast

⅓ cup/75 grams whole milk, scalded and cooled to 100°F

1 large egg, at room temperature

1 ⅔ cups/225 grams unbleached bread flour (spoon into dry-measure cup and level)

1 teaspoon/6 grams fine sea salt

7 tablespoons/100 grams unsalted butter, softened

INDIVIDUAL BRIOCHES

Individual brioches are a typical breakfast bread in France. Here I include descriptions and instructions for the principal ones, plus a few suggestions for inventing your own.

Brioche Rolls

Divide the dough into 60-gram pieces. Round them into perfect little spheres and place them, about 3 inches apart, on the prepared pan. Cover and let the rolls proof. Once almost doubled in size, brush the rolls with egg wash, using a very dry brush to avoid puddles, and leave plain or sprinkle with pearl sugar, coarse turbinado sugar, or coarsely chopped slivered almonds.

Raisin Brioches

When preparing the dough, add 1 cup currants or dark or golden raisins at the end of step 4, mixing them in for a minute or two on the lowest speed. Don't worry if they're not very evenly distributed; when the dough is turned in a later step, they will get mixed in. Proceed as for Brioche Rolls, above, but don't sprinkle with sugar or nuts before baking. If, when you're rounding the rolls, some raisins break through the top of the roll, poke them back in and pinch the dough over them; they'll burn if they stay on the surface.

Brioche Croissants

Press the finished dough out to a thick square on a floured cookie sheet and cover with plastic wrap. Chill until firm, about 1 hour. Roll the dough to a 12-inch square, then cut into 2 rectangles, each 12 x 6 inches. Join them together, overlapping the 6-inch sides by ¼ inch to make a 6 x 24-inch rectangle. Cut the dough into triangles with a 4-inch base, roll the crescents, and place in the prepared pans, following the instructions for shaping croissant dough on page 170. Cover the crescents with a lightweight flat-weave towel and proof until almost doubled in size, about 1 hour, depending on the temperature of the room. Brush with egg wash and sprinkle sparingly with pearl sugar; bake as above.

Brioches à Tête

These are a little tricky at first, but once you get the hang of forming them, they are quite easy. (And if this all seems too complicated, you can just use plain rounded pieces of dough . . .) Divide the dough into 40- to 60-gram pieces. Have ready 12 buttered fluted brioche pans that have about a ⅓ cup/80ml volume. Set the rounded piece of dough ① on its side with the smooth top facing to the right ②. Use the side of your hand, karate chop style, to indent the dough a third of the way in from the smooth side ③. Then roll back and forth at the indentation to make a little "neck" under the head ④. Turn the brioche so that the head is upward and use the fingers of one hand to make a trough in the body ⑤ so that the head is surrounded with an even doughnut-shaped piece of dough ⑥. Drop the brioches into the prepared pans as they're formed ⑦⑧. Cover, proof, and brush with egg wash. (Brioches à tête are not sprinkled with sugar or nuts.) Bake and cool.

BRIOCHE LOAVES

Makes 2 medium loaves

1 batch Brioche Mousseline Dough (page 184)

Egg wash: 1 egg whisked with a pinch of salt, optional

VARIATION

ROUND BRIOCHE LOAVES: Butter two 1½- to 2-inch deep, 8-inch round pans and line each with a disk of parchment. In step 1, divide each half of the dough into 10 pieces. Round and place them so that 6 pieces of dough line the perimeter of the pan and 4 are in the center. Continue with the recipe at step 3.

The lighter and richer Brioche Mousseline Dough is perfect for these. They can be baked in a standard loaf pan or in the same type of round pan used for cake layers. You can also make a single loaf and use the rest of the dough for one of the individual roll variations.

1. Butter two 8 x 4 x 2½-inch loaf pans. Divide the fully risen dough in half, making two 450-gram pieces. Divide each half into 5 pieces and round them all.

2. Stretching the dough balls slightly, place 5 pieces of dough in a line in each pan. Don't worry if the pans aren't full—they will be once the loaves have proofed.

3. Cover with a lightweight flat-weave kitchen towel and let rise until doubled and filling the pan.

4. Set a rack in the lower third of the oven and preheat to 375°F.

5. Once the dough has fully proofed, brush with egg wash if you like, being careful not to let any run between the loaf and the pan, which would make it stick.

6. Bake the loaves until well risen and deep golden, with an internal temperature of 200°F, 30 to 40 minutes.

7. Unmold the loaves onto a rack and cool them on their sides to prevent them from falling.

8. Wrap and keep the loaves at room temperature. For longer storage, freeze them; defrost and reheat briefly at 350°F and cool before serving.

SWISS BRIOCHE CREAM CAKE (NIDELKUCHEN)

This is a specialty of the Konditorei Aebersold in Murten, a charming walled medieval town in Switzerland's Canton Fribourg. After tasting and speaking with Hans Aebersold about the topping in 2005, I came home and worked out this version. While the original recipe remains a secret, my efforts got me pretty close. One difference is that the bakery uses a dough similar to a rich white bread, though this brioche dough version certainly makes for a delicate result. This is a great coffeecake to serve for breakfast or brunch.

1. Round the dough to a sphere. Cover with a towel or plastic wrap and let rest for 10 minutes. Butter and spray a 9-inch springform pan, buttering the sides thickly as the topping may run over while baking.

2. Using the floured palm of your hand, press the dough into the prepared pan. If it resists, cover for 10 minutes, then press again. Cover and let the dough proof until about 50 percent thicker, 30 to 40 minutes.

3. After about 20 minutes, set a rack at the middle level in the oven and preheat to 375°F. Slide a sheet of foil onto the bottom of the oven to catch any drips of butter.

4. For the topping, whisk the crème fraîche and yolks together. Use the palm of your hand to gently press an 8-inch round area in the enter of the dough to deflate it, leaving a ½-inch thicker rim at the side of the pan all around. Use a small offset spatula to spread the topping to within ½ inch of the side of the pan. Sprinkle with half the sugar.

5. Place the pan in the oven, decrease the temperature to 350°F and bake for 15 minutes. Open the oven and pull out the rack; quickly sprinkle on the remaining sugar.

6. Bake the cake until well risen and the topping is set and golden, about 20 minutes longer.

7. Cool the cake on a rack, then remove the side of the pan and slide the cake from the base onto a platter. Serve on the day it's baked.

Makes one 9-inch cake, 8 to 10 servings

½ batch Brioche Mousseline Dough
(page 184)

¼ cup crème fraîche or other thick cream

2 large egg yolks

3 tablespoons sugar

PRUNE PLUM TART IN A BRIOCHE CRUST

Makes one 11- or 12-inch tart, about 12 servings

½ batch Brioche Mousseline Dough
(page 184)

ALMOND FILLING

6 ounces canned almond paste

3 tablespoons sugar

1 large egg

6 tablespoons/¾ stick unsalted butter,
softened

2 teaspoons finely grated orange zest

1 large egg yolk

1 teaspoon vanilla extract

¼ cup unbleached all-purpose flour
(spoon into dry-measure cup and level)

¼ teaspoon baking powder

2½ pounds prune plums, rinsed, halved,
and pitted

2 tablespoons sugar for the plums

VARIATIONS

Substitute halves or quarters of small apricots
(pictured at right) or peaches (to cut the
peaches, see page 85). To use pears, peel,
halve, and slice them from stem to blossom
end, cutting each half into quarters or sixths.
If pear slices are too thick, they'll generate too
much water for the filling to absorb.

Brioche dough makes a perfect crust for a tart of juicy fruit like these plums—or apricots, peaches, or even small pears. A thin coating of almond filling helps to keep the crust drier, but the brioche can also absorb most of the fruit juices without becoming soggy. This is an excellent tart for brunch or tea, served with thick unwhipped cream like crème fraîche, or with some lightly sweetened whipped cream. The almond filling here is twice as much as you need; freeze the rest in a plastic container, covered tightly, and use within a few weeks.

1. Set a rack at the lowest level in the oven; preheat to 400°F. Butter a 9- or 10-inch tart pan.

2. Set the dough on a floured surface and lightly dust with flour. Roll to a disk a little larger than the pan. Fold the dough in half and transfer to the prepared pan, lining up the fold with the diameter of the pan. Unfold the dough and press into the pan. Cover and let rest at room temperature while preparing the filling.

3. For the almond filling, beat the almond paste and sugar on low speed in the bowl of a stand mixer fitted with the paddle attachment until reduced to fine crumbs. Add the whole egg and beat until completely smooth, 1 to 2 minutes. Beat in the butter until smooth, then stop and scrape the bowl and beater. Beat in the orange zest, yolk, and vanilla. Quickly mix the flour and baking powder together and fold into the filling using a rubber spatula.

4. Uncover the dough and press an 8-inch round area in the center of the dough to deflate it, leaving a ½-inch thicker rim at the side of the pan all around. Spread the almond filling on the dough—it will be a thin layer. Starting at the outside edge of the crust, arrange the plums, cut side upward, close to each other. Continue making concentric rows of plum halves until you reach the center of the crust. Sprinkle the plums with sugar.

5. Place the tart in the oven and decrease the heat to 375°F. Bake until the crust is well colored and dry, and the plums are softened and juicy, about 45 minutes.

6. Cool the tart on a rack and serve warm or at room temperature.

BOSTOCK

Makes about 8 bostocks

Eight 1¼-inch-thick slices of day-old brioche loaf

ALMOND SYRUP

⅔ cup water

⅓ cup sugar

2 strips orange zest, each 2 inches wide and 3 inches long, removed with a vegetable peeler

2 tablespoons orgeat (French almond syrup; see Note)

1 teaspoon vanilla extract

1 teaspoon orange flower water, optional

Almond Filling (page 192)

½ cup sliced almonds

Confectioners' sugar

NOTE

If you have no orgeat syrup, substitute ½ to 1 teaspoon almond extract (taste the syrup after adding ½ teaspoon and use more only if necessary).

Originally crafted from leftover brioche, bostock has taken its rightful place at the breakfast (or tea) table. A thick slice is moistened with an almond-flavored syrup, then spread with almond cream and sprinkled with sliced almonds. Moist, sweet, perfumed, and slightly crunchy around the edges, bostock always pleases. Traditionally, these were round because the slices were cut from a cylindrical loaf; you can use rectangular slices of brioche or trim them into rounds using a cutter.

1. Set a rack at the middle level in the oven and preheat to 375°F. Line a jelly-roll pan with buttered foil.

2. For the syrup, bring the water and sugar to a simmer, stirring to dissolve the sugar. Off the heat, add the orange zest; let the syrup cool. Remove the zest and stir in the orgeat, vanilla, and orange flower water, if using.

3. Arrange the brioche slices on the prepared pan and use a brush to moisten with the syrup.

4. Spread each slice with a tablespoon or two of the almond filling, then sprinkle the sliced almonds on top.

5. Place the pan in the oven and lower the temperature to 350°F. Bake until the filling is set and the bostocks are well toasted and crisp around the edges.

6. Dust with confectioners' sugar. Serve warm or cool on a rack and serve at room temperature.

VIENNESE BRIOCHE DUMPLINGS (BUCHTELN)

While Buchteln are originally from Bohemia, one of the countries that lost its national identity after being swallowed up by the Austrian Empire, today they're thought of as thoroughly Viennese. Small balls of rich dough (here I'm using brioche dough) usually filled with jam, Buchteln are baked in a heavily buttered pan so that the bottoms become quite crisp. They are served with just a sprinkling of confectioners' sugar or with a vanilla custard sauce. I love pastries like this that are made in coffeehouses as well as in the home.

1. Place the dough on a floured surface and press or pat it to a 12-inch square. Mark, then cut the dough into 2-inch squares.

2. Place a small dab of preserves or filling in the center of each square. Pull the corners upward, pinch together, and invert the little filled bun as it's formed. Work quickly so that the dough doesn't soften too much.

3. Once you've formed the dumplings, spread half the butter in the bottom of a 9-inch square baking pan, 2 inches deep, then brush the rest of the butter on the pastries. Place them in the pan in 6 rows of 6 pastries. Cover and let the dumplings proof while the oven is preheating.

4. Set a rack at the middle level in the oven and preheat to 400°F.

5. Once the oven is ready, uncover and place the dumplings inside. Decrease the temperature to 375°F and bake until well risen and deep golden, 20 to 25 minutes.

6. Serve the dumplings directly from the baking pan, placing a portion on a plate and dusting with confectioners' sugar. Serve the sauce on the side, if you like.

Makes about 36 small pastries, 3 or 4 to a portion

½ batch Brioche Mousseline Dough (page 184)

½ cup apricot preserves or any fruit preserves you like, prune butter, Poppy Seed Filling (page 200), or Walnut Filling (page 199), any large pieces chopped

8 tablespoons/1 stick unsalted butter, melted

Confectioners' sugar for finishing

Crème Anglaise (page 180) for serving, optional

RASPBERRY BRIOCHE SHORTCAKE

Back in the 1990s, we used to have a demonstration class every afternoon at Peter Kump's New York Cooking School. Occasionally the chef garde-manger or the pastry chef from the celebrated restaurant Le Cirque would do one of them. José, the young French pastry chef, once made this lovely take on a shortcake. I made it for a class soon after I tasted it and have always wanted to share the recipe as a memorial to his talent, because José passed away very young.

1. Round the brioche dough to a sphere and let it rest, covered, on the work surface for 10 minutes. Butter a 2-inch deep, 9-inch round pan and line with parchment.

2. Use the floured palm of your hand to evenly press the dough into the prepared pan. Cover and let proof until almost doubled in bulk, about 45 minutes.

3. Set a rack at the middle level in the oven and preheat to 350°F.

4. Bake the cake until well risen and deep golden, with an internal temperature of 200°F, 30 to 40 minutes. Unmold and cool on a rack.

5. Meanwhile, make the filling by whisking the granulated sugar, flour, and salt together in a nonreactive saucepan. Whisk in the milk and the yolks. Place the pan over low heat and whisk until the mixture thickens and comes to a full boil. Cook, whisking constantly, for 1 minute. Off the heat, whisk in 3 tablespoons of the orange liqueur and scrape the pastry cream into a bowl. Press plastic wrap directly against the surface and refrigerate until cold.

6. Use a sharp serrated knife to split the brioche cake horizontally into 2 layers. Place the bottom layer on a platter, cut side up, and sprinkle with half of the remaining orange liqueur.

7. Whip the cream and fold into the cooled pastry cream. Spread half the cream on the bottom layer. Top the cream with the raspberries, then spread the remaining cream over the berries.

8. Sprinkle the cut surface of the top layer with the remaining orange liqueur, then invert the cut side onto the filling.

9. Dust the cake with confectioners' sugar right before serving.

Makes one 9-inch cake, 8 to 10 servings

½ batch Brioche Mousseline Dough (page 184)

½ cup granulated sugar

⅓ cup unbleached all-purpose flour (spoon into dry-measure cup and level)

Pinch of salt

1½ cups whole milk

4 large egg yolks

6 tablespoons orange liqueur, divided use

¾ cup heavy whipping cream

2 half-pint baskets fresh raspberries, picked over but not washed

Confectioners' sugar for finishing

VARIATIONS

Tiny hulled strawberries or a mixture of different berries can replace the raspberries.

YEAST-RISEN WALNUT STRUDEL (NUSSBEUGELSTRUDEL)

Strudel made with a slightly sweet, buttery yeast dough is one of my favorite treats; in this recipe I'm using the Beugelteig on page 185 that's also used for the poppy seed and walnut horns that follow. One thing is important in preparing this: You have to be certain that the dough rolled into the center of the strudel is baked through. Testing the temperature of the strudel with an accurate thermometer ensures perfect results.

Don't be shocked at the method of baking the strudel sealed inside a tube of parchment paper—it's the best and easiest way to make it so that it doesn't spread out and burst. Thanks to my friend Brian Pansari for sharing this method for baking a similar type of strudel at his La Bonbonniere bakery in Edison, New Jersey.

1. For the filling, combine the butter, milk, and sugar in a medium saucepan and bring to a simmer. Stir in the walnuts and bread crumbs and cook, stirring constantly, for 1 to 2 minutes; the filling will be quite thick. Off the heat, stir in the vanilla, lemon zest, and cinnamon.

2. Scrape the filling onto a plate, press plastic wrap directly against the surface, and cool to room temperature.

3. Once the filling has cooled, invert the dough onto a floured surface and lightly flour the top. Press the dough into a rough square, then press or gently roll into a 10- x 12-inch rectangle. Evenly spread the cooled walnut filling all over the dough, leaving a 1-inch margin uncovered on each of the 12-inch sides.

4. Fold over the uncovered inch of dough at the top or bottom and roll the strudel jelly-roll style, ending seam side up. Thickly butter a 12 x 18-inch sheet of parchment paper.

5. Run the palms of both hands under the strudel and move it, without stretching it, and position it centered at one of the long edges of the buttered paper, seam side up. Tightly roll the paper around the strudel; wrap 4 or 5 pieces of masking tape around the paper to keep it firmly around the strudel while baking. Leave the ends of the paper open to let the strudel expand.

6. Transfer the strudel to a jelly-roll pan, seam side down, and let rest for 15 or 20 minutes.

7. Meanwhile, set a rack in the middle level of the oven and preheat to 375°F.

8. Place the strudel in the oven and decrease the temperature to 350°F. Bake until it reaches an internal temperature of 200°F on an instant-read thermometer, 45 to 55 minutes. (Pierce the strudel with the thermometer a little in from the ends, since they'll be trimmed away afterward.)

9. Slide the strudel to a rack and remove the paper. Cool, seam side down, on a rack. Trim the edges diagonally before serving. >>

Makes one 16-inch-long strudel, about 18 servings

1 batch chilled Viennese Sweet Yeast-Risen Dough (page 185)

WALNUT FILLING

2 tablespoons unsalted butter

½ cup whole milk

½ cup sugar

2 cups walnut pieces, finely ground

¾ cup fresh bread crumbs

1 teaspoon vanilla extract

Finely grated zest of 1 small lemon

⅛ teaspoon ground cinnamon

VARIATIONS

POPPYSEED BOWS (MOHNBEUGEL): These are given a slightly different final shaping from the walnut horns below, but use the same dough and a filling that's substantially the same.

In the walnut filling, page 199, substitute 6 ounces/about 1¼ cups ground poppy seeds for the walnuts and ¾ cup dark raisins, coarsely chopped, for the bread crumbs. Bring to a boil and cook, stirring, until no longer liquid, about 3 minutes. Cool, then divide the filling into 12 equal pieces, each about 40 grams. With lightly floured hands, roll each to a cylinder about 4½ inches long. Divide the dough into 12 pieces, each about 40 grams. Roll to the same size as the filling.

Place the dough on a floured surface and roll to an oval about 6 x 3½ inches. Brush the dough with water, place the filling on it, and wrap the dough around the filling ①. Roll the pastry under the palm of your hands and shape the ends into points ②. Arrange them on parchment-lined jellyroll pans and just curve an inch on each end inward to form an elongated crescent shape ③.

Brush the pastries with egg wash (1 egg whisked with a pinch of salt); wait 5 minutes, then brush again.

Place the pastries in the oven and decrease the temperature to 350°F. Bake until deep golden and baked through, 25 to 35 minutes. Cool on a rack and serve the day they are baked.

WALNUT BOWS (NUSSBEUGEL): Use the same dough and filling for this popular Viennese breakfast pastry. Shape as for the poppy seed bows above and use the side of your hand, karate-chop style, to make a crease in the middle of the pastry and bend it ③. Transfer to a parchment-covered jelly-roll pan. Repeat with the remaining dough and filling. Egg wash and bake.

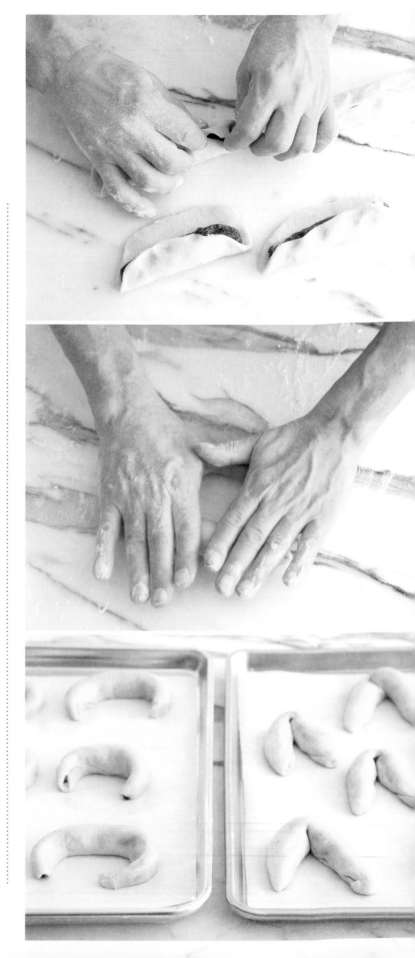

BRIOCHE FRUIT DUMPLINGS

These are a little like larger Buchteln and are served in a similar manner. While Buchteln may be left plain or filled with a jam or nut filling (see page 195), these dumplings are always filled with fresh fruit. This recipe is based on dumplings I recently tasted at Café Central in Vienna, one of the best places to enjoy traditional and contemporary Viennese pastry specialties.

1. Press or pat the dough on a floured surface to a 12-inch square. Mark, then cut the dough into 3-inch squares.

2. Place a small dab of preserves and an apricot half in the center of each square. Pull the corners upward, pinch them together, and invert the little filled bun as it's formed. Work quickly so that the dough doesn't soften too much.

3. Once you've formed the dumplings, spread half the butter in the bottom of a 2-inch-deep, 9-inch square pan, then brush the rest of the butter on the formed pastries. Place them in the pan in 4 rows of 4 dumplings in each. Cover and let proof while the oven is preheating.

4. Set a rack at the middle level in the oven and preheat to 400°F.

5. Once the oven is ready, uncover and place the dumplings inside. Decrease the temperature to 375°F and bake until well risen and deep golden, about 20 minutes.

6. Serve the dumplings directly from the baking pan, placing a portion on a plate and dusting with confectioners' sugar. Serve the sauce on the side, if you like.

Makes about 16 small pastries, 2 to a portion

½ batch Brioche Mousseline Dough (page 184)

¼ cup apricot preserves, any large pieces chopped

8 small apricots, rinsed, halved, and pitted

4 tablespoons unsalted butter, melted

Confectioners' sugar for finishing

Crème Anglaise (page 180) for serving, optional

VARIATIONS

Substitute halves of small prune plums, a couple of plump sweet pitted cherries, or even chunks of fresh pineapple or mango for the apricot halves.

NOTE

Traditional Viennese fruit dumplings are boiled, not baked, and are served with buttered bread crumbs and melted butter.

CHAPTER 9

PÂTE À CHOUX OR CREAM PUFF PASTRY

The only pastry dough that's actually cooked before it's baked, pâte à choux is not only versatile but also quite easy to prepare. Simple puffs, large or small, can be shaped by popping the dough onto a pan from a spoon, but more tailored shapes such as éclairs require piping. I've provided detailed instructions and photos on the techniques for piping, so with a little practice, the shapes should be easy to master.

Most desserts made from pâte à choux are filled with pastry cream. As you read through these recipes, you'll notice that the pastry cream fillings are similar but not exactly alike. Except for the crème Chiboust filling in the gâteau Saint-Honoré, you can pretty much use the fillings interchangeably, according to your taste. Further flavor variations for pastry cream are listed after the recipe for Petits Choux au Café on page 206.

Makes 1 pound, 8 ounces/780 grams

1 cup/243 grams whole milk

7 tablespoons/3½ ounces/100 grams unsalted butter

¼ teaspoon fine sea salt

½ teaspoon sugar

1 cup + 2½ tablespoons/5.5 ounces/156 grams unbleached all-purpose flour

1 cup/243 grams whole eggs

NOTE
For greatest accuracy weigh all the ingredients. For exact weight of the eggs, place a bowl on the scale and zero it. Add 4 eggs; if they're not enough, beat a fifth egg and add only enough for the exact weight. This base recipe for cream puff pastry will yield enough for any of the recipes in this chapter.

Makes 24 or more small choux, depending on the size they're piped

1 batch Pâte à Choux (above)

COFFEE PASTRY CREAM

1½ cups whole milk

½ cup heavy whipping cream

⅓ cup sugar

1 tablespoon instant espresso powder

3 tablespoons cornstarch

5 large egg yolks

2 teaspoons vanilla extract or dark rum

4 tablespoons unsalted butter, at room temperature

COFFEE GLAZE

3 cups confectioners' sugar, sifted after measuring

⅓ cup water

2 teaspoons instant espresso powder

2 tablespoons light corn syrup

2 tablespoons unsalted butter, softened

2 teaspoons vanilla extract

PÂTE À CHOUX

For the best leavening, plan on getting the piped shapes into the oven as soon as possible after the paste is mixed and the shapes are formed. Thanks to Jeff Yoskowitz for sharing his excellent recipe.

1. Combine the milk, butter, salt, and sugar in a 2-quart saucepan and place over medium heat. Bring the mixture to a boil, stirring occasionally, to make sure the butter melts.

2. Once the liquid has come to a full rolling boil, remove the pan from the heat and add the flour all at once. Use a wooden spoon or silicon spatula to smoothly stir it in. Return the pan to the heat and beat the paste just until the bottom of the pan is filmed, 20 to 30 seconds.

3. Pour the paste into the bowl of a stand mixer and fit it with the paddle attachment. Beat on the lowest speed for half a minute to cool slightly. Add the eggs one at a time, beating smooth after each addition. Stop and scrape the bowl and beater after the second and third eggs.

COFFEE FILLED & ICED CREAM PUFFS (PETITS CHOUX AU CAFÉ)

Small puffs like these were used to form part of the assortment of petits fours served at the Sporting Club in Monte Carlo when I worked there several summers in the 1970s. Since the recipe makes quite a few, these would be a perfect dessert to serve, along with some cookies or plainer pastries, for a large party.

1. Set racks in the upper and lower thirds of the oven and preheat to 375°F. Prepare two cookie sheets: use a dab of the dough in each corner ① to hold parchment in place for piping ②.

2. Using a pastry bag fitted with a ⅜-inch fine French star tube (#4B, Ateco #864), pipe the pâte à choux to make twenty-four ¾-inch-diameter choux on the prepared pans. Hold the bag at a 45-degree angle to the pan, touch the tube to the paper, squeeze quickly to make a small sphere, then stop squeezing and lift upward ③. If you leave a point, moisten your fingertip and smooth it away.

3. Bake the choux until golden and dry, 20 to 25 minutes. Completely cool the pans on racks.

4. For the pastry cream, set aside ½ cup of the milk in a medium bowl. Combine the remaining 1 cup milk with the cream, sugar, and espresso powder in a medium nonreactive saucepan and whisk to mix. Place the pan over low heat and bring to a full boil.

5. Meanwhile, whisk the cornstarch into the reserved ½ cup milk and whisk in the yolks.

6. Once the milk boils, whisk about a third of it into the yolk mixture. Return the remaining milk to a full boil. Beginning to whisk before pouring, add the yolk to the pan mixture in a quick stream, whisking constantly. >>

FLAVORING PASTRY CREAM

In each of the following variations, omit the coffee and rum from the recipe.

VANILLA PASTRY CREAM: Flavor the pastry cream with 2 teaspoons vanilla extract instead of the rum.

LEMON OR ORANGE PASTRY CREAM: Add the grated zest of 1 large lemon or orange to the milk mixture. For lemon, add 2 tablespoons lemon juice to the yolk mixture; for orange, add 2 tablespoons orange juice and 1 tablespoon lemon juice. Reduce the vanilla extract to 1 teaspoon.

CHOCOLATE PASTRY CREAM: Bring an additional ½ cup milk to a boil and stir in 8 ounces bittersweet chocolate off the heat. Whisk smooth and add to the pastry cream along with the vanilla and butter.

CARAMEL PASTRY CREAM: Mix ½ cup sugar and 2 tablespoons water in a large saucepan. Set the pan over medium heat and cook, stirring occasionally, until the sugar melts and caramelizes to a deep amber color. Reduce the sugar in the pastry cream recipe to ¼ cup; heat the milk, cream, and sugar in a separate pan while you are cooking the caramel. Once the caramel is cooked, remove the pan from the heat and pour the hot milk mixture into the caramel, shielding the hand you use to hold the handle of the milk pan with a towel and averting your face. Afterward, bring the mixture to a boil and continue with the recipe.

LIQUEUR PASTRY CREAM: Add 1 to 2 tablespoons sweet liqueur, such as triple sec, or 1 tablespoon nonsugared liquor, such as rum or kirsch, to the cream along with the butter and vanilla.

7. Cook, whisking constantly, until the pastry cream thickens, comes to a full boil, and boils for 30 seconds.

8. Off the heat, whisk in the vanilla and butter. Pour the pastry cream into a shallow bowl so it cools quickly and press plastic wrap directly against the surface. Refrigerate immediately and use it as soon as it's cold or within 24 hours.

9. Fill the choux puffs completely with the pastry cream using a pastry bag and a ¼-inch plain tube, inserting the tube through the bottom flat side of the choux; it will feel noticeably heavier once it's fully filled ①. Set aside.

10. For the glaze, half-fill a saucepan with water and bring to a boil over medium heat.

11. Meanwhile, use a silicon spatula to mix the confectioners' sugar, water, and espresso powder in a heatproof bowl larger than the top of the saucepan—it will be very thick. Beat in the corn syrup, butter, and vanilla.

12. Lower the heat so that the water just simmers gently, then set the bowl over the pan. Warm the icing, beating constantly, until it is lukewarm, about 100°F. Use the glaze immediately or reheat it carefully if necessary.

13. Once the glaze is ready, quickly dip the top third of each choux puff into it, letting the excess glaze drip back into the bowl and setting the puff right side up on a paper-covered pan ②.

14. Arrange the choux on a platter to serve. Refrigerate them if they have to sit more than a couple of hours—but don't chill for too long, or the pastry will get soggy.

①

②

CHOCOLATE ÉCLAIRS

Makes about eighteen 4-inch éclairs

1 batch Pâte à Choux (page 204)

VANILLA BEAN PASTRY CREAM

1½ cups whole milk

½ cup heavy cream

⅓ cup sugar

1 vanilla bean, split lengthwise

3 tablespoons cornstarch

5 large egg yolks

2 tablespoons unsalted butter, at room temperature

CHOCOLATE GLAZE

⅓ cup water

⅓ cup light corn syrup or golden syrup

1 cup sugar

8 ounces bittersweet chocolate in pellets or cut into ¼-inch pieces

VARIATION

For éclairs with a chocolate filling, use the chocolate pastry cream variation on page 206.

No one seems to agree as to whether the "chocolate" in "chocolate éclair" refers only to the icing or to the pastry cream filling as well. I'm partial to vanilla pastry cream with chocolate icing, but you can use chocolate or any other flavor of pastry cream you like.

1. For the pastry cream, set aside ½ cup of the milk in a medium bowl. Combine the remaining 1 cup milk with the cream, sugar, and vanilla bean in a medium nonreactive saucepan and whisk together. Bring to a full boil over low heat.

2. Meanwhile, whisk the cornstarch into the reserved ½ cup milk, then whisk in the yolks.

3. Once the milk boils, whisk about a third of it into the yolk mixture. Return the remaining milk to a full boil. While whisking constantly, add the yolk mixture in a quick stream. Cook, whisking constantly, until the pastry cream thickens, comes to a full boil, and boils for 30 seconds more. Use tongs to discard the vanilla bean and, off the heat, whisk in the butter. Pour the pastry cream into a shallow bowl to cool quickly and press plastic wrap directly against the surface. Refrigerate immediately until ready to use.

4. Set a rack at the middle level in the oven and preheat to 425°F. Line a cookie sheet with parchment paper.

5. Use a pastry bag fitted with a ½-inch fine French star tube (#6B, Ateco #866) to pipe 4-inch éclairs 2 inches apart on the prepared pan. Hold the bag at a 45-degree angle with the tube touching the paper and pull while squeezing the bag. When you reach the end, stop squeezing and lift toward the éclair to avoid leaving a point—see page 202. (If you do, moisten your fingertip and rub it smooth.)

6. Bake the éclairs for 10 minutes, then decrease the heat to 350°F and bake until dark golden and dry, about 20 minutes more. Cool the éclairs on a rack.

7. Using a pastry bag fitted with a ¼-inch plain tube, pierce the bottom of each éclair in a couple of places and squeeze in the filling. Set the éclairs, filled side up, on a clean paper-lined pan.

8. For the glaze, stir the water, corn syrup, and sugar together in a medium saucepan. Bring to a boil over medium heat, stirring occasionally so that the sugar dissolves. When you reach a full rolling boil, boil for 30 seconds more. Off the heat, add the chocolate, and shake the pan so that it submerges. Let stand for a couple of minutes, then whisk the glaze only until just smooth; too much agitation will introduce air bubbles.

9. Test the coating ability of the glaze by dipping the handle of a wooden spoon into it. If the glaze isn't covering well, let cool for a few minutes, gently stir with a spatula, and test again.

10. Pick up an éclair, filled side up, and dip the unpierced side into the glaze. Hold for the excess to drip off, then turn glazed side up and place back on the pan. Repeat with the remaining éclairs (if the glaze cools, reheat over simmering water without stirring too much). Let the glaze set and serve within several hours.

BIGNÈ DI RICOTTA

Makes about eighteen 2½- to 3-inch cream puffs

1 batch Pâte à Choux (page 204)

2 pounds firm, dry ricotta

1½ cups confectioners' sugar, sifted after measuring, plus more for dusting

1 teaspoon vanilla extract

1 teaspoon finely grated orange zest

¼ teaspoon ground cinnamon

4 ounces semisweet chocolate, cut into ¼-inch pieces, or ⅔ cup semisweet mini chips

⅓ cup candied orange peel, cut into ¼-inch dice, optional

VARIATIONS

Half fill the choux with any flavor of pastry cream, then top them by piping on a large rosette of sweetened whipped cream. Finish with the top and confectioners' sugar.

Or fill the puffs with a thin layer of vanilla pastry cream, add some sliced sugared strawberries or lightly sugared raspberries, and top those with a rosette of whipped cream.

These cream puffs are split and filled with the same type of cream that you find inside Sicilian cannoli. Look for freshly made ricotta for the filling—the supermarket variety is too wet and loose to hold its shape. Pastry shops use a very dry ricotta called *impastata*, and it's available nationally but only in large quantities. Maybe a friendly local grocer will order some for you.

1. Set a rack at the middle level in the oven and preheat to 425°F. Line a cookie sheet with parchment paper.

2. Use a pastry bag fitted with a ½-inch fine French star tube (#6B, Ateco #866) to pipe the pâte à choux in 1½-inch mounds 2 inches apart all around on the prepared pan. Hold the pastry bag perpendicular to the pan and about an inch above it, then squeeze out a half sphere. Stop squeezing and pull away sideways to avoid leaving a point. If you do, wet a fingertip and "erase" the point by gently smearing over it.

3. Bake the choux for 10 minutes, then lower the heat to 350°F and bake until well risen, deep golden, and fairly dry, about 20 minutes more. Slice off the top third of one of the choux, as in step 5, to determine doneness. Cool on a rack.

4. While the choux are baking and cooling, beat the ricotta and sugar together on low-medium speed in a stand mixer fitted with the paddle attachment. Remove the bowl from the mixer and use a rubber spatula to beat in the vanilla, orange zest, and cinnamon. If you chopped the chocolate, sift away any small dusty particles in a small open-mesh strainer, then add the chocolate and, if you like, the orange peel.

5. Line the pastries up on a clean pan and use a sharp serrated knife to slice off the top third of each. Pipe or spoon the filling into the choux puffs, overfilling slightly so that the ricotta shows when the top is replaced. Dust with confectioners' sugar before serving.

PARIS–BREST PRALINÉ

This tire-shaped pastry was supposedly invented in honor of a bicycle race of the same name. Today, it's more common to make it as a series of separate large spheres of dough that grow together while the pastry is baking, whether in the traditional round shape or as a rectangular strip, rather than piping the dough into rings. The crunchy topping has recently become popular in fancy pastry shops in Paris.

1. For the crunch topping, beat the butter and sugar on low speed with a rubber spatula. Beat in the flour until absorbed. Set aside at room temperature.

2. Set a rack at the middle level in the oven and preheat to 425°F. Line a cookie sheet with parchment paper.

3. Trace a 9-inch circle on the paper lining the pan and turn it over. Use a pastry bag fitted with a 1-inch opening and no tube to pipe 2-inch spheres of the choux paste close together just inside the circle.

4. Divide the crunch topping into as many pieces as there are spheres of pâte à choux and roll the topping pieces ⅛ inch thick; cut them into even rounds using a 1½-inch plain or fluted cutter.

5. Paint the pastry with egg wash and top each mound of pâte à choux with the topping.

6. Bake the pastries for 10 minutes, then lower the temperature to 350°F and bake until they are well risen, deeply colored, and crisp, 20 to 30 minutes more; cool on a rack.

7. When you're ready to assemble the pastry, beat the butter and praline paste on medium speed in a stand mixer with the paddle attached until smooth. Add the chilled pastry cream all at once, then beat until the filling is soft and smooth, about 5 minutes.

8. Use a serrated knife to slice off the top third of each chou. Slide the bottom to a platter and pipe in the filling in a series of large rosettes using a pastry bag fitted with a ½-inch star tube.

9. Replace the top choux and serve it within a couple of hours.

Makes one 9-inch round pastry, about 10 servings

½ batch Pâte à Choux (page 204)

CRUNCH TOPPING

2½ tablespoons unsalted butter, cool but slightly soft

¼ cup granulated or turbinado sugar

⅓ cup unbleached all-purpose flour (spoon into dry-measure cup and level)

Egg wash: 1 egg whisked with a pinch of salt

FILLING

8 ounces/2 sticks unsalted butter, softened

½ cup hazelnut praline paste

1 batch Vanilla Bean Pastry Cream (page 208)

VARIATIONS

For a change of shape, pipe the pâte à choux in 2 straight lines of spheres next to each other instead of a circle; everything else remains the same. Brush egg wash onto the pastry and sprinkle with sliced almonds or hazelnuts instead of using the crunch topping.

GÂTEAU SAINT-HONORÉ

Possibly the most elegant and impressive-looking dessert made from pâte à choux, gâteau Saint-Honoré has a double pedigree: it is named in honor of a seventh-century bishop of Amiens who is venerated as the patron saint of pastry cooks, and it was first made in Paris pastry shops in 1884 to celebrate the centennial of the birth of Antonin Carême, the greatest French chef of the nineteenth century. The crème Chiboust filling, named for the nineteenth-century Parisian pastry shop in which it originated, uses a cooked meringue to lighten the pastry cream. This cake is really a combination of quite easy preparations, and I've changed the round shape to a rectangular one that's even simpler to put together.

1. Set racks in the upper and lower thirds of the oven and preheat to 375°F. Line 2 cookie sheets with parchment paper.

2. Place the flaky dough on a floured surface, roll to a rectangle a bit larger than 16 x 5 inches, and place on one of the prepared pans. Use a ruler and a sharp pastry wheel to trim the pastry to exactly 16 x 5 inches. Use a fork to pierce the pastry all over at ½-inch intervals.

3. Brush the long edges of the pastry base with water. Using a pastry bag fitted with a ⅜-inch fine French star tube (#4B, Ateco #864), pipe the pâte à choux in a straight line onto the moistened edges, holding the bag at a 45-degree angle to the strip of dough and squeezing out a line equal to the diameter of the tube. Don't worry about the short edges—they will be trimmed.

4. Use the remaining pâte à choux to make twenty-four 1-inch puffs on the second prepared pan. Hold the bag at a 45-degree angle to the pan, touch the tube to the paper, and squeeze quickly to make a small sphere, then stop squeezing and lift upward. If you leave a point, moisten a fingertip and smooth it away (see photos on page 205).

5. Bake the base and choux until golden and dry, 20 to 25 minutes. Cool in the pans on racks.

6. For the filling, set aside ½ cup of the milk in a medium bowl. Combine the remaining 1½ cups milk with ¼ cup of the sugar and the vanilla bean in a medium nonreactive saucepan and whisk well. Place over low heat and bring to a full boil.

7. Meanwhile, whisk the cornstarch into the reserved ½ cup milk and whisk in the yolks.

8. Once the milk boils, whisk about a third of it into the yolk mixture. Return the remaining milk to a full boil. Whisk in the yolk mixture in a quick stream and cook, whisking constantly, until the pastry cream thickens, comes to a full boil, and boils for 30 seconds. Discard the vanilla bean.

9. Off the heat, whisk in the butter. Pour the pastry cream into a shallow bowl to cool quickly and press plastic directly against the surface. Chill until cold and use within 24 hours.

10. Whisk the pastry cream smooth in a large bowl and set aside. Use a fork to stir the gelatin into the water in a small heatproof bowl. Half-fill a saucepan with water and bring to a boil. Whisk the egg whites and the remaining ⅓ cup sugar together in the bowl of an electric mixer and place over the pan of boiling water. Whisk gently but constantly until the egg whites are >>

Makes one 16-inch-long dessert, about 8 servings

½ batch/10 ounces/300 grams Flaky Buttery Dough (page 14) or ⅓ batch/10 ounces/300 grams Puff Pastry (page 155)

1 batch Pâte à Choux (page 204)

CRÈME CHIBOUST FILLING

2 cups whole milk

¼ cup plus ⅓ cup sugar

1 vanilla bean, split lengthwise

3 tablespoons cornstarch

5 large egg yolks

2 tablespoons unsalted butter, soft

1½ envelopes unflavored granulated gelatin

⅓ cup water

3 large egg whites

CARAMEL GLAZE

1½ cups sugar

2 tablespoons water

½ teaspoon distilled white vinegar

WHIPPED CREAM

1 cup heavy whipping cream

2 tablespoons sugar

1 teaspoon vanilla extract

SPINNING THE CARAMEL

To spin the caramel in the choux, gently reheat the caramel and dip a spoon into it. Hold the spoon perpendicular to the pan and let the caramel begin to fall in a thin stream and then quickly run the spoon back and forth over the choux on one side of the pastry, holding the spoon about 2 inches above them.

hot, about 140°F, and the sugar dissolves. Place the bowl on the mixer with the whisk attachment and whip on medium-high speed until well risen in volume but not dry. Once you start whipping, place the bowl of soaked gelatin over the pan of water off the heat until it becomes a clear liquid. When the egg whites are ready, quickly whisk the gelatin into the pastry cream and then fold in the meringue.

11. Fill the small choux puffs using a pastry bag and a ¼-inch plain tube, inserting the tube through the bottom flat side of the choux. Set aside. Spread the remaining filling in the rectangular base between the two side walls of pâte à choux.

12. For the caramel glaze, stir the sugar, water, and vinegar together in a medium saucepan and place over medium heat. Have a bowl of ice water ready. Make sure the bowl is wide enough for the bottom of your saucepan to be submerged in the water by a couple of inches.

13. Once the sugar starts to melt, stir occasionally with a metal spoon, but don't stir too much, or it might start to crystallize in large lumps. If a lot of sugar sticks to the side of the pan, use a clean pastry brush dipped in hot water to dissolve it. As the sugar liquefies and starts to become an even, light caramel color, move the pan off the heat and continue cooking in the heat retained by the pan. When finished, the caramel should be clear (without any visible sugar granules) and a deep amber color. Usually it takes a few times removing the pan from the heat and putting it back again before the caramel is the correct color. Test by letting a few drops fall from a spoon onto a sheet of white paper—it should be a clear dark amber color. Once the caramel has reached the right shade, immerse the bottom of the pan in the ice water for just a few seconds to cool the pan so that it won't keep darkening the caramel. Don't let the caramel itself cool or it will become too thick to use.

14. Immediately glaze the puffs: quickly dip the top third of each into the caramel, turning it right side up and setting it on a parchment-lined pan. Take care to prevent any crumbs or dabs of filling from dropping into the caramel—this might cause it to become lumpy and crystallized before you have glazed all your pastries. Once all the puffs are glazed, gently reheat the caramel. Carefully dip a single spot on the bottom of each choux and affix it to one of the side walls on the pastry base.

15. Whip the cream with the sugar and vanilla to a soft peak and spread over the pastry cream. Trim the edges of the pastry before serving. Keep the gâteau at a cool room temperature (but not in the refrigerator) until serving time.

ITALIAN CREAM PUFF FRITTERS (SFINCI)

My maternal grandmother loved to make these, and I can understand why—they're light, luscious, and easy to whip up from very little in the way of ingredients. The standard coating is cinnamon sugar, but sugar mixed with grated lemon or orange zest is delicious too.

Makes about 40 small fritters

1 batch Pâte à Choux (page 204)

½ cup sugar

½ teaspoon ground cinnamon

2 cups safflower oil or light olive oil for frying

1. Combine the sugar and cinnamon in a medium bowl.

2. Heat the oil in deep pan or wok over medium heat to 350°F. Line a jellyroll pan with paper towels.

3. Use a teaspoon to scoop up a spoonful of the dough, then use a second spoon to scrape it out into the hot oil. Work with the spoons close to the surface of the oil so it doesn't splatter.

4. Use a skimmer or slotted spoon to stir the fritters around for a few seconds until they become inflated and golden. Wait to see that they split, then that the split area colors too, as a sign of doneness.

5. Transfer the fritters to the prepared pan to drain, then, one at a time, roll them in the cinnamon sugar.

6. Continue frying and sugaring the fritters; as you finish each fritter, arrange it on a serving platter.

GOUGÈRE WITH GRUYÈRE, BACON & PECANS

Hardly a French classic, this bacony and nutty version of the traditional Burgundian pastry always wins admirers. If you buy a large gougère in a pastry shop, it's piped as a series of spheres in a ring, but you can also make individual smaller puffs to serve as an hors d'oeuvre to nibble with drinks.

1. Scatter the diced bacon in a sauté pan and place over low heat. Cook until the fat has melted and the pieces are beginning to crisp, about 10 minutes, stirring occasionally. Using a slotted spoon, transfer the bacon to a plate covered with paper towels to drain.

2. Set a rack at the middle level in the oven and preheat to 425°F. Line a cookie sheet with parchment paper.

3. Bring the water, butter, and salt to a boil in a small saucepan. Remove from the heat and stir in the flour all at once. Return the pan to the heat and beat the paste until the bottom of the pan is filmed, about 20 seconds.

4. Scrape the paste into a mixing bowl and stir for 1 minute to cool it down. Beat in the eggs, one at a time, then beat in the pepper, nutmeg, cheese, and cooked bacon.

5. Trace a 9-inch circle on the paper lining the prepared pan and turn it over. Use a pastry bag fitted with a 1-inch opening and no tube to pipe large spheres of the paste close together on the traced circle.

6. Brush the pastry with the egg wash and scatter the pecans all over the surface.

7. Bake for 10 minutes, then lower the temperature to 350°F and bake until well risen, deeply colored, and crisp, about 20 minutes more. A good gougère is still moist inside.

8. Cool the pastry on a rack and serve warm, or cool completely and reheat it at 350°F for 10 minutes before serving.

Makes one 9-inch ring or 24 small puffs

2 ounces thick-cut bacon, cut into ¼-inch dice

⅓ cup water, milk, or a combination

3 tablespoons unsalted butter, cubed

½ teaspoon fine sea salt

½ cup unbleached all-purpose flour (spoon into dry-measure cup and level)

2 large eggs, at room temperature

¼ teaspoon freshly ground black pepper

Large pinch of freshly grated nutmeg

1 cup coarsely grated Swiss Gruyère

Egg wash: 1 egg whisked with a pinch of salt

½ cup pecan pieces, coarsely chopped

VARIATIONS

Substitute walnuts or pistachios for the pecans. Or for a traditional gougère, omit the bacon and pecans.

To make small gougères, pipe like the petits choux on page 204, using a ½-inch plain tube (Ateco #806), and resume at step 6, above, baking for only about 5 minutes after lowering the temperature; taste one to check doneness.

AFTERWORD

This pastry book has marked several important milestones in my life and my career. My first book, *Nick Malgieri's Perfect Pastry*, was published in 1989, exactly twenty-five years before the appearance of this book. While there are a few similarities between the two books, the present one is 90 percent new material, the result of many years spent teaching and writing about baking and desserts.

While this book was in the editing process, about a year before publication, I had the joyful experience of visiting with some friends I had met exactly forty years prior, when I arrived in Switzerland to work at my first job after culinary school. My friend and mentor, Albert Kumin, who was my pastry teacher at the Culinary Institute of America, had urged me to work in Switzerland if I was serious about becoming a pastry chef. The start of that process was a foundation for many opportunities to learn first hand about pastries, desserts, chocolates, breads, and a whole world of baking and desserts that continues to fascinate me.

I've been fortunate that through my work over the years, I've been able to indulge my passion to learn more and more about my craft and share it with readers like you.

Today, because of all the computer technology within everyone's easy reach, I can even provide video tutorials for some of the more complex parts of this book: look for them at my website, www.nickmalgieri.com.

It's my hope that you use this book to learn new techniques and recipes and that you delight yourself as well as your family and friends with the results.

And remember, bake something!

BIBLIOGRAPHY

Bachmann, Walter. *Swiss Bakery and Confectionery.* London:
    Maclaren & Sons Limited, 1949.

Calvel, Raymond, *Le Goût du Pain.* Paris: Éditions Jérôme Villette,
    1990.

Darenne, E., and E. Duval. *Traité de Pâtisserie Moderne* (rev. ed.).
    Paris: Flammarion, 1974.

Fance, Wilfred James. *The New International Confectioner.* London
    and Coulsdon, England:
    Virtue & Company, 1981.

Ferber, Christine. *Mes Tartes Sucrées et Salées.* Paris: Payot, 1998.

Gouffé, Jules. *Le Livre de Pâtisserie.* Paris: Hachette, 1873.

Grigson, Jane. *Jane Grigson's Fruit Book.* New York: Atheneum,
    1982.

Kaltenbach, Marianne. *Aus Schweizer Küchen.* Bern, Switzerland:
    Hallwag, 1977.

Lacam, Pierre. *Memorial Historique et Géographique de la
    Pâtisserie.* Paris: Chez l'Auteur, 1895.

Mayer, Eduard. *Wiener Süßspeisen.* Linz, Austria: Trauner Verlag,
    1968.

Nutt, Frederick. *The Complete Confectioner; or, the Whole Art of
    Confectionary Made Easy.*
    London: L. Harrison & J.C. Leigh, 1815.

Polshenke, Paul. *Gebäck aus Deutschen Landen.* Alfeld, Germany:
    Gildeverlag, 1949.

Schumacher, Karl. *Wiener Süßspeisen.* Linz: Trauner Verlag, 1990.

Skrach, Hans. *Die Wiener Konditorei.* Vienna, Austria: Verlag Für
    Jugend und Volk, 1949.

Spriano, Carlos. *Mi Cocina.* Buenos Aires: Sociedad Impresora
    Americana, 1939.

Thuries, Yves. *Le Livre de Recettes d'un Compagnon du Tour de
    France* (3 vols.). Cordes-
    sur-Ciel, France: Société Éditar, 1980.

Vogt, Ernst, et al. *Der Schweizer Bäcker-Konditor* (3 vols.). Thun,
    Switzerland: Ott Verlag, 1944.

Witzelsberger, Richard. *Das Österreichesche Mehlspeisen
    Kochbuch.* Vienna: Verlag Kremayr
    & Scheriau, 1979.

INDEX

A

almond 180
    cookie dough 20
    cream filling 179, 181
    crunch topping, apple tarts with 57
    filling 176, 192–4
    meringue, with sour cherry tart 52–3
    & orange tart 40–1
    & pear dumplings 168–9
    syrup 194
    Viennese crescents 181
apple
    bacon & Gruyère quiche 104
    & blueberry pie 82–3
    & Calvados cream tart 42
    & Cheddar pie 88
    & cranberry granola crisp 96
    "French" pie 90–1
    individual tarts, with almond crunch 57
    Old Vienna strudel 132
    old-fashioned applesauce tart 46
apricot 178–9
    & almond dumplings 169
    brioche fruit dumplings 201
    & cheese strudel 133
    dried, pie 86–7
    tart, in a brioche crust 192
    Viennese pockets 180

B

bacon
    goat cheese and greens strudel 137
    Gruyère & apple quiche 104
    pecan & Gruyère gougère 216–17
    quiche Lorraine 100, 102
baking powder/soda 9
baklava 127, 140–3
    Turkish "carrot slice" 144–5
banana cream pie 73
beef
    börek 149
    Cornish-style pasties 125
    French Canadian meat pie 121
berries
    mixed, cobbler 97
    see also specific berries

bignè di ricotta 210
biscuit
    cream crust 92-3
    nut, batter 22
blackberry pie 82
blind baking 37
blueberry
    & apple pie 82-3
    deep-dish pie 92-3
börek, feta and mint 148-9
bostock 194
bow ties, puff pastry 171
bows
    poppy seed 200
    walnut 200
brioche 183
    brioches à tête 187-8
    croissants 186
    crust, prune plum tart in a 192-3
    fruit dumplings 201
    loaves 188-9
    mousseline dough 184, 186-97, 201
    raisin 186
    raspberry shortcake 196-7
    rolls 186
    round loaves 188
    Swiss cream cake 190-1
butter 9
buttermilk 10
butternut squash old-fashioned pie 80
butterscotch custard pie 76-7

C

Calvados cream & apple tart 42
caramel
    cashew filling 58
    glaze 212-14
    pastry cream 206
    salted, chocolate tartlets 58-9
    sauce 166-7
    spun 212-13
caramelized puff pastry layers 160
cashew caramel filling 58
Cheddar
    & apple pie 88
    & potato quiche 105
cheese
    & apricot strudel 133
    bianco family pizza chiena 115
    cornmeal dough with 18
    Mexican, tartlets 64-5
    pizza rustica alla Parmigiana 114
    Provençal spinach pie 120
    see also specific cheeses

cherry
    sour, tart, and almond meringue 52-3
    sweet, & rhubarb pie 84
chess pie, Mississippi 75
chicken
    Argentine empanadas 122-4
    Cornish-style pasties 125
    Mexican pie 112-13
chiltomate 113
chocolate
    bignè di ricotta 210
    cinnamon twists 176
    cookie dough 21
    custard filling 62-3
    éclairs 208-9
    ganache filling 56-7
    ganache glaze 62-3
    glaze 62-3, 208-9
    Lesley's individual double tarts 62-3
    pains au chocolat 172-3
    pastry cream 206
    raspberry tart 56
    salted caramel tartlets 58-9
    sweet cocoa dough 21
"cigarette" pastries, Turkish fried 150-1
cinnamon
    chocolate twists 176
    walnut Viennese crescents 177
citron tartlets, Moravian 61
cobblers 92-7
    mixed berry 97
cocoa, sweet dough 21
coconut
    cream pie 72-3
    & pineapple tart 44-5
coffee
    glaze 204-7
    pastry cream 204-7
confit, pineapple 45
cookie dough
    almond 20
    chocolate 21
    crusts 22
    French-style 20
    gluten-free 23
Cornish-style pasties 16, 122, 125
cornmeal dough 18
    with cheese or herbs 18
cornstarch 81
cottage cheese pie 74
crabmeat curried tart 108
cranberry
    & apple granola crisp 96
    Osgood pie 71
    pecan pie 68-9

cream 10
    banana 73
    Calvados 42
    "carrot slice" Turkish baklava 144-5
    coconut 45, 72-3
    gâteau Saint-Honoré 212-14
    lemon 48
    raspberry brioche shortcake 196-7
    raspberry cream pie 78-9
    strawberry raspberry mille-feuille 162-3
    Swiss brioche cake 190-1
    vanilla orange pastry 162
    see also pastry cream
cream biscuit crust 92-3
cream cheese-filled Viennese squares 174-5
cream puff fritters, Italian 214-15
cream puff pastry 203-7
cream puffs, coffee filled & iced 204-7
crème Anglaise 180
crème chiboust 212-14
crisps 92-7
    apple & cranberry granola 96
    plum & raspberry 94-5
croissants 153-4, 170
    brioche 186
    Professor Calvel's dough 158, 170, 172-3,
        176
crusts
    double 32, 81-91
    empty pie 37
    finishing a 36
    forming mini rectangular, square or
        barquette 30-1
    full top 32
    prerolled 27
    see also lattice work; tart crusts
currant & pear pie 89
curried crabmeat tart 108
custard
    butterscotch 76-7
    chocolate 62-3

D-F

dairy products 10
Danish dough
    coffeecake 178-9
    Viennese 154, 159, 174-5, 177-81
dough scraps 22
dried fruit 86-7, 136, 174-5, 178-9
dumplings
    brioche fruit 201
    pear & almond 168-9
    Viennese brioche 195

Easter Swiss rice tart 47
èclairs, chocolate 208–9
egg 10, 122–4
    hard-boiled 114–15, 122
empanadas 17, 122–4
equipment 7, 11

fats 9
feta and mint börek 148–9
flaky dough 14–15
flours 8
fritters, Italian cream puff 214–15
fruit juices, overflowing 81

G–I
ganache
    filling 56–7
    glaze 62–3
gâteau Saint-Honoré 212–14
ginger & peach pie 85
glaze
    caramel 212–14
    chocolate 208–9
    coffee 204–7
gluten-free dough 23–5
goat cheese
    greens and bacon strudel 137
    summery tomato tarts 110–11
gougère with Gruyère, bacon & pecan
    216–17
granola crisp, apple & cranberry 96
Gruyère
    apple & bacon quiche 104
    bacon & pecan with gougère 216–17

hazelnut
    Appenzell tart 43
    individual pithiviers 166–7
    Paris-Brest praliné 211

icing 90–1, 179
ingredients 7–10

K–M
kale pie, Italian 116–17
katmer dough 138–9
kaymak 138–9, 144–5

lamb
    börek 149
    Cornish-style pasties 125
laminated doughs 153–81
lard 9, 15
lassi mango tart 54–5

lattice work 84–7
    diagonal 33, 84–5
    perpendicular 33, 84–5
    woven 34–5
leaveners 9
leek & mushroom quiche 101, 103
lemon
    cottage cheese pie 74
    curd 48
    French meringue tart 48–9
    mille-feuille 161
    Moravian citron tartlets 61
    Osgood pie 71
    pastry cream 206
lining pans 28, 29
liqueur pastry cream 206
liquids 10

mango lassi tart 54–5
meringue
    almond, with sour cherry tart 52–3
    French lemon tart 48–9
milk 10
mille-feuille
    strawberry raspberry 162–3
    traditional vanilla 161
mint
    and feta börek 148–9
    strawberry & raspberry tart with 50–1
Mississippi chess pie 75
molasses pecan pie 70
mushroom & leek quiche 101, 103

N–O
nut(s)
    biscuit batter 22
    Tyrolean strudel 136
    see also specific nuts

oil(s) 9
    olive 9, 14
    sweet pastry dough made with 18
olive oil 9
    dough 14
orange
    & almond tart 40–1
    pastry cream 206
    vanilla pastry cream 162
Osgood pie 71
oven position 81

P
pains au chocolat 172–3
pans 11
    lining 28, 29

Paris-Brest praliné 211
pasties, Cornish-style 16, 122, 125
pastry cream 51, 79, 161, 162, 204–7, 210
    common flavorings 206
    vanilla bean 161, 208–9, 211
pâte à choux 203–15
peas & salmon, quiche of 106–7
peach
    & almond dumplings 169
    & ginger pie 85
    tart, in a brioche crust 192
pear
    & almond dumplings 168–9
    & currant pie 89
    tart, in a brioche crust 192
    Tyrolean strudel 136
pecan
    cranberry pie 68–9
    Gruyère & bacon with gougère 216–17
    molasses pie 70
    Osgood pie 71
    traditional pie 70
phyllo dough 127, 144, 146
pies
    apple & Cheddar 88
    baking an empty crust for 37
    blueberry & apple 82–3
    butterscotch custard 76–7
    coconut cream 72–3
    cottage cheese 74
    cranberry pecan 68–9
    deep-dish blueberry 92–3
    diagonal lattice top 33
    double crust 32, 81–91
    dried apricot 86–7
    finishing piecrusts 36
    "French" apple 90–1
    French Canadian meat 121
    full tops for 32
    Italian kale 116–17
    Mexican chicken 112–13
    Mississippi chess 75
    molasses pecan 70
    old-fashioned sweet potato 80
    Osgood 71
    peach & ginger 85
    pear & currant 89
    Provençal spinach 120
    raspberry cream 78–9
    summer vegetable 118–19
    sweet cherry & rhubarb 84
pineapple
    & coconut tart 44–5
    confit 45

pistachio
    "carrot slice" Turkish baklava 144–5
    & raspberry individual tarts 60
    Turkish pastry 138–9
    Turkish rolls 146
pithiviers, individual hazelnut 166–7
pizza
    chiena, bianco family 115
    rustica 99
    rustica alla Parmigiana 114
plum & raspberry crisp 94–5
poppy seed
    bows 200
    strudel 130–1
potato
    & Cheddar quiche 105
    Cornish-style pasties 125
praliné, Paris-Brest 211
prerolled crusts 27
prune plum
    & almond dumplings 169
    & apricot pie 87
    brioche fruit dumplings 201
    tart in a brioche crust 192–3
puff pastry 153, 154–7, 160–9
    bow ties 171
    caramelized layers 160
    quick 154, 157
    tart crust 164–5

Q–R

quiche 99
    apple, bacon & Gruyère 104
    leek & mushroom 101, 103
    Lorraine 100, 102
    potato & Cheddar 105
    of salmon & peas 106–7

raisin 71
    brioche 186
    & cheese strudel 133
    pie 87
raspberry
    brioche shortcake 196–7
    chocolate tart 56
    cream pie 78–9
    pie 82
    & pistachio individual tarts 60
    & plum crisp 94–5
    strawberry mille-feuille 162–3
    & strawberry tart with mint 50–1
red pepper & zucchini tart 109
rhubarb & sweet cherry pie 84

rice tart, Swiss Easter 47
ricotta, bignè di 210
rolling dough 24–7
rolls, brioche 186

S

salmon & peas, quiche of 106–7
salt 9
salted caramel chocolate tartlets 58–9
sausage
    bianco family pizza chiena 115
    empanadas 124
shortcake, raspberry brioche 196–7
sour cream 10
    dough 16
spinach Provençal pie 120
strawberry
    raspberry mille-feuille 162–3
    & raspberry tart with mint 50–1
    & rhubarb pie 84
strudel
    apricot & cheese 133
    dough 128–9
    of greens, bacon & goat cheese 137
    Old Vienna apple 132
    poppy seed 130–1
    Tyrolean 136
    yeast-risen walnut 198–200
sugars 8
sweet pastry dough 19
    made with oil 18
sweet potato old-fashioned pie 80
syrup 144–6, 194

T

tart crusts
    forming from gluten-free dough 24–5
    forming individual 28
    forming mini round 29
    puff pastry 164–5
tartlets
    Mexican cheese 64–5
    Moravian citron 61
    salted caramel chocolate 58–9
tarts
    Appenzell hazelnut 43
    apple & Calvados cream 42
    baking an empty crust for 37
    chocolate raspberry 56
    curried crabmeat 108
    French lemon meringue 48–9
    individual apple, and almond crunch 57
    individual raspberry & pistachio 60
    Lesley's individual double chocolate 62–3

mango lassi 54–5
old-fashioned applesauce 46
orange & almond 40–1
pineapple & coconut 44–5
prune plum, in a brioche crust 192–3
sour cherry, with almond meringue 52–3
strawberry & raspberry, with mint 50–1
summery tomato 110–11
Swiss Easter rice 47
zucchini & red pepper 109
thickening agents 81
thin doughs 140–51
tomato
    chiltomate 113
    summery tarts 110–11
tools 11
torta salata 99

V–Z

vanilla
    bean, pastry cream 161, 208–9, 211
    crème chiboust 212–14
    icing 179
    orange pastry cream 162
    pastry cream 206, 210
    traditional mille-feuille 161
vegetable summer pie 118–19
Viennese
    layered dough 154, 159, 174–5, 177–81
    sweet yeast-risen dough 185, 198–200

walnut 68
    bows 200
    cinnamon Viennese crescents 177
    yeast-risen strudel 198–200
water 10

yeast 9
    yeast-risen doughs 17, 183–201
yufka 127, 147–51

zucchini & red pepper tart 109

ACKNOWLEDGMENTS

Enormous thanks to all my colleagues and friends whose kindness and support contributed to this book:

Phyllis Wender, my agent, and her team Susie Cohen and Allison Cohen;

At Kyle Books: Kyle Cathie, owner; Anja Schmidt, US publisher; Ron Longe, publicist; and Judith Hannam and Vicki Murrell in the London office;

Natalie Danford, my 24/7 writing advisor;

Our production team: Dirk Kaufman, designer; Romulo Yanes, photographer; Paul Grimes, food stylist; PJ Mehaffey, prop stylist; Ana Deboo, copyeditor and Liana Krissoff, proofreader;

For recipe testing: Kyra Effren, Jeff Yoskowitz, and Sandy Gluck;

At the Institute of Culinary Education: Rick Smilow, owner; Andrea Tutunjian, director of education; and director of purchasing Shawona Jones and all her staff;

For sharing recipes and their experience with various recipes and processes: Rhonda Caplan, Lesley Chesterman, Philippe Conticini, Rachel Fletcher and Stephen Fagg, Gunther Heiland, Albert Kumin, Sandy Leonard, Ben Mims, Nancy Nicholas, Ann Nurse, Brian Pansari, Hermann Reiner, Roberto Santibañez and Marco Diaz, Chef Somsak, Michelle Tampakis, Barbara Bianco Tutunjian, and Jeff Yoskowitz;

In Austria: Hans Diglas, Erik Goeller, and Astrid Pockfuss of Vienna Tourism;

In Switzerland: Aurelia Carlen of Zurich Tourism, Brian Jaeger, Ivo Jud, Fredi Nussbaum, Kerrin Rousset, Michaela Ruoss of the Switzerland Tourism New York office, and Claudia Schmid;

In Turkey: Aylin Öney Tan, Cenk Sönmeszoy, Seraç Deniz Akgüneş, Sitare Baras, Cem Erol, Nadir Güllü, Ömer Güllü, Murat Güney, Filiz Hösükoğlu, Mary İşin, Dinçer Oruçoğlu, Mustafa Özgüler, and Ahmed Sevim.